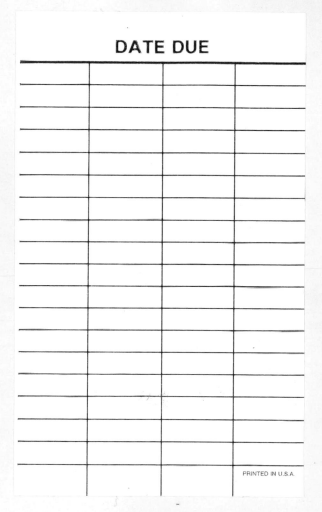

DATE DUE

			PRINTED IN U.S.A.

This study explores the relationship between China's foreign trade reforms and the domestic economic reforms that undergird China's policy of openness in the 1980s and 1990s. It provides the first comprehensive analysis, in any language, of how China has emerged since reform began in 1978 as one of the most dynamic trading nations in the world. It examines both the external policy changes, such as the decentralization of trading authority and the devaluation of the domestic currency, and internal economic reforms such as the increased use of markets and prices that underlie China's dramatic transformation.

The book argues that China's prereform trade system is best understood as an extreme example of the import substitution trade regime that was common in developing countries in the 1950s. And it explains how trade reforms of the 1980s, particularly the systematic devaluation of the domestic currency and the introduction of limited convertibility, have reduced the bias against exports characteristic of the prereform foreign trade and exchange rate system.

The author concludes with an analysis of the sources of China's export growth and outlines further domestic economic reforms that he believes will be required to sustain China's increasing integration into the world economy.

Foreign trade and
economic reform in China, 1978–1990

Foreign trade and
economic reform in China, 1978–1990

NICHOLAS R. LARDY
University of Washington

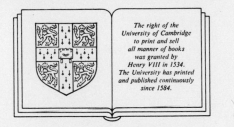

The right of the
University of Cambridge
to print and sell
all manner of books
was granted by
Henry VIII in 1534.
The University has printed
and published continuously
since 1584.

CAMBRIDGE UNIVERSITY PRESS

Cambridge
New York   Port Chester   Melbourne   Sydney

Published by the Press Syndicate of the University of Cambridge
The Pitt Building, Trumpington Street, Cambridge CB2 1RP
40 West 20th Street, New York, NY 10011, USA
10 Stamford Road, Oakleigh, Melbourne 3166, Australia

First published 1992

Printed in the United States of America

Library of Congress Cataloging-in-Publication Data
Lardy, Nicholas R.
Foreign trade and economic reform in China, 1978–1990 / Nicholas R. Lardy.
    p.   cm.
Includes bibliographical references and index.
1. China – Commercial policy.   2. China – Economic policy – 1976–
HF1604.L37   1991
338.951′009′048–dc20   91-15693
                                                                    CIP

A catalogue record for this book is available from the British Library.
ISBN 0 521 41495 4   hardback

Contents

Tables

Preface

In the decade of the 1980s China emerged as one of the most dynamic trading countries in the world. The Maoist legacy of economic and financial self-reliance was overthrown in favor of a policy of "openness" that welcomed direct foreign investment, created special export processing zones on the coast, encouraged dramatically higher levels of foreign trade, and utilized foreign borrowing to accelerate the inflow of foreign capital and technology. By 1990 China's trade volume was larger than all but a dozen of the most advanced industrial economies. China is the only socialist or former socialist country that became a more significant participant in the international economy in the 1980s.

Although China's growing role as an international trading country and as a site for direct foreign investment has been widely noted, much less has been written about the reforms that undergird the policy of openness that China has followed since the late 1970s. These reforms – including the adoption of a more realistic exchange rate and other measures that reduce the bias against exporting – in many respects are similar to policies pursued by other developing countries as they move away from policies of protection of domestic industries and import substitution toward more open, externally oriented development policies.

Yet, as this book seeks to show, the legacy of the system of economic planning adopted in the 1950s posed a special set of problems as China sought to enter the international trading system. In particular the systematic separation of domestic from foreign prices over a period of several decades and the complete reliance on a handful of state-run foreign trading companies to transact all import and export business combined to insulate Chinese firms from the world economy in a way that surpassed that found in even the most inward-looking developing countries. This volume traces how this legacy of economic planning was substantially reduced in the 1980s, making it possible for external sector reforms to transform China's role in the international economy.

This study was made possible by many institutions and individuals. I am particularly grateful to the Joint Committee on Chinese Studies of the American Council of Learned Societies and the Social Science Research Council for the fellowship that supported my sabbatical from the University of Washington in the 1989–90 academic year. This provided me with unencumbered time for research and writing. The Henry M. Jackson School of International Studies provided support for a part-time research assistant over a period of several years facilitating my review of the ever-growing number of Chinese periodicals addressing issues of trade reform. In the late spring and early summer of 1990 I was fortunate to be able to spend six weeks in China at the invitation of the Institute of Economics of the Chinese Academy of Social Sciences. The Institute was instrumental in arranging interviews with specialists in many institutes and organizations who have written extensively on China's foreign trade reforms in the 1980s. These interviews helped me to understand something of the process of foreign trade reform, particularly its complex linkages to China's internal economic reforms. The staff of the library of the Institute was also especially helpful during my visit.

I am indebted to many colleagues who have read drafts of this study and offered numerous suggestions for improvements. The comments of David Denny, Dwight Perkins, Thomas G. Rawski, and Shahid Yusuf, each of whom read the entire manuscript, were especially valued.

1

Trade policy and economic development

Introduction

Since economic reform began in 1978 China has emerged as a major trading nation and foreign trade has begun to exert a greater influence on the domestic economy than at any other period in China's history. Its enhanced role in the world economy is evident both in China's participation in international economic organizations and its volume and pattern of trade. In the early 1980s China joined both the World Bank and the International Monetary Fund. In the mid-1980s China became a member of the Asian Development Bank and initiated the process of becoming what is called a contracting party of the General Agreement on Tariffs and Trade.[1]

Over the same years China's trade volume expanded dramatically. In 1978, on the eve of reform, China was the world's thirty-second ranked exporting country. By 1989 it was the world's thirteenth largest trading nation. In the process its share of world trade almost doubled. Moreover, more than 90 percent of China's trade was with market economies. In both its rapid trade growth and its orientation toward market economies, China poses a sharp contrast with the Soviet Union and the states of Eastern Europe. Despite their reforms, some of which significantly predate those of China, none of these states have become more important participants in the world economy. The foreign trade of the Soviet Union and the countries of Eastern Europe remains heavily skewed toward trade with one another and none of these states increased its hard currency exports substantially in the 1980s.

Equally significant as the increased importance of China's trade in the world economy is the greatly heightened influence of foreign trade on China's domestic economy. In both 1989 and 1990 trade turnover (imports plus exports valued at world prices) exceeded $110 billion.* China's imports,

*All references in dollars are to United States dollars.

1

which consist overwhelmingly of industrial goods, now contribute significantly to increased levels of technological sophistication and production capacity in a number of key domestic industries. And, at the same time, international markets are a growing source of demand for Chinese goods. China's textile industry, for example, is the world's largest and in 1990 exported products worth $13.5 billion, about one-third of its output. Because foreign trade has grown far more rapidly than the domestic economy over the past decade it is possible that in some sense trade has served as an engine of growth. According to Chinese data the rate of expansion of the domestic economy also has increased significantly to approximately 9 percent per annum in the first decade of reform compared to 6 percent prior to reform.

To what extent has China's shift toward a more open trade policy contributed to the growth acceleration observed in the first decade of reform? Economists have long argued that the shift away from a closed to a more open economy should improve the efficiency of resource allocation in developing economies and contribute to more rapid growth. This has been borne out by empirical studies showing trade liberalization tends to lead to an acceleration of economic growth, particularly in economies where severe prereform trade restrictions were countered with strong liberalization measures (Michaely, Papageorgiou, and Choksi, 85–92). What is sometimes overlooked is that the gains from trade liberalization are likely to be limited unless domestic economic policies are also liberalized. This linkage would appear to be even more important for a reforming socialist economy where various forms of government control have imposed more severe distortions in a larger number of domestic markets than in most developing countries.

In short, the issue is the extent to which reforms of China's domestic economy have been sufficient for trade liberalization to have improved the allocation of resources domestically and to have contributed to the faster growth of the Chinese economy since the late 1970s. Ultimately that focus will shed light on the sustainability of China's increasing participation in the world economy. Continued domestic economic distortions could limit the improvement in the allocation of domestic resources usually associated with increased openness and trade. Under these conditions expanding trade would fall short of its potential to increase the rate of growth of the economy and improve welfare. Trade liberalization and reform would likely be curtailed by a government weighing the limited positive economic benefits against the negative political effects of openness and trade expansion.

What are the lessons of the first decade or so of reforms in China for other economies seeking to alleviate the negative consequences of decades of central planning? Many economists believe that the only hope of saving the Soviet economy from an utter collapse is a program of comprehensive reform instituted within a span of only a year or two. Key elements include slashing subsidies to loss-making enterprises and to consumers, freeing of prices, reducing the fiscal deficit, shrinking the monetary overhang, privatizing state assets, drastically devaluing the ruble, opening the economy to international competition, and so on. The economic challenge in Poland is similar but the demise of the Communist Party made it possible to initiate a radical reform strategy beginning in 1990, whereas Soviet reforms in many critical areas are still being debated.

China's economic reform program, begun cautiously in the late 1970s, seems almost quaint by comparison with either the dramatic reform blueprints advanced in the Soviet Union or Poland's "big bang" reform program instituted in 1990. Although the Chinese Communist Party over the first decade of reform approved dozens of major reform measures, no comprehensive reform blueprint with a specific timetable for implementation has ever been approved. Reform has been both incremental and ad hoc. Moreover, even prior to the tragedy of Tiananmen in June 1989, many observers felt that the impetus for economic reform in China had waned. A coalition of conservative party and state bureaucratic forces seemingly had undermined the reform process. China seemed to be following the Hungarian path, where the incremental reforms adopted under the rubric of the New Economic Mechanism in the later half of the 1960s had, within a decade, stalled out. The ascendency of political conservatives and the ouster of Zhao Ziyang in 1989 only deepened the pessimism felt in many quarters regarding the future of China's economic reform.

Yet China's foreign trade reforms by no means floundered after mid-1989. This study discusses several critical areas where reform continued in 1989 and 1990: a renewed devaluation of the official exchange rate to promote exports relative to imports; a further relaxation of exchange control, reflected in a continued rapid expansion in both 1989 and 1990 in the volume of transactions on the parallel, open market for foreign exchange; and further significant reforms in the domestic pricing of traded goods that more closely linked domestic and international prices for almost all imports and for a growing share of exports as well.

It is too soon to say that these reforms can be sustained. Indeed a principal argument in the concluding chapter is that China must soon deepen a broad range of domestic reforms, particularly in areas where elements of the traditional system of central planning seem least changed. Without these reforms it seems unlikely that further reforms in the foreign trade and exchange control regimes would be warranted. However, it would be too soon to assert that China's more incremental approach to economic reform has or must fail.

Finally, to what extent is China's trade regime consistent with principles of the General Agreement on Tariffs and Trade? In early 1989 it appeared as if the working party appointed by the GATT Secretariat to examine the merits of China's request to participate in the world trade body would agree to an accession document setting forth the conditions under which that could be accomplished. But in the wake of the Tiananmen tragedy China's accession became a moot issue. To many participating countries, particularly major industrial states that imposed a variety of economic sanctions against China, accession was out of the question.

The official position of the Chinese government is that its economic and trade systems are already close to achieving "GATT compatibility" and that negotiations on China's accession should resume at an early date. Although serious negotiations may not resume for some time, when they do it is likely China will undergo a much closer scrutiny of its trade regime than it had received prior to June 1989. It probably will be expected to conform much more closely to GATT principles prior to its accession. Before mid-1989 China received a great deal of credit for the direction of its reform (Jacobson and Oksenberg 1990, 102–3). When negotiations resume the GATT working party likely will expect concrete evidence of compatibility rather than simply examine the trajectory of China's reforms. Thus the issue of GATT compatibility probably will be examined for some time. A thorough discussion of the degree to which China's trade regime is consistent with GATT principles is best left to someone better versed in the intricacies of the various codes and agreements negotiated in recent decades over several rounds of multilateral trade negotiations within the GATT. This study has the more modest aim of simply pointing out a few of the areas where China's trading system appears still to fall short of GATT expectations.

An analysis of the issues sketched in this introduction is best undertaken in a comparative framework. What were the central characteristics of the trade regimes adopted by most developing countries in the 1950s? How did these characteristics affect the allocation of resources and the patterns of growth and development?

Alternative trade regimes

In the years following World War II developing countries faced two basic alternatives as they shaped their international trade policies to support their broader development objectives. One alternative, the outwardly-oriented strategy, sought to link the domestic economy to the world economy in order to foster industrialization. Regimes of this type generally offered only modest protection to domestic industries and imposed few controls on trade and foreign exchange. By contrast, the inwardly-oriented strategy sought to spur industrialization through policies that replaced imports with domestically produced manufactures. These regimes generally were characterized by high levels of protection for domestic manufacturing, direct controls on imports and investments, and overvalued exchange rates (World Bank 1987, 78–83).

The choice between these two strategies, while often not explicit, was shaped by assessments of both the nature of the international economic environment and the particular characteristics of individual economies (Little, 60–76). Many developing countries specialized in the production of agricultural and other primary commodities, which they exported in exchange for manufactured goods. Because of the widespread view in the 1940s and 1950s that world market prospects for the traditional exports of developing countries were dim, most developing countries' economic strategies focused on increasing the pace of industrial growth as the primary means of raising national income. For many that led to what came to be known as inwardly oriented or import substitution trade strategies.

The logic of import substitution was simple. If the prospects for traditional exports were limited, the foreign exchange available to import industrial goods would be limited, far less than necessary to satisfy the demand for the full range of industrial goods that could not be produced at home. It would thus be necessary to use the limited capability to earn foreign exchange to import the machinery and equipment required to produce a broad range of manufactured goods domestically. Thus the phrase import substitution: a strategy designed to develop the indigenous capacity to produce domestically the manufactured goods initially acquired through imports.

Import substitution regimes

The premises of the import substitution strategy dictated the character of government intervention in foreign trade. Above all, the prospect was for a shortage of foreign exchange. If the income elasticity of demand for traditional exports was low, rising incomes in the developed world could not be counted on to lead to rising demand for developing country exports. Moreover, technological innovations in developed countries were expected to reduce the demand for many raw materials, lowering the price the developing countries would receive for each unit of exports. On the other hand, the expectation was that demand would push up the prices of manufactured goods and the machinery and equipment used to produce them. Thus, the expectation was for a secular unfavorable shift in the terms of trade of developing countries.

The expectation of a persistent "shortage" of foreign exchange led to a panoply of policy instruments to conserve foreign exchange and to insure its allocation to priority uses. These included import licenses and quotas, to influence the structure of imports; import tariffs, to restrict the import of goods that could be produced at home; domestic content requirements for industrial products, to encourage the replacement of imported parts and components; and frequently public ownership of firms in critical industries, to provide even more direct government control.

These policies on the trade side were complemented and reinforced by exchange rate policy. First, various forms of exchange control were common. These generally required exporters to relinquish some or all of their foreign exchange earnings to an agency of the state, typically a specialized state-owned bank. Foreign exchange thus gathered could then be allocated by the government to priority imports. Second, the government established an overvalued exchange rate as a mechanism to provide imported machinery and equipment to priority industries at a relatively lower domestic currency cost than would otherwise be possible. Because world prices of these goods could be assumed to be given to the developing country, when these prices were converted to domestic currency at the overvalued exchange rate (i.e., too few units of domestic currency per unit of foreign currency), the internal domestic currency price of imports would be less than the levels that would prevail at a more realistic exchange rate.

That overvaluation of the domestic currency invariably turned the internal terms of trade against producers of agricultural goods, raw materials, and other traditional export goods. Again prices for most of these goods would be established in the world market. Because the magnitude of exports of an individual country would not influence the world price, the developing country would usually be a price taker. Because the establishment of an exchange rate that overvalued the domestic currency would reduce the domestic currency earnings received by exporters, they, in turn, would be able to sustain exports only if they were able to purchase these goods at a lower domestic price than would prevail at a more realistic exchange rate. Thus the domestic market prices of all export goods tended to fall, turning the internal terms of trade against this sector and thus lowering the real incomes of individuals producing export goods.

Although advocates of import substitution strategies were aware that an overvalued exchange rate would turn the internal terms of trade against producers of traditional exports, they did not regard this as a significant problem for three reasons. First, as already noted, they were pessimistic about the long-term prospects for the growth of traditional exports. They believed the income elasticity of demand for these products was low so rising incomes in the developed world would not increase the world market for these goods. Second, they did not believe that producers of traditional export goods, particularly agricultural goods, were very responsive to changes in relative domestic market prices. Declining relative farm prices, for example, would not necessarily lead to declining farm output because traditional peasants were believed not to be very responsive to price incentives (Little, 159–60).

Finally, advocates of import substitution strategies overwhelmingly represented the interests of urban elites. Policies that shifted the internal terms of trade against agriculture raised the relative real incomes of largely urban workers in manufacturing and other modern activities at the expense of the rural peasant class. Thus an antirural bias is one of the most salient characteristics of the import substitution development strategy.

The key features of the import substitution strategies adopted by many developing countries – a high degree of protectionism and an overvalued exchange rate – resulted in an inwardly-oriented development strategy in which trade and other incentives were biased in favor of production for the domestic market and against production for export. The bias against production for export arose because an overvalued exchange rate reduced the domestic currency earnings received by export producers and high tariffs increased the price of imported inputs and thus the cost of export goods that required such inputs.

Export promotion regimes

The alternative approach, an outwardly-oriented development strategy, is simply one in which trade and industrial policies are neutral and do not promote the production of goods for the domestic market at the expense of export goods or vice versa. Although the phrase export promotion strategy is sometimes used to describe this alternative, it obscures the key feature of the alternative regime which is to avoid discrimination either against or for exports.

Countries pursuing externally-oriented development strategies above all provide substantially lower protection of their domestic industries. Trade controls, such as quotas and import licensing arrangements, are minimal to nonexistent. Tariff rates are relatively low and their structure relatively uniform to avoid the distorting effects of highly variable rates of protection across sectors. Moreover, in the case of the most strongly outwardly-oriented strategies whatever modest import barriers do exist as a result of tariffs and controls are more or less counterbalanced by export incentives (World Bank 1987, 82). The exchange rate is maintained at a reasonable level, so that exporters are not penalized, and the exchange controls required due to excess demand for foreign exchange that arises in the case of an overvalued domestic currency can be largely avoided.

A wide range of empirical studies supports the view that more outwardly-oriented economies in the 1960s, 1970s, and 1980s achieved significantly higher rates of real growth of gross domestic product. These studies show that this was because more open economies achieved both higher rates of saving and investment as well as more efficient use of investment resources. These efficiencies arise from greater utilization of existing plants, economies of scale that are sometimes achieved when production is not for the domestic market alone, and from the stimulus that competitive pressures from abroad provides for technological change and management efficiencies (Feder, 51). It is important to recognize that these efficiencies stem not only from substantially higher marginal factor productivities in export than in nonexport-oriented industries. In addition, the export sector confers positive effects on productivity in the nonexport sector through externalities that include the development of more efficient management, improved production techniques, training of higher quality labor, and an improved supply of imported inputs and so forth (Feder, 60–1). In one estimate based on a sample of developing countries, the positive effect of increased exports on productivity in the nonexport sector contributed more to higher growth than did the shift of resources into the higher productivity export sector (Feder, 69–70).

Thus even on the more narrow criterion of industrial development, as opposed to more broadly based growth, the import substitution strategy did not succeed. By several measures more outwardly oriented economies not only grew more rapidly overall but also were more successful in industrialization. Their growth of manufacturing output (measured in value-added terms) was more rapid; their shares of manufacturing in gross domestic product expanded more rapidly and finished at a higher level; and both their manufacturing employment and their shares of labor employed in industry grew more rapidly than in the countries where inwardly-oriented development strategies prevailed (World Bank 1987, 83–8; Balassa 1989).

Finally, there is even evidence, although less conclusive, that countries following outwardly-oriented strategies achieved more equitable growth than countries following inwardly-oriented strategies. Put alternatively, the outwardly-oriented countries did not, on average, have to accept relatively inferior distributive outcomes to achieve higher rates of growth and more rapid industrialization (World Bank 1987, 85).

Although trade policy is only one of several influences on the dimensions of performance discussed above, there is a growing consensus that trade policies have a decisive influence both on the efficiency with which an economy employs its resources and on the distribution of income. Protection associated with inwardly-oriented regimes, by redistributing resources from more to less efficient sectors, imposed real efficiency costs which, in the aggregate, outweighed the benefits to the protected sector. Typically, as import substitution policies persisted and domestic production replaced an ever broader range of increasingly capital-intensive imported goods, incremental capital-output ratios for the economy as a whole rose more rapidly than one would have expected. This meant that an ever increasing rate of savings and investment was required to sustain growth at previous levels (Balassa 1989, 1,660; Krueger 1988, 359). Efficiency was further reduced because the distortions of the inwardly-oriented regime, such as an overvalued exchange rate, discouraged domestic producers from exporting. But without the export market, the scale of production was sometimes too small to reap advantages of scale economies, resulting in inefficient, high-cost production.

These sources of inefficiency reduced the real output of the economy and thus usually reduced savings and investment as well. Savings and investment were further discouraged under inwardly-oriented trade strategies. First, capital markets frequently were more distorted in countries pursuing import substitution policies. That often depressed real interest rates, discouraging savings. Second, the overvalued exchange rates common in these regimes discouraged foreign capital inflows in the form of direct investments (World Bank 1987, 91).

Even more serious, inwardly-oriented regimes appear to have discouraged innovation and thus productivity growth. Over time, this compounded the static inefficiency associated with import substitution. One major cause was that the high protection afforded by tariffs and other restrictive policies limited competition in the domestic market. Protection under import substitution regimes frequently increased the market power of domestic firms and sometimes converted domestic industries to monopolies. This increased static inefficiency, as these producers sought to increase their profits by cutting output and raising prices. Because these goods in turn were frequently used as inputs in the production of export goods, increased market power raised the domestic cost of goods produced for the export market, compounding the initial bias of the trade regime against exports. Moreover, increased market power in these industries discouraged innovations that would increase productivity over time.

The linkages between trade policy and income distribution were also criti-cal. Import substitution regimes, because they indirectly subsidized capital goods imports, encouraged more capital-intensive production, which meant lower levels of employment. Moreover, real wages tended to increase more rapidly in countries pursuing outwardly-oriented strategies where export growth tended to be more rapid (Balassa 1989, 1,679). Import substitution regimes also increased inequality because the import licenses and other instru-ments of trade control frequently generated economic rents that were cap-tured by favorably positioned urban elites. But, most importantly, import substitution regimes had a strong antirural bias that reduced agricultural incomes relative to those of urban wage earners. The overvalued exchange rate reduced the real return to producing and exporting traditional agricul-tural goods and other primary products. As a result, these developing coun-tries suffered sharp declines in their shares of world markets for these products (Balassa 1989, 1,669–70). That reduced the rate of growth of employment in rural areas, widening the gap between rural and urban incomes.

Given the accumulation over time of evidence of the advantages of an outwardly-oriented trade and development strategy, many developing coun-tries have sought to reform their trade regimes and to introduce more realistic exchange rates as well. These liberalizations, begun in the 1960s, generally were successful in enhancing economic growth and employment. However, given the varying initial conditions and the differences in specific liberaliza-tion measures pursued, there are, of course, varying interpretations of the precise mechanisms through which changes in trade regimes affected macroeconomic performance (Krueger 1988, 360).

Part of the difficulty in reaching a consensus on these causal linkages stems from the fundamentally different approaches taken to trade liberalization. Broadly speaking, there were two alternatives. The first was to move toward free trade by dismantling the import substitution policies initiated decades earlier. Obvious measures of that type include reducing or eliminating im-port tariffs and quotas, reducing the degree of overvaluation of the domestic currency, and dismantling other measures protecting domestic industries.

An alternative strategy was to initially leave most of the protective mea-sures in place but to add policies promoting exports to overcome, at least in part, the bias against exports that is characteristic of the import substitution regime. South Korea was one of the more notable examples of this latter approach to trade liberalization. A panoply of policies – export finance guarantees, preferential provision of infrastructure and utilities for export producers, export tax incentives, and so forth – was adopted in the 1960s to promote exports. The net effect of these policies was to provide increasing export incentives that amounted to almost a third the value of exports by 1971 (Bhattacharya and Linn, 79–80). Beginning in the mid-1970s, as elements of the import substitution regime were removed, export promotion measures were simultaneously reduced.

In practice, most states adopted some of both of these two approaches to trade liberalization. The balance is quite important because, with excessive export promotion, there is as much potential for resource misallocation from increased international sale of inappropriate exports as there is potential resource misallocation from import substitution policies (Bruton, 1,627).

The case of China

China is the largest developing economy to embark on a strategy of trade liberalization. And the results appear to be nothing short of spectacular. As reflected in Table 1.1, after languishing at about $4 billion in the 1960s and the early part of the 1970s, China's trade jumped sharply beginning in 1972 in China's initial turn toward the outside world. The latter was reflected in the historic trip of President Richard Nixon to China in 1972 and the ending of the U.S. trade embargo against China in the same year.

However, China's opening to the outside world in the early 1970s was motivated largely by geopolitical and strategic considerations not by economic factors. Relations with the West, particularly with the United States, were improved to enhance China's leverage vis-à-vis the Soviet Union not because there was a high-level political consensus that China should abandon its long-time policy of economic self-sufficiency. Thus the process of economic opening stalled out in 1974–7 when trade turnover remained on a plateau just under $15 billion. These were the years in which a radical resurgence in domestic Chinese politics fundamentally challenged the initial outward turn that had been largely orchestrated by Zhou Enlai. However, with the arrest of the leading Cultural Revolution radicals in the fall of 1976 and Deng Xiaoping's return to sustained political power by mid-1977, the ground was laid for the rapid growth of China's foreign trade in the decade of the 1980s. Between 1978 and 1990, the average annual pace of trade expansion was in excess of 15 percent, over three times the rate of growth of world trade.

Moreover, this trade acceleration was not heavily dependent on external

Table 1.1. *China's foreign trade, 1952–90 (billions of $)*

	Series A	Series B
1952	1.94	–
1957	3.11	–
1959	4.38	–
1960	3.81	–
1962	2.66	–
1965	4.25	–
1970	4.59	–
1971	4.84	–
1972	6.30	–
1973	11.00	–
1974	14.57	–
1975	14.75	–
1976	13.43	–
1977	14.80	–
1978	20.64	–
1979	29.33	–
1980	37.82	38.14
1981	40.38	44.03
1982	39.30	41.61
1983	40.73	43.62
1984	49.77	53.55
1985	60.25	69.60
1986	60.10	73.85
1987	68.11	82.65
1988	80.49	102.79
1989	82.58	111.68
1990	84.05	115.41

Notes: Dash means figure not available. Series A is compiled by the Ministry of Foreign Economic Relations and Trade and Series B is compiled by the General Customs Administration. The two series differ in coverage, valuation, and recording times. For example, customs data are generally more comprehensive reflecting all goods moving into or out of China, regardless of whether this leads to payments to, or the receipt of income from, foreign parties. The Ministry generally only records imports that lead to payments to foreigners or exports that generate foreign exchange income. Thus customs data include the value of goods imported into China by foreign embassies in China or exported from China to Chinese embassies abroad. Similarly, in export processing, customs data record the full value of imported raw materials and parts and the full value of exports. Ministry data, in principle, record only the value added in export processing activities, as reflected by the labor costs of the exported finished goods. Similarly, the Ministry would not record the value of machinery brought into China under a compensation trade contract. Nor would it record the value of the export goods produced using the machinery when such exports were the form of payment for imported machinery, as in compensation trade contracts. On the other hand, the value of such machinery and the value of the related exported products would be reflected in the customs data on imports and exports, respectively. Customs data are recorded when the goods clear cus-

borrowing. China's current account was in deficit in 1978–81, 1985–6, and 1988–9.[2] The surpluses in other years were far from sufficient to carry China through the deficits. But the deficits were readily financed largely by official bilateral credits, loans from international organizations, commercial borrowing, and direct foreign investment. At mid-1990, China's external debt (excluding short-term credits) stood at $45.4 billion whereas foreign exchange reserves were in excess of $23 billion (China Daily News). China's ratio of debt to exports stood at less than one, a comfortable ratio by international standards and far far below the ratios of 3:1 or more prevailing in the severely indebted countries either of Latin America or of Eastern Europe.

Hungary and Poland, for example, borrowed heavily in the early 1970s as they sought to upgrade their manufacturing technology in order to increase their trade with the capitalist world. This strategy failed. Their exports to developed market economies stagnated through most of the 1980s. Their technological lag behind Western economies continued to widen and their exports actually lost market share as they came under increasing competitive pressure from the exports of the newly industrialized economies of East Asia (Poznanski). Moreover, at the end of the 1980s they were saddled with external debts of roughly $15 billion and $34 billion, respectively (World Bank 1990b, 219). These comparisons understate China's relatively favorable position because the other countries just mentioned had foreign exchange reserves that were negligible, whereas China's reserves were equivalent to about five months of imports. In short, the vast majority of China's increased imports during the decade were paid for with earnings from increased exports of goods and services.[3]

During this decade of rapid trade growth, China's role in the world economy grew significantly. In the latter half of the 1970s, thirty or more other countries regularly exported more goods onto world markets than China. China shot up to become the sixteenth largest exporting country in the world by 1987 and the thirteenth largest by 1989.[4] That means that the only countries exporting more than China were Japan, most of the advanced industrial economies of North America and Western Europe, South Korea, and Tai-

Notes to Table 1.1. *(cont.)*
toms. The Ministry records exports on the shipping date listed on the export shipping document and imports on the arrival date listed in the notice of arrival provided by the firm transporting the goods. For more detail see Jia Huaijin (1988, 51–6) and Clarke (1987, 15–16).
Sources: Series A: Ministry of Foreign Economic Relations and Trade (1989, 353); Yao Jianguo (1990, 43); "News in Brief" (1991, 43).
Series B: State Statistical Bureau (1989a, 633; 1990b, 641; 1991, 4).

Table 1.2. *China's foreign trade and economic output, 1952–89 (average annual rate of growth in percent)*

	National income (1)	Trade (2)
1952–77	5.7	8.5
1978–89	8.7	13.3

Note: National income is measured according to the net material product concept, which omits portions of the service sector. The growth rate of national income is calculated in terms of comparable prices, which is the methodology used by the State Statistical Bureau to remove the influence of changes in the price level on the level of output. The growth rate of foreign trade is calculated based on data reported in current prices. The Chinese have published data on the prices of imports and exports since 1978 that allow one to calculate the growth of trade, measured in constant prices, during the 1980s. However, such data have not been published for the prereform period.
Sources: Column 1 – State Statistical Bureau (1984, 30; 1990a, 7).
Column 2 – Calculated from date in Table 1.1, Series A.

wan. During the decade, China's exports surpassed those of several industrial market economies such as Australia, Spain, Finland, Norway, and Denmark as well as several upper middle-income developing countries such as those of Brazil, Mexico, South Africa, Singapore, and Hong Kong.

China's outward turn was successful not simply in terms of the sustained growth of foreign trade. Like other liberalizing import substitution regimes, expanded foreign trade led to, or at least coincided with, a spectacular increase in the growth of China's economy. As reflected in Table 1.2, in the first decade or so of economic reform, the growth rate of national income in China increased by more than half. Indeed, according to figures compiled by the World Bank, China's economy was the fastest growing economy in the world. At the same time the rate of growth of China's foreign trade also accelerated by just over half.

This book examines the nature of the relationship between China's turn outward and improved macroeconomic performance in the decade of the 1980s. Chapter 2 examines the prereform foreign trade system. It shows that China's traditional foreign trade system, borrowed in large part from the Soviet Union, has many points of similarity with the import substitution trade regime sketched above. Chapter 3 provides a detailed examination of the reforms of the foreign trade and exchange rate systems adopted in the first decade of reform. Chapter 4 analyzes the economic consequences of the expansion of trade in the semireformed economic system of the 1980s. Chapter 5 evaluates the extent to which the foreign trade reforms contributed to the growth acceleration evident in the decade of the 1980s and explains why further reform of China's foreign trade system is constrained by the lagging pace of reform of the domestic economy.

Although foreign direct investment in China is discussed briefly at several points, the focus of this volume is on foreign trade and the relationship between trade and foreign exchange control reform, on the one hand, and the reform of the domestic economy, on the other. This is not because I believe that foreign direct investment has not contributed significantly to the acceleration of economic growth and the improvement of the levels of production technology in several important branches of Chinese industry. It clearly has. However, the lesson from the experience of other developing countries of East and Southeast Asia is that substantial flows of foreign direct investment are neither a sufficient nor a necessary condition for successful foreign trade liberalization and rapid modernization. Direct foreign investment in South Korea, for example, has been severely restricted. Yet its trade policy reform and liberalization are judged to be among the most successful and its aggregate economic performance compares extremely well with other economies in the region. Malaysia and Indonesia have been much more open to and have attracted relatively large amounts of direct foreign investment. But their growth rates have lagged well behind that of South Korea. Most importantly, the East Asian experience suggests that the contribution of foreign direct investment to domestic economic development is greatest if it takes place in an economy with an outwardly-oriented trade regime (Bhattacharya and Linn, 118).

Finally, it is particularly important in analyzing the reforms of centrally planned economies to focus initially on the reforms of the trade regime and the domestic economy rather than on foreign direct investment. Foreign direct investment may be seen simply as a means of obtaining foreign technology and capital to revive a socialist country's flagging economic performance. It could thus become, as it may have in the Soviet Union, a substitute for reform rather than part of a far-reaching program of foreign trade and domestic market liberalization (Ericson, 325).

2

The prereform foreign trade system

China's prereform foreign trade regime, which was borrowed from the Soviet Union in the 1950s, should be regarded as an extreme example of import substitution. This is evident in official policy statements, the organization of foreign trade, the domestic pricing of traded goods, the role of the exchange rate, the system of centralized control of foreign exchange, and in the pattern of imports and exports. The Minister of Foreign Trade summed it up in 1955 when he said "Export is for import and import is for the country's socialist industrialization" (Ye Jizhuang in Mah 1968, 672). The director of the Ministry's Import Bureau was even more specific, stating in 1955 that "the purpose of importing more industrial equipment from the Soviet Union is to lay the foundation of China's industrial independence, so that in the future China can produce all of the producer goods it needs and will not have to rely on imports from the outside" (Zhang Huadong in Mah 1968, 672–3). Seldom has an import substitution strategy been set forth so explicitly.

Organization of foreign trade

The organization of foreign trade reflected the import substitution regime adopted in the 1950s. Foreign trade was heavily controlled by the state even in the early 1950s, because the communist regime took over the foreign trade corporations, which had played a significant role in China's foreign trade under the Nationalist Party. By 1956, with the nationalization of the few remaining nonstate firms engaged in trade, international trade became a complete monopoly of the central government. The Ministry of Foreign Trade, created in 1952 when it was split off from the Ministry of Trade[1], was the executive department responsible for China's foreign trade and economic relations, including technical cooperation with other countries.[2] The Ministry exercised control of foreign trade through a number of corporations that specialized in trade in defined product areas. As early as March 1950, less

16

than six months after the creation of the People's Republic of China, six specialized foreign trade corporations were established – five for export goods and one for imports. By the mid-1950s the number had increased to sixteen. The number rose and fell over the ensuing more than two decades prior to the reform beginning in the late 1970s. But the range was narrow, from ten to around sixteen (Donnithorne, 325).

Foreign trade corporations were responsible for implementing the state's foreign trade plan. The annual foreign trade plan was an integral part of the economic planning process. The Chinese adopted the method of material balances from the Soviet Union to coordinate the flow of raw materials and intermediate goods among enterprises and to insure that production of each good was sufficient to meet interindustry demands and final demand for consumption, investment, and export.[3]

Foreign trade was one of the key factors in the iterative process of drawing up a consistent materials balance. Typically the planned demand for some products initially exceeded domestic production capability. In a centrally planned economy such as China's in the 1950s, in which emphasis was placed on the development of heavy industry rather than consumer goods, excess demand was common for machinery, equipment, and industrial raw materials and intermediate goods such as steel products. Rather than reduce the final demand for these goods, which in most cases would have meant scaling back the level of investment, planners sought to use imports to increase available supplies. Exports sufficient to pay for these imports (at anticipated world market prices for both exports and imports) were then identified. Goods for which domestic supplies exceeded planned demands were the most obvious potential exports. But if these were not sufficient to finance planned imports further iterative adjustments were undertaken. Because of the reluctance to reduce investment these adjustments usually took the form of cutting back planned final consumption (not investment) to free up more goods for export.

Once the iterative balancing process was completed the lists of import and export commodities were assigned to specific foreign trade corporations. That assignment was facilitated by the emergence by the mid-1950s of a structure of foreign trade corporations that generally paralleled China's industrial production ministries. For example, the China National Chemicals Import and Export Corporation handled goods produced by the Ministry of Chemical Industry; the China National Textiles Import and Export Corporation handled goods produced by the Ministry of Textile Industry, and so forth.

Several points should be noted about foreign trade in this material balance process. First, the purpose of imports was primarily to overcome bottlenecks due to limited domestic production capability. Exports were perceived mainly, if not exclusively, as a means of financing imports. At the firm level, export activities were not the result of decentralized profit maximizing behavior by producers who found higher returns from international than domestic market sales. At the macro-level planners did not envisage international demand for specific products as a potential source of growth of output of that sector nor did they consider rising production for export in the aggregate as a potential engine of growth for the economy as a whole.

The second characteristic of material balance planning was that it led to a plan that, at best, was consistent. Consistency meant that the planned supplies of each good included in the balance were equal to planned demands, both intermediate and final. For traded commodities it meant that the exports and imports, measured at anticipated international prices, were in balance except to the extent that available international trade credits and other capital inflows as well as foreign remittances and other service income allowed a merchandise trade deficit. But planners had no mechanism to assure that any particular level of imports was acquired efficiently. A comparison of the real domestic resource cost of alternative bundles of exports could be based on their costs if those cost measures were based on market determined prices reflecting real economic scarcities or opportunity costs. Alternatively, planners could use shadow prices, which reflect social costs and benefits, to evaluate alternative mixes of export goods. However, as discussed in the next section of this chapter, Chinese prices were fixed by the state and bore no necessary relationship to real economic scarcities. And there is no evidence that Chinese planners in the prereform period used either shadow prices or world market prices to evaluate systematically the real cost of alternative exports. Thus, there was no way of knowing whether export earnings sufficient to purchase the planned imports might have been achieved at a lower real resource cost. In short, there was no mechanism to assure that the goods exported exploited China's comparative advantage in the sense that they were goods for which the relative production cost in China was less than it was abroad. As discussed below in this chapter (see *Commodity composition of foreign trade*), the situation actually seemed to have worsened by the 1960s, because export decisions increasingly were made taking distorted domestic prices into account.

Third, in practice planned export supplies were not always assured to the foreign trade corporations so that they had to scramble to locate goods to meet their export quotas, a process that further diminished the relevance of economic costs in determining the pattern of exports. There were several reasons for this. In the first instance material balance planning was of limited scope. At most, only a few hundred commodities were balanced centrally in China compared to several thousand, for example, in the Soviet Union (Naughton 1988a, 181). Moreover, even for the sectors of the economy included within the plan, the degree of aggregation within individual balances was fairly high. For example, a single balance might be drawn for the textile industry as a whole. It would specify the quantities of inputs such as raw cotton, chemical fibers, electricity, and so forth that would be supplied to the industry. And it would establish an aggregate output target and further allocate this output among alternative final uses, in this case consumption, export, or additions to inventories. However, the precise commodities to be exported were determined through further discussion and negotiation between the China National Textiles Import and Export Corporation and the Ministry of Textile Industry whose firms produced the goods. Even if they had had some knowledge of real economic as opposed to financial costs of various textile products, central planners had little if any opportunity at that stage to influence the selection of export goods. In addition, unexpected production shortfalls during the year could reduce the availability of goods for export. In principle, priority was to be given to export commodities, meaning that domestic consumption would be cut when production fell below the planned target. But in practice the foreign trade corporations frequently were not able to purchase the planned quantity of export goods (Mah 1968, 680). Because of pressure to fulfill their export quotas, foreign trade corporations sometimes would be forced to acquire higher cost goods not included in the original export plan, which could be sold on international markets only at a loss.

Pricing of traded goods

As the description above indicates, the system of foreign trade planning provided little room for prices to serve their allocative and incentive functions, particularly on the export side. Foreign trade corporations purchased goods prespecified by the plan from domestic producers at officially established prices, either ex-factory prices in the case of manufactured goods or procurement prices in the case of agricultural goods. Thus producers received the same price for a good whether it was sold domestically or in the international market.[4] Moreover, producers received none of the foreign exchange income from the sale of the goods abroad nor did they have any indirect claim on that foreign exchange to purchase goods abroad for their own use. Under these circumstances producers had little incentive either to sell on the international market or to expand production of goods for which there was strong international demand.

These problems were compounded by the virtually complete separation, by the mid-1950s, between domestic and world market prices. The so-called socialist transformation of private industry and commerce, completed in 1955, substantially curtailed the role of supply and demand in determining the prices of a broad range of goods and services (Perkins, 110). In place of the market, which had determined prices of most industrial goods in the early 1950s, the state began to fix the prices of thousands of individual commodities.

From the outset the government set prices with a variety of objectives, of which accurately reflecting real opportunity costs of alternative goods was secondary, at best. Moreover, even if prices initially bore some relation to underlying scarcities, this would have been eroded over time because Chinese prices remained fixed, sometimes for decades. Because prices in international markets continued to respond to changes in supply and demand, China's price structure appears to have diverged increasingly over time from world prices. Indeed one of the objectives of China's price fixing was to insulate China from the influence of price fluctuations in the world market (Ye Jizhuang, 92). That separation of Chinese domestic prices from international prices is one of the reasons that the World Bank (1985, 97) characterized China's pre-1978 foreign trade organization as an "airlock system."

The separation of domestic and world prices gave rise to a concern that is unknown in open, market-oriented economies – the foreign trade balance measured in domestic currency. In an open economy, if trade is balanced when measured at international prices there will be no imbalance when the trade is measured in domestic currency. However, when domestic prices diverge from international prices it is possible that a country whose international trade is in balance (i.e. the value of exports equals the value of imports, both measured at international prices) could experience either a surplus or a deficit measured in terms of domestic currency. As discussed below in this chapter and again in Chapter 3, reforms of China's foreign trade system frequently have been stimulated by the occurrence of domestic currency losses on foreign trade.

The pricing of imported goods sold on the domestic market was more complex than export pricing and changed more over time, even prior to the reforms of the foreign trade system initiated in the late 1970s. But import pricing policies generally reflected the import substitution character of the trade regime. That was apparent particularly in the 1950s and early 1960s when imported producer goods were made available to domestic users at relatively low prices. From 1953 through 1963 the domestic prices of almost all imported machinery, equipment, industrial raw materials and intermediate goods such as steel were determined by converting the import price valued in foreign exchange, including cost, insurance, and freight (CIF) to renminbi using the official exchange rate (Ye Jizhuang, 92–3; Wang and Qiao, 195).* Frequently the foreign trade corporation handling the import charged a commission of 2 to 3 percent that covered their own costs of handling the transaction (Ye Jizhuang, 93). However, as will be established later in this chapter, the official exchange rate significantly overvalued the renminbi (i.e. too few yuan were needed to purchase a unit of foreign currency). That caused the domestic prices of these imported goods to be substantially lower than they would have been at an equilibrium exchange rate. Thus the users of imported machinery, equipment, and industrial raw materials received implicit subsidies.

The domestic prices of a much smaller portion of imported goods were established with reference to the prices of comparable domestic products. In most cases that meant that the lower world price was marked up to the price of similar domestic goods, providing protection for domestic production. For a few goods that were sold at subsidized prices the sale of imports was also subsidized.

The overvaluation of the domestic currency, which made imported steel, machinery, and equipment, and so forth cheaper on the domestic market than would have been the case with an equilibrium exchange rate, became more problematic by the 1960s for two reasons. First, by the mid-1960s, the gross value of output produced by China's own machinery industry had expanded more than twenty-fold compared to 1952.[5] The rate of growth of this sector, more than 25 percent per annum, was well above the pace of expansion of industry as a whole, reflecting the priority the planners assigned to machine tools. The machine tool industry had improved qualitatively as well because a broad range of new models incorporating multiple spindles, numerical controls, and other advanced techniques were available by the mid-1960s (Rawski, 65–6). Similarly, domestic steel production, only 1.35 million tons in 1957, reached 7.62 million tons in 1963 and the range and variety of domestic steel products was much broader. By the mid-1960s, for example, China's steel industry was producing many kinds of high-grade alloy steels resistant to corrosion, high temperature, and pressure (Clark, 81). As a result of these quantitative and qualitative developments in Chinese industry, imports and domestic goods were increasingly in competition.

*China's currency is the renminbi. The unit of account is the yuan.

Underpricing of imports was "influencing the development of domestic industry" as Chinese firms competed to purchase cheap imports (Wang and Qiao, 195).

Second, beginning in the late 1950s and continuing in the early 1960s the foreign trade corporations under the Ministry of Foreign Trade for the first time incurred financial losses, measured in domestic currency, on their trade transactions (Xiang Yin, 15). Their renminbi earnings from the sale of imports on the domestic market no longer covered the costs of purchasing goods from domestic producers for export.

Beginning in 1964 the state substantially changed the domestic pricing of imported goods in order both to protect domestic producers and to alleviate the domestic financial losses being incurred on external transactions. The State Council stipulated that most imported goods should be sold at prices comparable to similar domestic goods with "appropriate" adjustment either upward or downward to reflect differences in quality (State Council 1963).[6] From 1964 through 1980, 80 percent of all China's imports were priced on this principle.

When either there was no similar domestically produced good or the volume of domestic production was very limited, imports continued to be priced on the basis of import cost.[7] Whole plant imports as well as machinery and electronic equipment were the principal imports priced on this basis beginning in 1964 (Contemporary China Series Editorial Board, 226). The import price on a CIF basis was converted to domestic currency. Tariffs, appropriate industrial and commercial taxes, and import fees then were added to determine the domestic price. But conversion from the CIF to the domestic price no longer occurred at the official exchange rate but at a rate that was a specified premium over the official rate. Under the provisions of the State Price Commission's regulation, the premium was to be set in part to increase earnings from the domestic sale of imports by an amount sufficient to cover the domestic currency losses incurred on exports (Contemporary China Series Editorial Board, 226). The premium over the official rate initially was 103 percent. That meant the international price in dollars was converted to yuan not at the then prevailing official rate of 2.46 but at 5 yuan per dollar (= 2.46 × 2.03).[8] That premium lasted until 1975 when it was reduced to 60 percent for two years (State Council 1975, 75). Then in 1977 the State Council raised the rate to 80 percent where it remained through 1980 (Hu Changnuan, 502–3).

The introduction in 1964 of the practice of converting the import cost to domestic currency at a premium over the official exchange rate effectively devalued the yuan for roughly one fifth of China's imports. That meant prices paid by domestic users of these goods roughly doubled, substantially increasing the protection afforded to China's rapidly emerging producer goods sector, particularly machinery and other equipment.

Interestingly, all goods imported by the military were exempt from paying the premium and continued to be priced by converting the CIF price to renminbi at the official exchange rate with no added premium. For example, the Chinese navy was exempt from paying higher prices for its imports, ranging from petroleum to refined sugar (State Price Commission 1964a, 68). This appears to be the beginning of a pattern of providing preferred treatment to China's entire military system (zhunshi xitong) in all of their import and export transactions. As is noted in Chapter 3, these preferences expanded further in the 1980s.

Effectively doubling the domestic currency prices for imports for which there was no similar domestic good and increasing the domestic currency prices for a broader range of goods by lesser proportions raised substantial additional domestic resources for the foreign trade corporations (Wang and Qiao, 195). In 1964, the first year the new pricing methods were used, financial losses on external transactions fell by 500 million yuan and by 1966 foreign trade was again profitable. However, when the premium was reduced to 60 percent in 1975 the foreign trade sector again moved into the red, a situation that was resolved by raising the premium to 80 percent in 1977 (Xiang Yin, 18).

An alternative approach to dealing with domestic currency losses would have been to devalue the yuan explicitly by changing the official exchange rate and to have continued to price most imports based on import cost. Converting the price of imported goods to domestic currency at a higher number of yuan per dollar would have increased the domestic revenues of the foreign trade corporations by an amount sufficient to compensate for the higher price they would pay the Bank of China to purchase the dollars to use to buy goods internationally. But they would increase their profits on exporting because their domestic costs of procuring goods for export would be unchanged, while their export earnings in dollars would be converted to yuan at a more favorable (i.e. higher) rate. But according to Xue Muqiao (1986, 5), who had served as Director of the State Statistical Bureau in the 1950s and was the Director of the State Price Commission in 1963, the People's Bank of China would not agree to a devaluation. They apparently subscribed to the traditional view of central bankers that devaluation entails a loss of national prestige and may contribute to domestic price inflation. Changing the procedures for import pricing was adopted as a second best solution for reducing the domestic currency deficit of the foreign trade system.

The net result of the changes in the pricing of imports initiated in 1964 was to reduce the role of relative prices in resource allocation and to increase substantially the degree of protection offered to China's domestic industry, particularly the machinery sector. For roughly 80 percent of all imports the foreign price became irrelevant to the domestic end user in China because the goods were priced with reference to the price of similar domestic goods. That was a sharp departure from the period 1953–63 when changes in foreign prices were transmitted to domestic users in China through price conversion at the official exchange rate. The degree of protection of domestic industry rose, however, because foreign goods with relatively low production costs and thus relatively low prices were less able to compete with domestic goods because their prices were marked up to at least the price level of Chinese producers. And the pricing of imported goods for which domestic production volume was small or nonexistent at a 103 percent premium over the official exchange rate provide substantially increased protection for both existing and potential Chinese producers of import goods. Protection of domestic industry was an explicit goal of the import pricing reform (Wang and Qiao, 195).

Chinese policy of initially low but then rising protection of producer goods was similar to other developing countries pursuing import substitution trade strategies. They frequently provide little protection against imported capital goods until after they have largely exhausted the import substitution possibilities in consumer durables. But in China the switch came sooner both because the initial period of industrialization in the 1950s was so rapid and because consumer durables were a relatively low priority.

Role of the exchange rate and exchange control

Just as international prices had only the most modest influence on Chinese decisions on individual import and export commodities, there was little role for the price of foreign exchange to influence the volume of either imports or exports in the prereform era. Thus, as in other centrally planned economies, the exchange rate was a largely passive instrument in the formulation of trade policy (van Brabant, 5). However, as seen above, it played a major role in subsidizing certain categories of imported goods, at least through 1963. The official exchange rate was fixed at 2.46 yuan per U.S. dollar in 1955 and remained virtually unchanged for almost two decades (see Appendix A). The yuan was highly overvalued (i.e. the domestic currency price of foreign exchange was far too low) so that in the 1950s exports, particularly manufactured goods, were usually sold at a financial loss (Ye Jizhuang, 92). That

Table 2.1. *Financial losses on China's Exports*

Year	Domestic currency cost of earning $1 in export sales (yuan) (1)	Exchange rate (yuan/$) (2)	Losses per $1 exports (yuan) (3)
1952	3.08	2.26	.82
1962	6.65	2.46	4.19
1963	>5	2.46	>2.54
1971	ca.5	2.46	ca.2.54
1975	3	1.85	1.15
1978	2.5	1.68	.82
1979	2.4	1.55	.85
1981	2.31	2.80	(.49)
1982	2.66	2.80	(.14)
1983	3.02	2.80	.22
1984	2.79	2.33	.46
1985	3.67	2.94	.73
1986	3.9 (August)	3.45	.45
1987	4.20	3.72	.48
1988	5.80	3.72	2.08

Notes: Except where noted the data in column 1 are annual averages. Except in 1981–3 the exchange rate is the average official exchange rate prevailing during each year. For 1981, 1982, and 1983 the rate is the internal settlement rate, a rate applied to all trade transactions.
Sources: Column 1 – 1952, 1962, 1971, 1978, 1981, 1982, and *1985:* Wu and Chen (1989, 15–16, 32, 36, 49, 71, 75, 180).
1963, 1975: Hu Changnuan (1982, 502).
1979: Compiliation Group (1982, 177); Yu Xingfa (1982, 51).
1983, 1984: Ren Long (1988, 22).
1986: Jing Ji (1987, 38).
1987: Li Lanqing (1988b, 5).
1988: Jiao Wuliang and Zhou Zhuangen (1989, 59).
Column 2 – Appendix A.
Column 3 – Column 1 minus column 2.

meant that when the dollar earnings from the sale of exports were converted into yuan at the official rate they were less than the domestic price the foreign trade corporation originally paid the producer for the goods. A few financially profitable agricultural exports, such as soybeans, peanut oil, and frozen pork, have been identified in the literature, but in the aggregate exports were money losers when the results were measured in domestic currency (Donnithorne, 327).

The overvaluation of the domestic currency is borne out in Table 2.1, which provides data on the domestic currency cost of earning foreign exchange. In 1952, when the average exchange rate was 2.26, the average cost of earning one U.S. dollar in foreign exchange was 3.08 yuan, exceeding the exchange rate by over a third. By the early 1960s, the degree of overvaluation appears to have increased substantially. The average cost of earning one U.S. dollar was 6.65 yuan, a premium of 170 percent over the official rate of 2.46.

As discussed in the previous section of this chapter, up until 1964 a large quantity of imported machinery and equipment was sold at a price determined by converting the foreign exchange cost to yuan via the official exchange rate, with the addition of a small commission in many cases to cover direct importing costs of the foreign trade corporations. Although this practice would appear to leave no room for domestic currency profits the Minister of Foreign Trade stated that import transactions in the 1950s were generally profitable (Ye Jizhuang, 92). That was because high profits were made on the portion of import goods for which prices were set on the basis of a markup over the price of similar domestic goods. The markup was to protect the domestic industry and to generate revenue to cover domestic currency losses on exports (Ye Jizhuang, 93).

As long as the foreign trade sector as a whole generated financial profits, the profits and losses on individual commodities had little short-run effect on the pattern of trade, which was determined by the planning process described in the first section of this chapter. The losses, which were common on export products, had little or no influence on the financial status of the firms producing the loss-making exports (Hu Changnuan, 464–5). Similarly, profits had little direct effect on the pattern of imports. The individual trade corporations too, frequently were not sensitive to the profits or losses of individual traded commodities. Because many corporations handled both imports and exports within a given sector of industry, profits on imported goods could be used to offset losses on the exports, a method referred to as "taking imports to subsidize exports" (yi jin tie chu) (Wu and Chen, 16). If an individual foreign trade corporation sustained a net loss, the Ministry of Foreign Trade simply reallocated financial profits from another money-making corporation. This usually was feasible because in the prereform period the foreign trade system as a whole was profitable. Between 1953 and 1980, in addition to generating 29.8 billion yuan in customs duties, the foreign trade system cumulated a domestic currency profit of 16.3 billion yuan (Hu Changnuan, 496). These profits, as well as the customs revenues, routinely were handed over to the state treasury and included in government receipts.[9]

This basic system of cross subsidies within the system of foreign trade corporations seems to have changed little in the decades prior to reform.

Export losses were common in the mid-1950s, when the exchange rate of 2.46 yuan per dollar was established, and widened significantly in the early 1960s. As shown in Table 2.1, the cost of earning a dollar in foreign markets in 1962 reached a peak of 6.65 yuan. Because the exchange rate was still 2.46 the foreign trade corporations lost over four yuan for every dollar's worth of international sales. These financial losses on exports continued after the early 1960s, because the cost of earning foreign exchange remained consistently around 5 yuan and the exchange rate remained unchanged (Wu and Chen, 48–9). By 1975 the situation was not quite so extreme because the relative stability of prices in China after the early 1960s compared to the rest of the world had reduced the domestic currency cost of earning a dollar in foreign markets to 3 yuan. However, by 1975 the official exchange rate had been revalued to well under 2 yuan per dollar. Thus export losses were reduced, but not by as much as would have been the case if the exchange rate had remained at 2.46.

As can be seen from Table 2.1, these trends continued right up to the beginning of the reform period. The domestic cost of earning foreign exchange continued to fall, the yuan was revalued further (i.e. fewer renminbi were needed to purchase a dollar of foreign exchange) and high losses on export sales persisted. In the years just prior to 1980, 70 percent of China's exports accrued financial losses (Zhou and Zhao, 46).

The overvaluation of the domestic currency and the system of cross subsidies within and among the foreign trade corporations had major implications for China's exchange regime. First, as in the case of most states pursuing a strategy of import substitution with an overvalued currency, China had to establish a stringent system of foreign exchange control. Both firms and individuals earning foreign exchange through export activities or otherwise owning foreign exchange would not willingly sell it at the undervalued price established by the government. Thus, Chinese law, as early as 1950, required that all foreign exchange holdings, including those of overseas Chinese, foreign travelers, and foreign embassies and missions, be deposited with the Bank of China, the sole bank authorized to deal in foreign exchange (Hsiao, 24). Withdrawal of these funds within China was possible only after converting the foreign exchange into domestic currency at the official exchange rate. On the buying side of the foreign exchange market, the overvaluation of the domestic currency (i.e. undervaluation of foreign exchange) assured excess demand for foreign exchange. The limited supply of foreign exchange was allocated bureaucratically by the Bank of China to priority uses established by the state through the economic planning process. Thus the Chinese domestic currency from the early 1950s was inconvertible.

Second, the system of extensive cross subsidies meant that China had a de facto multiple exchange rate system. The system in effect allowed the determination of the exchange rate on a product-by-product basis. There were three economic consequences of this system.

First, the changes in the official exchange rate had little effect on the trade balance. A devaluation would simply reduce losses on exports at the expense of reduced profits on imports. A revaluation would increase profits on imports at the expense of increased losses on exports. If trade were initially balanced a devaluation or a revaluation would simply redistribute financial profits and losses among different import and export products and thus among various individual foreign trade corporations. But, because the volumes of imports and exports were fixed by the plan, a change in the exchange rate would not affect the overall balance of trade.

Second, the exchange rate was relevant only for a few relatively small nontrade items in the balance of payments – earnings from tourism, remittances from overseas Chinese, expenditures for services, and so forth. Indeed, beginning in the 1950s, the Bank of China set the exchange rate at least in part on the basis of the relative domestic and world prices of consumer goods (Chen Jianliang, 18). In this respect China was similar to other centrally planned economies where trade flows were determined largely by plan but where the exchange rate was set with an eye on its influence on tourism expenditures, private remittances, and other nontrade expenditures (van Brabant, 9). Regular surveys of prices of consumer goods purchased by Chinese diplomats abroad and by overseas Chinese visiting their relatives in China were undertaken. These surveys revealed that a basket of consumer goods that cost the equivalent of a dollar abroad could be purchased in China for 1.43 yuan in 1952 and 1.92 yuan in 1962 (Wu and Chen, 16). The official exchange rate that was set appears to be some sort of compromise between the cost of earning foreign exchange in trade transactions on the one hand, and the purchasing power of the Chinese currency on the other. But the purchasing power measure was based on a relatively narrow range of commodities that was not representative of Chinese trade, which included few consumer goods, particularly on the import side. Thus, in 1952 the average official exchange rate of 2.26 yuan was far less than the 3.08 yuan cost of earning a dollar in international trade but far more than the 1.43 yuan cost of a dollar's worth of consumer goods.[10]

Third, the system is likely to lead to irrationalities in foreign trade that are greater than in conventional multiple rate systems. Multiple exchange rate systems, which were once quite common in Latin America, can take several forms. For example, one rate may apply to trade transactions and another to invisibles such as services and capital movements. Or one rate may apply to exports and another to imports. W. M. Corden (1971, 87–92) has pointed out that these conventional multiple exchange rate systems can be analyzed in terms of their protective effects. A system, for example, in which exporters receive 8 pesos per dollar while importers pay 12 pesos per dollar has the same effect as a system combining a uniform exchange rate of 8 pesos per dollar and a 50 percent duty on all imports. The only difference is that in the former arrangement the treasury would collect the tariff revenue whereas under the latter arrangement the central bank would receive the exchange profits. But in most multiple exchange rate systems, exporters would all receive the same exchange rate, although in some cases a more favorable rate may apply to certain "new" exports as opposed to "traditional" exports that would have effects similar to a unified export rate combined with a subsidy of "new" exports.

However, in the Chinese case virtually every product could have had a different exchange rate. In practice dozens, if not hundreds, of different rates applied to different categories of exports. The potential for inefficiency in such a system arises because products with widely varying domestic resource costs per unit of foreign exchange earnings may all be exported when widely varying exchange rates apply to different categories of exports. In short, widely varying commodity specific rates are not consistent with an effort to minimize the quantity of domestic resources required to earn foreign exchange and do not facilitate a more efficient allocation of resources through foreign trade (Mah 1971, 37).

Commodity composition of foreign trade

The pattern of international commodity flows also reflected China's import substitution development strategy. In the First Five-Year Plan this bias was especially strong. Imported producer goods, a category that includes machinery and equipment, industrial raw materials and intermediate goods such as steel, were critical to China's industrialization drive. Over 90 percent of all imports were producer goods, leaving less than 10 percent for consumer goods (State Statistical Bureau 1982, 354). This was a marked contrast with the precommunist era. In the first half of the twentieth century producer goods comprised a relatively small share of imports. The largest imports were typically cotton goods, cotton yarn, and raw cotton followed by grain, flour, sugar, and tobacco. The major producer goods categories of petroleum, transport equipment, chemicals, and metals totaled only 10–14 percent of total imports in the Teens, Twenties, and early Thirties. By 1936 they comprised about one third of all imports. Most important, machinery imports were only 2–3 percent and even in 1936 were only 6 percent of all imports (Feuerwerker, 124).[11]

Within the category of imported producer goods in the 1950s machinery and equipment was the single largest category, reflecting the importance of the 156 (later 166) key Soviet-aided complete plant projects that formed the core of the First Five-Year Plan. Those projects, which were concentrated in the ferrous metallurgy, machinery, and electric power industries, absorbed almost half of all industrial investment in the First Five-Year Plan. They were intended to make China self-sufficient in a broad range of industrial commodities.

The bias toward producer goods was even more apparent in the Great Leap Forward (1958–60). Total trade turnover rose sharply and the share of producer goods in Chinese imports hit a record in excess of 95 percent in both 1959 and 1960.

The share of producer goods in Chinese imports dropped significantly as food imports, particularly grain, rose sharply and China's total trade turnover plummeted in the early 1960s in the wake of China's disastrous Great Leap Forward. The share of consumer goods in total imports exceeded 40 percent in 1962, 1963, and 1964.

Yet the underlying strategy of import substitution changed little. Food imports were required to mitigate a massive famine (Lardy 1987, 378–86) and were scaled back as domestic grain production began to recover. The break with the Soviet Union in 1960 led to the withdrawal of Soviet technical advisors from China and a precipitous decline in Sino-Soviet trade. But as early as 1963 China initiated a new, although much smaller, program of complete plant imports, this time largely from Japan. These plants were for synthetic fiber and chemical fertilizers. China's imports of chemical fertilizer grew rapidly in the early 1960s, as part of a program to spur agricultural recovery following the debacle of the Great Leap Forward. The import of a urea factory from Japan was intended to reduce the need for imported fertilizer. Similarly, raw cotton imports soared in the early 1960s, in part because cultivated land in China had been shifted into grain production. Two synthetic fiber plants imported from Japan were intended to produce synthetic cloth that would substitute for the cloth made with imported cotton. This strategy was made feasible by the discovery, in the late 1950s, and exploitation, beginning in the early 1960s, of a vast oilfield at Daqing in the Songliao Basin in northeast China. This field would end China's dependence on imported petroleum and provide the petroleum feedstocks and petrochemical products necessary for urea and synthetic fiber production, respectively.

Thus, while there was a surge in imports of food, particularly grain and sugar, and other consumer goods in the early 1960s, the underlying strategy of import substitution adopted during the First Five-Year Plan changed relatively little right up to the eve of the reform period of the 1980s. The commitment to this strategy is evident in a sharp increase in the domestic supplies of producer goods as a share of total producer durable goods consumption. China relied on imports for more than 40 percent of all durables used in 1957. This figure dropped to 10 percent by 1965 and only 8 percent by 1973 (Rawski, 101).

The structure of Chinese exports, to a lesser degree, also reflected the character of China's domestic development strategy in the prereform era. As noted in Chapter 1, an import substitution strategy inevitably turns the domestic terms of trade against producers of traditional exports, frequently agricultural goods and raw materials, relative to producers of finished industrial goods. As discussed above, in the 1950s export planning in the short run in principle was carried out in physical terms with little regard to the financial profitability of specific transactions. However, in the 1960s the situation began to change. The underlying problem was that, as discussed above, foreign trade transactions in the early 1960s were no longer profitable, measured in terms of domestic currency. Thus the Ministry of Foreign Trade had to negotiate with the planners to receive direct financial subsidies through the government budget. However, the collapse of domestic economic production in the wake of the disastrous Great Leap Forward had left the state in a perilous financial condition. Per capita national income in China by 1962 had declined by one third from its peak in the 1950s, roughly comparable to the peak to trough fall in per capita gross national product in the United States during the first four years of the Depression (Lardy 1987, 395). Fiscal revenue proportionally fell even further and the government in the early 1960s struggled to bring large budgetary deficits of 1958–61 under control.

Thus in the early 1960s there was growing pressure to hold down financial losses on foreign trade transactions. Foreign trade corporations, to the extent they had flexibility, sought out export goods that would have financial profits if possible or at least relatively low losses. These pressures recurred and grew in intensity when the foreign trade system as a whole incurred losses measured in domestic currency as in 1975–6. And in 1980, when the foreign trade system again was in the red, foreign trade corporations "were not allowed without exception to export goods that incurred losses beyond 70 percent," implying they were prohibited from exporting or had to seek special approval to export commodities for which the loss rate exceeded 70 percent (Chen Jiaqin et al., 57).[12] These informal pressures and formal regulations would increase the overall financial profitability of foreign trade or, in some years, reduce the magnitude of domestic currency losses for which the Ministry of Foreign Trade would have to seek offsetting financial subsidies from the Ministry of Finance.

Thus over time planners and foreign trade corporations increasingly considered the domestic financial profitability of foreign trade transactions. There was a growing incentive to increase the exports of agricultural and other primary products that were relatively underpriced on the domestic market. There was a growing parallel incentive to reduce the exports of industrial goods that were relatively overpriced on the domestic market.

These financial pressures apparently did affect the commodity composition of China's trade, particularly exports. But judging how rapidly the structure of exports would have evolved under an alternative trade and domestic price regime is problematic at best. But some Chinese authors have argued that China's domestic price structure inappropriately encouraged exports of agricultural and primary products and discouraged exports of manufactured goods, resulting in a very slow increase over time in the share of total exports accounted for by finished industrial products (Feng, Li, and Zhou, 15; Zhou Xiaochuan 1987, 6).

The share of primary product exports in China's total exports did fall sharply from almost 80 percent in 1953 to 64 percent in 1957, and then 56 percent in 1965–6.[13] However, in the rest of the 1960s and throughout the 1970s the share of primary goods remained fairly constant at around 53 to 54 percent (Ministry of Foreign Economic Relations and Trade 1989, 361). That meant manufactured goods as a share of total exports were on a plateau even though manufactured goods output as a share of China's national income was rising rapidly.[14]

Economic consequences

The economic consequences for China of the import substitution strategy of the 1950s, 1960s, and 1970s were, in many respects, similar if not more extreme than those observed in other developing countries pursuing comparable strategies. Most obvious was the sharply rising incremental capital output ratio (ICOR). This measure, the ratio of gross investment to the absolute increase in output, is widely used as a rough and ready indicator of the efficiency of investment. This ratio normally rises during the process of economic development as the savings rate rises and capital deepening increases the capital stock per worker (Krueger 1988, 359). Thus, comparisons of incremental capital output ratios across countries at different levels of economic development are hardly an unambiguous indicator of relative efficiency.

What is striking, however, is how rapidly the incremental capital output ratio rose in China between the 1950s and the 1970s. Investment relative to national income rose from about one fourth in the 1950s to around one third in the 1970s. On the other hand, the rate of growth of output fell significantly from just over 8 percent in the 1950s to 6 percent in the 1970s (World Bank 1983, vol. 1, 273).

These data suggest that incremental capital output ratio rose by more than 80 percent, from 3.0 to 5.5 between the 1950s and the 1970s. The World Bank (1983, I, 88) judged that the increase was "unusually steep" particularly in light of the reduced share of investment in the 1970s, as compared to the 1950s, Chinese planners allocated to housing and other "nonproductive" investments that would not contribute directly to increased output.

In part, the decline in the incremental capital output ratio reflects a lengthening of the gestation period of the average investment project. That was a consequence of periodic campaigns that led to excessive investment. As more and more investment projects were undertaken, the average time required to complete each project lengthened, resulting in more and more assets being tied up in projects not contributing to final output. Because the rough and ready ratios of the type reported above do not take into account the lag between the time an investment is initiated and when the project begins to contribute to output, the rising ICOR may overstate the decline in underlying efficiency of assets that are actually contributing to final output. The delayed completion, in the 1980s, of many projects initiated in the 1970s may have contributed to the acceleration of economic growth in the 1980s, discussed in Chapter 1. If this were investigated and confirmed by new economic research it would imply that the World Bank overestimated the decline in the ICOR between the 1950s and the 1970s.

The possibility that the declining ICOR reflects a lengthening of the gestation period of the average investment project rather than a decline in the underlying efficiency of capital actually contributing to final output can be investigated by examining the ratio of incremental installed capital to output. That measure is not influenced by the lengthening gestation period of the average project and thus more accurately reflects the influence of import substitution and other policies on productivity. According to the World Bank (1983, vol. 1, 273) that ratio also rose sharply, about 60 percent, during the decades of the 1960s and 1970s compared to the 1950s.

A large part of the rise in the ICOR was due to the shift of domestic production into ever more capital-intensive sectors.[15] This process began in the 1950s with the program of complete plant imports from the Soviet Union. As discussed above, those investments were concentrated in ferrous metallurgy and machinery, both very capital-intensive sectors. But emphasis on capital-intensive sectors continued in the 1960s as Chinese industrial production emphasized more complex products within these sectors and the petro-chemical industry, also very capital-intensive, became a major contributor to industrial output in the 1960s and 1970s. The share of industrial output produced by less capital-intensive industries, such as textiles and other light industries, fell steadily for three decades. Like other countries that pursued import substitution strategies for sustained periods, the incremental capital output ratio rose steadily as domestic production shifted into ever more capital-intensive sectors.

The rising capital intensity of domestic production was basically the consequence of China's attempt to achieve self-sufficiency over an ever broader range of industrial products – the import substitution strategy. But it was no doubt compounded, beginning in the mid-1960s and continuing into the early 1970s, as Mao Zedong promoted what came to be called the third front strategy. That strategy called for the creation of a large self-sufficient industrial base in southwest and western China – remote regions to which the Chinese could withdraw in the event of a military invasion (Naughton 1988b, 351). The high capital intensity of this program was inevitable given its focus on steel, armaments, machinery, chemicals, and railroad development. But it was exacerbated by the decision to locate these new facilities in especially remote places in the deep interior of China. The capital costs of development in interior regions, even in well-chosen locations, were well above those of eastern and northeastern China. The selection of particularly remote sites increased the capital costs further because they lacked transport and other infrastructure. Poor project design and the haste with which these new industrial facilities were constructed further magnified the capital intensity of the third front (Naughton 1988b, 375–6).

One consequence of this rising capital intensity of production was that gains in per capita consumption were very modest for a country in which per capita output grew relatively rapidly. Between 1957 and 1977 per capita national income rose at an average annual compound rate of 3.4 percent in real terms. Yet, because the share of output that had to be reinvested to sustain that rate of growth rose by fully one third (from 25 percent in 1957 to an average of 33 percent in the 1970s), improvements in real living standards were quite modest. In large part that was because China's development policy was biased against agriculture for most of this period. The domestic terms of trade shifted against farm producers, as in other countries pursuing import substitution strategies. Partly as a result the growth of agricultural output averaged only 2.3 percent per annum between 1952 and 1978, barely keeping up with the expansion of the population (Lardy 1983, 3). Per capita consumption of basic food grains, edible vegetable oils, and cotton cloth all declined between 1957 and 1978. Moreover, the shift in the terms of trade against agricultural commodities had negative consequences for traditional agriculture exports. For example, production of soybeans recovered very slowly after World War II and it was not until well into the 1980s, when more reasonable agricultural policies were adopted, that China regained the volume of soybean exports it had achieved in the 1930s. Even then China's once dominant world market position had been lost to Brazil and other new producers that emerged in the decades in which antiagrarian polices held sway.

In another respect, the growth of employment in the modern sector, China's performance paralleled that of other countries pursuing import substitution strategies. Between the 1950s and the 1970s the growth of employment in the modern sector, particularly in state-owned manufacturing, was relatively modest given the rate of growth of output in manufacturing. The real value of output that was produced by state factories in 1978 was more than seven times that of 1957 but the workforce of these factories only quadrupled (State Statistical Bureau 1984, 195; State Statistical Bureau Social Statistics Office, 26).

To prevent widespread open urban unemployment, the state maintained a comparatively draconian policy on rural to urban migration during this period. Opportunities for rural residents to freely migrate on a permanent basis to urban centers were practically nonexistent. Rural residents were kept out of cities by regulations that comprised a catch 22 situation. Urban housing, virtually all state controlled, was available only to those classified as permanent urban residents and who held urban jobs.[16] The jobs, however, were open only to those who already were classified as permanent urban residents. Rural male heads of household frequently were able to find nominally temporary or contract jobs in urban areas, typically in construction. Even if the male's urban job was made formally permanent, his family generally was not able to follow him. That was because the conversion of the worker's household registration status from rural to permanent urban provided no right for his spouse or his children to permanent urban residence status or access to subsidized urban housing or subsidized staple foodstuffs. Their residence status followed that of their mother's (Potter, 481).[17]

Finally, the persistent shortage of foreign exchange in China paralleled that in other developing countries following an import substitution strategy.

That strategy was designed to alleviate the excess demand for foreign exchange by producing domestically an ever-growing share of goods that were once imported. That strategy anticipated that as domestic production displaced imports, the demand for foreign exchange would fall. What proponents of the strategy failed to anticipate was that the disincentives for exporting would reduce the supply of foreign exchange, i.e. the sale of domestic goods on international markets, so substantially relative to what otherwise would have been achieved that the demand–supply imbalance actually worsened. China was no exception. As a result, China's system of foreign exchange control in the 1970s was as stringent as when it was established in the early 1950s. It had not been possible to relax, even partially, the requirement that all earnings from the sale of goods on international markets be turned over to the Bank of China. And the Bank continued to act as the agent of the state in allocating foreign exchange to importers in accordance with the priorities established by the state plan. There was little opportunity for decentralized trading to emerge in that environment. As a result, the renminbi remained inconvertible and the national foreign trade corporations continued to exercise their monopolistic control of both imports and exports.

3

Reforming the foreign trade system

The traditional foreign trade system was entirely unsuited to the opening of the Chinese economy to the outside world and the new development strategy that began to emerge in the late 1970s. As early as 1975, after he had been named a vice-chairman of the party and first vice-premier, Deng Xiaoping took the lead in drafting three major party documents that, if formally adopted, would have launched China on a reform course as early as the mid-1970s (Harding, 49). Among other changes, Deng proposed a major transformation of China's foreign trade and investment policies.[1] Most important, Deng decisively rejected the Maoist policy, most obvious during the Cultural Revolution, of pursuing a course of technological and financial self-reliance. Deng believed accelerating the pace of industrial development would require the selective import of advanced technologies from abroad. This strategy had far-reaching implications for Chinese strategies for both exports and for international finance. The document Deng drafted unequivocally advocated a rapid acceleration of exports, concentrating on industrial and mining products. In contrast with the then prevailing Chinese practice of eschewing foreign credits, except for short-term trade finance, Deng advocated the utilization of both conventional long-term credits and long-term credits to be repaid by the export of coal and petroleum.

The Cultural Revolution radicals, who had engineered Deng's purge in the mid-1960s and opposed his rehabilitation in 1973, learned of the substance of his program (Lieberthal, 33–49). By the spring of 1976 Deng's opponents launched a formal campaign against him. Deng's views on trade policy quickly became a central issue (Fenwick). Deng fell from sight shortly after the death of Zhou Enlai, who had groomed him to be his successor as premier. Soon thereafter the party newspaper, *People's Daily*, marked a new stage in the campaign against Deng and others. In language reminiscent of the height of the Cultural Revolution, the party organ attacked the "unrepentant" power holders who "were taking the capitalist road" (Hsu 1990, 6).

Following a public demonstration simultaneously memorializing the death of Zhou Enlai and supporting Deng Xiaoping, the campaign against Deng reached its height and the Central Committee formally stripped Deng of all of his government, party, and army posts.

However, the arrest of Jiang Qing and the other members of the "gang of four" within a month of Mao's death in September 1976 set the stage for Deng's official political rehabilitation. By the spring of 1977 Deng's return to power was arranged, and in July the Central Committee restored the party, government, and army positions he had held in 1976. Although it would take several years for Deng to achieve complete success in stripping his rival Hua Guofeng of his position as premier and Party Chairman, Deng and his supporters began to implement their reformist economic program almost immediately.

This was reflected in the promulgation by the State Council, China's highest executive organ, of a series of reforms of the traditional foreign trade system. Some – such as the law on joint ventures and the creation of special economic zones along China's southeast coast – were dramatic and captured the immediate attention of the outside world. Ultimately more important, however, were a series of domestic reforms which over the decade of the 1980s began to erode the bias against exports inherent in China's traditional trade policy and began to conform China's foreign trade system with standard international practices. These policy reforms included a decentralization of foreign trading authority, a reduction in the degree to which the official exchange rate overvalued the domestic currency and a reduction in direct import subsidies. The latter two measures tended to bring the price of imports more into line with their true economic cost. Devaluation, the rebate of various domestic taxes on exported goods, and a relaxation of the state's monopoly control over the allocation of foreign exchange reduced the bias against exports of the traditional foreign trade system.

The pace of foreign trade reform over the decade was highly uneven and frequently uncoordinated with other domestic economic reforms. In part this was inevitable given the lack of an overall economic reform blueprint. Reform, rather was incremental, frequently undertaken in response to pressure from lower levels of the administrative hierarchy rather than being designed and implemented unilaterally from the center. But initial reform steps only created pressures for further reform, frequently to alleviate unanticipated consequences of the initial measures. As traced in some detail in this chapter, this led to a highly incremental and perhaps paradoxically a very bureaucratized process of reform. More importantly, as is discussed in Chapter 4, the insufficient coordination with domestic reform meant that the economic benefits of China's vastly increased foreign trade were below their potential.

Decentralization of foreign trade authority

The central government, as one of its first steps to stimulate the growth of exports, decentralized the authority to engage in foreign trade transactions. In effect it relinquished the monopoly on foreign trade it had exercised, through its subordinate foreign trade corporations, since the mid-1950s. In 1979 a dozen national foreign trade corporations handled all foreign trade transactions. By the mid-1980s the Ministry of Foreign Economic Relations and Trade had approved the creation of 800 separate import and export corporations, each authorized to engage in international trade transactions within specified product ranges (Ministry of Foreign Economic Relations and Trade 1987). Only a few years later the number of trading companies had soared to more than 5,000 (Reporter 1990).

The new corporations were of several types. First, some national production ministries created their own foreign trade corporations, enabling them to bypass the national foreign trade corporations of the Ministry of Foreign Economic Relations and Trade. For example, in January 1980 the Ministry of Metallurgical Industry established its own foreign trade corporation, the China National Metallurgical Import and Export Corporation, enabling it to bypass the China National Metals and Minerals Import and Export Corporation (Minmetals), one of China's oldest and largest foreign trade corporations. Similarly, China's military production ministries established six new foreign trade corporations to handle the international sale of both military hardware and consumer durable goods turned out by the extensive network of enterprises under their control.

Second, provincial governments established hundreds of foreign trade corporations to handle trade in their regions. In some cases this was accomplished by converting existing provincial branches of national foreign trade corporations into local trading companies. For example, the thirty-eight local branches of China National Machinery Import and Export Corporation (Machimpex) became financially independent in 1988 and were placed under the authority of the provinces and large cities where they were located, ending the monopoly role of Machimpex in machinery trade. In other cases new corporations were formed. For example, Guangdong established the Guangdong Province Foreign Trade Corporation in July 1980. By the end of 1987 there were nearly 900 foreign trade enterprises in Guangdong province alone (Vogel 1989, 377).

Finally, in a few cases large enterprises set up their own trading companies. In principle this was possible for firms that supplied $3 million or more annually in export products. In practice it appears to have been far more limited, except in Guangdong where the provincial authorities approved direct international sales rights for some firms exporting as little as $1 million.

Although the proliferation of new corporations authorized to trade was impressive, the monopoly position of the national trade corporations of the Ministry of Foreign Economic Relations and Trade eroded slowly. In 1981 they handled 91 percent of exports and 87 percent of imports. Three years later their shares had dropped, but were still quite high – 79 percent for exports and 65 percent for imports (World Bank 1988a, 102–3). As discussed below in this chapter (see *Pricing of traded goods*), the initially slow pace of displacement of the national corporations appears to have been a consequence of insufficient economic incentives to undertake decentralized exports and a consequent shortage of foreign exchange to finance local imports.

Simultaneous with the decentralization of trading authority the State Council reduced the scope of the national foreign trade plan. Prior to the reforms of the 1980s all trade, in principle, was included in the national foreign trade plan. The export plan alone specified the quantities of some 3,000 individual commodities that were to be procured by the state for export (Sun Wenxiu, 53). The State Planning Commission, the highest planning authority, took the direct responsibility for 500 of these commodities while ministries and other state agencies were responsible for the remaining export commodities (Yang and Song, 31). The import plan was similarly comprehensive, covering more than 90 percent of Chinese imports. As discussed in Chapter 2, the handful of national foreign trade corporations were responsible for importing and exporting each of the goods specified in physical terms in the foreign trade plan.

In the decade of the 1980s, the State Council modified this traditional system in several ways. First, the scope of the national foreign trade plan was reduced successively in January 1982, September 1984, and February 1988 (Sun Wenxiu, 53–4). On the export side that led to a substantial diminution in the role of the plan in determining the pattern of exports. As early as January 1982 the number of planned export commodities fell to 199. It was further reduced to about 100 in 1984 and stood at 112 commodities by 1988. Of these 112 export commodities only twenty-one, comprising about 20 percent of the total quantity of exports, were directly under the control of the State Planning Commission (Yang and Song, 31). As a result, by 1988 the planned share of exports fell to 45 percent. Progress was even more rapid on the import side. In the same year only seventeen import commodities fell into the planned category (Sun Wenxiu, 54). The share of planned imports in China's total imports fell from more than 90 percent at the beginning of the decade to only 40 percent by 1988 (Working Party 1988, 21).

Second, the foreign trade plan was divided into mandatory and guidance plan components. As implied by the language, targets in the mandatory plan (zhilingxing jihua) were specified in physical terms and were orders of a legally compulsory nature. In most cases the responsibility for fulfilling command plan targets for exports and imports lay with the head offices of the national foreign trade corporations, although for some commodities this responsibility was shared with local import and export companies. By contrast, targets in the guidance plan (zhidaoxing jihua) were said to be noncompulsory and generally specified in value terms, providing local trading corporations, which are generally responsible for implementing these plans, with more flexibility in determining the precise mix of import and export products.

Third, the state promoted the use of the agency system (daili zhi) in foreign trade. That marked a significant departure from the traditionally prevailing arrangements. Under the agency system foreign trade corporations, both national and local, provided international trade services to enterprises producing goods for export or importing goods from abroad. But under the agency system domestic prices of both imported and exported commodities were linked to international prices via the exchange rate. Thus the most critical component of the traditional "airlock system" was eliminated. Moreover, the enterprises themselves, rather than the foreign trade corporations, bore the responsibility for all profits and losses of the transaction. Adoption of the agency system, particularly in import transactions, was a major element of the foreign trade reform approved by the State Council in 1984.[2] In principle, the agency system meant that the prices of imports, with few exceptions, would be linked to international market prices for the first time in more than twenty years (Yao Jinguan, 232).[3]

New forms of trade

Even as the decentralization of foreign trade authority and the reduction in the scope of the state foreign trade plan proceeded, the state introduced new forms of trade, primarily as means of promoting exports. Among the most important of these were export processing and compensation trade.

The legal framework for export processing, which the first official document on the subject called "taking imports to support exports" (yi jin yang chu), was established in 1979 (State Planning Commission, State Economic

Commission, and Ministry of Foreign Trade 1979, 181–4). Export processing is a rather broad concept encompassing both the processing of imported raw materials for export, the assembly of imported components to produce exportable final goods, and certain other types of exports.[4] Beginning in 1979, the state sought to promote export processing via several policies. First, the state promised to make foreign exchange for the necessary imports available on a priority basis by incorporating it into the annual state foreign exchange import plan. Moreover, raw materials and components imported under the plan were allocated directly to the relevant export producing firms in China rather than being allocated indirectly through the existing materials balance planning process. Finally, the state guaranteed appropriate supplies of domestic raw materials, fuel, and electricity for these firms.

However, the state initially stopped short of guaranteeing that required imports would be available at world prices. Rather, the domestic prices of imported inputs were subject to the same rules of domestic pricing as other imported goods. As discussed in detail later in this chapter, that meant most imported inputs were priced at the same level as comparable domestic goods. The import processing regulations implicitly recognized that the inability to obtain imports at world market prices would handicap exporters. But the relief offered was highly bureaucratic and it is difficult to know how many export processing firms were able to utilize it. According to the regulations, if the price export producers had to pay for imported inputs was so high that they actually incurred financial losses on their exports, the state would allow them to purchase the imports at import cost plus a small commission or they would exempt them from paying certain indirect taxes on their final goods. Either method would reduce their costs and make their goods more competitive on world markets.

Compensation trade (buchang maoyi) was also introduced in the late 1970s. Under these contracts a foreign firm supplies technology or equipment to a Chinese enterprise in exchange for goods produced with that technology or equipment. Compensation trade thus involves deferred payment in kind, making it possible for Chinese enterprises without access to foreign exchange to acquire foreign capital goods.

The development of these new forms of trade, in turn, was linked closely to the promulgation of a joint-venture law in 1979, the establishment of special economic zones on the southeast coast of China in 1980, and the subsequent development of several other types of special arrangements to promote China's economic openness to the world economy. The four special economic zones (jingji tequ) were Shenzhen, Zhuhai, and Shantou in Guangdong, and Xiamen in Fujian. The other special arrangements included the fourteen coastal cities designated as open cities (duiwai kaifeng chengshi) in 1984[5]; the subsequent opening up of the Yangtse Delta, the Pearl River Delta, the Southern Fujian Triangle Area (Xiamen–Zhangzhou–Quanzhou), the Liaodong Peninsula, and the Jiaodong Peninsula; the establishment of coastal economic and technological development zones (jingji jishu kaifa qu) in 1985; the administrative separation of Hainan Island from Guandong to form a separate province in 1988; and the designation of the Pudong District of Shanghai as a new development zone in 1990. Under each of these arrangements there were special tax provisions and other incentives to attract foreign direct investment.

Import and export licensing

As the scope of foreign trade planning shrank and new forms of trade expanded, the state instituted a system of import and export licensing to control the volume and commodity composition of trade. Actually these systems were not new, because the state relied on licensing to regulate both imports and exports in the first half of the 1950s, before the monopoly powers of the national foreign trade corporations were established fully. The main purpose of licensing is to control unplanned imports financed through retained foreign exchange earnings (discussed below in this chapter, see *Relaxation of exchange control*). This includes the over-plan portion of commodities that are also brought into China under the import plan.

Whereas in market economies the introduction of import and export licenses is frequently viewed as a step away from freer trade toward more managed trade, the adoption of licensing in China should be regarded as a measure reflecting a transition from a stage one to a stage two liberalization of an import substitution trade regime (Krueger 1978, 24–6). The previous direct monopoly on all trade transactions exercised by the Ministry of Foreign Trade corresponds to Kreuger's stage one in which there is heavy reliance on quantitative restrictions. Stage two is characterized by increasingly complex quantitative restrictions rather than the across-the-board restrictions of phase one. Moreover, as discussed below, China's increasing use of import duties, export subsidies, and other types of price measures designed to buttress quantitative restrictions, is also common in phase two.

After a hiatus of more than twenty years the state restored licensing beginning in 1980 (Sun Wenxiu, 57; State Import and Export Commission and Ministry of Foreign Trade 1980). As shown in Table 3.1, initially the number of commodities for which licenses were required was small. But as the scope of planning shrank, more commodities were added to the schedule of im-

Table 3.1. *Commodities subject to licensing*

	Import goods	Export goods
1981		24
1982	21	74
1983		99
1984	18	129
1985		127
1986	45	235
1987	45	159
1988	53	166
1989	53	173

Notes: Because changes in the schedules of goods subject to import and export licensing are instituted during the year, different sources frequently give differing values for the number of goods subject to licensing in any year. In these cases the table lists the data for the latest month in the year in question.
Sources: State Import and Export Commission and Ministry of Foreign Trade (1980, 408–14); Sun Wenxiu (1989, 57–8); Ministry of Foreign Economic Relations and Trade and the Customs General Administration (1984, 439); Da Chansong (1987); Ministry of Foreign Economic Relations and Trade (1987, 17–19); Working Party on China's Status as a Contracting Party (1988, 29–31); Yuan Zhou (1988); Qu Yingpu (1989).

ports and exports for which licenses were required. Even more significantly, the share of trade regulated by licenses rose sharply. By 1987 licensed exports exceeded \$23 billion, fully two thirds of China's exports as reported by the Ministry of Foreign Economic Relations and Trade (Yuan Zhou 1988). Even though the number of export commodities requiring licenses subsequently declined sharply, the share of exports under license was still 55 percent in 1989. The share of imports under license in the same year was 46 percent (Qu Yingpu 1989).

This extensive use of licensing serves several economic functions. On the import side a key role is to balance the disequilibrium between rising demand for imports and limited sources of foreign exchange. Despite several devaluations in the 1980s, the domestic currency remained overvalued, creating excess demand for imports. That excess demand is controlled in part through import licensing.

Licensing is also used to protect specific domestic industries. For example, in the mid-1980s the State Economic Commission announced it would no longer approve any licenses for the import of additional assembly lines to produce seven types of consumer durables (World Bank 1988a, 139). This was a measure to protect the market of existing producers of televisions, refrigerators, washing machines, radio cassette recorders, room air conditioners, motorcycles, and light motor vehicles. The list of prohibited imports expanded significantly in the late 1980s, in part to protect a broader range of domestic producers and in part for balance of payments purposes (Liu Dizhong).

Finally, combined with other reforms discussed in this chapter, licensing in principle could contribute to a more rational choice of and domestic distribution of imports. As pricing and exchange rate reforms, analyzed later in this chapter, raised the prices of many imported goods closer to world prices, making imported goods available to a wide range of domestic end users via licensing made it likely that only firms whose economic gains from the use of such imports could cover their cost would apply for such licenses. That would be a vast improvement over the traditional system in which a few priority users received underpriced imports and were not concerned about the underlying economic rationale of imports.

Licenses also serve several economic functions on the export side. First, they are used to prevent "excessive" exports of goods that remain significantly underpriced on the domestic market. Because the domestic prices of these goods were fixed by the state with insufficient regard for world market conditions, in the absence of export controls these goods would be sold largely on the international market. Normally, sharply higher international sales would tend to raise the domestic price of an exported good, increasing the profitability of domestic market sales and thus partially counteracting flows of the good abroad. However, because the domestic prices of many of China's exported goods are controlled there would be no price rise to signal the domestic shortage of these goods. Thus, as the state decentralized trade in the 1980s, it increasingly used export licenses to alleviate or forestall potential domestic market shortages.

This was most obvious in the case of raw materials and mineral products, which remained underpriced on the domestic market. For example, the state in late 1988 banned the export of copper and copper-based alloys, aluminum and aluminum-based alloys, and several other metals effective beginning January 1, 1989 (Zhou Hongqi). Rising prices on the international market had led to huge runups in the volume of export of these commodities. Exports of copper, which have been subject to export licensing since 1982, soared twenty-five-fold between 1985 and 1987. The ban was implemented by the Ministry of Foreign Economic Relations and Trade, which announced that, except in very unusual circumstances, it would refuse to issue the export licenses required for these products.

On the other hand, export licenses are not required for the sale abroad of manufactured goods such as machinery and electronics. These goods are not generally underpriced by world standards.

A second economic function of export licenses is to restrict exports of those products where China is a dominant supplier to the world market and can exercise market power. For example, China is a major supplier to the world market of some minerals such as tungsten, antimony, and tin, and of certain rare earths. For these commodities, for which China is not a price-taker in international markets, China may be able to maximize its foreign exchange earnings by using licenses to restrict the quantity of the product sold internationally. China is also the predominant supplier of fresh vegetables and of many speciality foodstuffs to Hong Kong and Macao. China closely monitors price conditions for these products in the Hong Kong market and uses export licenses to control the volume of exports so as to maximize profits in that market. Indeed, the importance of the Hong Kong market largely explains why the number of licensed export goods exceeded the number of licensed import goods in the 1980s (Table 3.1). For example, in early 1987, only 45 imports were licensed but 212 commodities were subject to export licensing. But licenses for 175 of these products were required only when they were sold to Hong Kong or Macao. Export licenses were required for all international markets for only thirty-seven commodities.

Finally, export licenses are used to ensure that China does not exceed quota restrictions on specific products, such as textile products, that are imposed by most developed market economies.

Tariffs and domestic tax rebates

Just as the use of licensing expanded as the scope of foreign trade planning diminished, the state also began to make more active use of tariffs and taxes as trade policy instruments beginning in the early 1980s. This development was foreshadowed by the elevation, in 1980, of the bureaucratic status of the former Customs Bureau of the Ministry of Foreign Trade to a ministerial level entity, the General Administration of Customs. The new agency, directly under the State Council, became responsible for formulation and administration of policies, laws, and regulations concerning tariffs (Li Cheng-xun, 91). The concern to shape a tariff system congruent with standard international practices was reflected in China's joining the Customs Cooperation Council, an international organization, in 1983 (Chan, 48). In a further development the Customs Tariff Rate Commission, an organ under the Ministry of Finance, was abolished in 1987 and replaced with a new Customs Tariff

Commission. Chaired by the Minister of Finance, the Commission was a more high-powered body directly under the State Council. The membership included the chief of the General Administration of Customs and a vice-minister of the Ministry of Foreign Economic Relations and Trade. Finally, also in 1987, the Chinese promulgated a comprehensive customs law to replace the interim law that had governed customs since 1951 (Chan and Levy, 44).

All of these developments reflected a change in the underlying purpose of the tariff system. In the prereform era tariffs were simply regarded as one of several sources of government revenues. They were collected by the Ministry of Foreign Trade based on tariff rates that were seldom, if ever, adjusted. In any case tariff rates had little if any effect on trade decisions because prices paid by end users of most imported goods, particularly after 1963, were tied to the price of domestic substitute goods rather than the international price adjusted for tariffs. The role of tariffs was thus redundant, just as in other centrally planned economies (Holzman, 240).

Beginning in 1980 changes in tariff rates became more frequent and of greater importance in influencing the volume and commodity composition of both exports and imports. In the early 1980s duties on imported consumer durables, such as television sets, radio recorders, and electronic calculators, were raised sharply to control the volume of these imports. More systematic revisions of a large number of import tariffs were undertaken in 1982. Tariffs ranging between 10 and 60 percent on various exports were introduced in mid-1982. In 1985 the various import and export tariffs that had been announced in the previous five years were published in the first comprehensive tariff schedule released since 1951. Subsequent changes also have occurred. These details are readily followed in periodic announcements in the monthly journal of the General Customs Administration, *Chinese Customs* (Zhongguo haiguan) or, in summary form, in the annual reports of the International Monetary Fund. And a comprehensive customs schedule, the first in several years, was released in September 1989 (General Administration of Customs Tariff Office 1989).

As a result of these changes and the growing volume of trade, customs revenues rose rapidly in the first half of the 1980s. Tariff revenues collected in 1980–5, 49.7 billion yuan, were more than twice the entire amount collected during 1953–79 (Ministry of Finance General Planning Department, 42–3). Even adjusting for the sharply higher annual trade volume in the first half of the 1980s, tariff revenues as a share of the value of imports rose sharply from 11 percent in the prereform era to 15 percent in 1980–5. However, customs revenues reached a peak of over 20 billion yuan in 1985 and then dropped to about 15 billion yuan annually in the second half of the decade. Thus average tariff rates fell sharply in the second half of the 1980s.

China also designed changes in its domestic tax structure to bring its practices into greater conformity with international conventions. The most important change of this type was the State Council decision in principle in 1984 to rebate to producers a portion of the indirect taxes paid on export goods (Sun Wenxiu, 56). Like many other countries, China relies heavily on indirect taxes to finance government expenditures. These taxes are usually levied each time products are transferred from one enterprise to another. Thus the prices of final goods have a tax component that varies significantly depending on the number of stages in the production process. In contrast, some countries, such as the United States and Japan, rely primarily on direct taxes, such as corporate and personal income taxes, which typically fall more uniformly on all goods. Moreover, in most countries that rely on indirect taxes, such as a value-added tax or indirect taxes levied only on final sales, taxes do not accumulate or cascade. Thus their indirect taxes also tend to fall relatively uniformly on all goods. It has long been common, and allowed under the regulations of the General Agreement on Tariffs and Trade, to rebate the indirect taxes levied on exported goods so that exports from countries that rely heavily on indirect taxes can compete with exports of other countries on international markets.

Rebate of these taxes was also closely tied to the question of the financial profitability of exports. When Chinese firms suffered financial losses from exporting in the early 1980s, it was sometimes argued that these were "false losses" in part because the taxes collected by the state at several earlier stages of processing exceeded the financial losses sustained by the enterprise exporting the final good (Ji Chongwei, 1; Xu and Meng; Ye and Xu; Zhou and Zhao, 48). Thus, it was argued the state could afford to subsidize the losses enterprises incurred on these exports.

Because this system was cumbersome and undermined decentralized decision-making on exports, the State Council formally approved a system of indirect tax rebates that began in April of 1985 (State Countil 1985a). Compared to states with a uniform value-added tax, however, the rebate calculation in China was extremely complex. China had several indirect taxes that were either levied directly on export goods or which affected the prices of export goods. These include a business tax (yingye shui), levied on gross sales of commercial enterprises; a product tax (shangpin shui), essentially a turnover tax levied on products of state-owned and collective enterprises; and, since the early 1980s, a value-added tax (zengzhi shui) levied on selected industrial commodities (World Bank 1988b, 402–3). Indirect taxes accounted for more than 60 percent of government financial revenue (Zhou Xiaochuan 1988b, 59). Moreover, the rates varied widely by commodity so rebates could not be uniform. For example, 400 different commodity groups were subject to the turnover tax at rates that varied from 3 percent to 66 percent. The spread of value-added tax rates in 1986 was roughly four to one.

As a result of these complexities in the structure of indirect taxes, administration of the rebate program was a bureaucratic nightmare that took several years to institute. Teams formed by experts from the Tax Bureau of the Ministry of Finance, the Ministry of Foreign Economic Relations and Trade, the State Economic Commission, and the State Statistical Bureau carried out commodity-by-commodity investigations to determine the indirect tax component in the prices of exported goods.

The problem of measuring the magnitude of indirect taxes embedded in each export commodity was compounded by conflicting economic interests, both between different levels of government and among bureaucratic interests at the center. The central–local conflict arose because the revenues from different taxes historically had been assigned to different levels of government administration. In principle whoever controls the revenue should rebate the taxes. But reality was quite different. Provincial and local governments resisted rebating any indirect taxes they had previously been assigned as a local revenue source. To sell the program the central government had to agree to absorb the entire cost of the rebates, even for taxes it did not receive (Zhou Xiaochuan 1988b, 64).

Bureaucratic conflicts within the central level were also severe. The main split was between the Ministry of Foreign Economic Relations and Trade and the Tax Bureau of the Ministry of Finance. The former was one of the key advocates of tax rebates on exported products because rebates made export goods more competitive internationally and, for any given level of domestic resources available to subsidize exports, made it easier for the Ministry to achieve targeted levels of exports. The Tax Bureau's interests were diametrically opposed because the rebates reduced the revenues flowing to the Ministry of Finance. The same attitude was also occasionally evident at the State Planning Commission. One article analyzing the finances of foreign trade, published in the Commission's journal, actually lumped together direct export subsidies and the rebate on taxes to form a single measure that the authors advanced as reflecting the deteriorating finances of foreign trade (Jiao and Zhou, 59). From an economic perspective, of course, rebates of the indirect taxes imposed on exports and the direct fiscal subsidy of financially unprofitable exports were quite different. But from the short-term perspective of the bottom line the effect of the two was the same.

In the end various compromises were made. For example, for processed goods subject to value-added taxes, the rebate was based on the value-added rate that applied to the final good, ignoring the product taxes that were sometimes levied on the earlier stages of processing. For foreign trade, transport, and other service enterprises an additional 3 percent, above the product or value-added tax, was rebated. That was intended to offset product taxes built into inputs, such as electricity and fuel, which these enterprises used intensively, but for which it was difficult to determine the specific tax burden on each product. The product tax on certain goods, such as crude oil, was not to be refunded on the grounds that the prices of these products had been fixed at such low levels that sufficient profit was already assured on export sales (Zhou Xiaochuan 1988b, 65–6). Finally, no attempt was made to rebate the business tax that was paid by foreign trade enterprises (Li Lanqing 1988b, 8).

As the system was carried out, the magnitude of rebates increased. In the first year, 1.8 billion yuan was rebated. By 1986 more investigations of the indirect burden on specific export commodities had been completed and rebates of the indirect taxes on half of all exports were made. The amount rebated rose to 4.2 billion yuan. The scope of rebates expanded further in 1987 and 1988 and rebates rose to 7.4 billion yuan and 12.0 billion yuan, respectively (Zhou Xiaochuan 1990a, 302–3).[6]

Although the magnitude of the rebates was relatively small in the aggregate, only about 7 percent of the value of exports in 1988, for example, the rebate system was nonetheless important both economically and politically. First, because indirect tax rates were uneven across products, the rebates probably were quite important in improving the international competitive position of some export goods. Resource allocation could improve because world demand would allow expanded production of some products whose comparative advantage previously was partially obscured by the effect of cumulative layers of indirect taxes on the final price. Second, the rebates presumably facilitated, at least at the margin, the emergence of more decentralized decision-making with regard to export. Other things being equal, the rebates must have reduced the financial losses sustained on some exported goods. Finally, the rebate of indirect taxes on exports was an attempt to bring China's foreign trade system into conformity with the GATT charter. Article XVI strongly condemns the use of export subsidies because of the potential distortions they introduce. But rebates of indirect taxes are clearly allowed. As will be seen later in this chapter, this attempt in the mid-1980s to end export subsidies was feeble because it was not supplemented with either a sufficiently realistic official exchange rate or a sufficiently far-reaching reform of domestic prices. Nonetheless, the intention was basically sound.

Relaxation of exchange control

One of the first steps the state took to stimulate exports was to modify the stringent system of exchange control that had been in effect since the early 1950s. Superficially, the interim regulations for exchange control issued by the State Council in 1980, to take effect March 1, 1981, seem every bit as stringent as the 1950 regulations they replaced.[7] The regulations stipulated that foreign exchange was subject to centralized control and unified management by the State General Administration of Exchange Control and that the Bank of China was to serve as the specialized state bank engaging in foreign exchange business (State Countil 1980a, 119). The provision that "all Chinese and foreign institutions and individuals in the People's Republic of China must sell their foreign exchange receipts to the Bank of China, and that any foreign exchange required is to be sold to them by the Bank of China in accordance with the plans approved by the State" is very similar to the document of three decades earlier.

However, there were two critical differences. First, the regulations authorized the State General Administration of Exchange Control to allow other banking institutions to engage in foreign exchange business.[8] Thus the regulations forecast the potential erosion of the Bank of China's historic monopoly control of foreign exchange. Indeed, only a few years later there were about a dozen banks and other institutions that borrowed funds from abroad, sold bonds on international financial markets, and so forth. Moreover, by 1988 ninety banks and financial institutions, including affiliates of nonresident banks, were authorized to handle foreign exchange transactions in China (International Monetary Fund 1989, 100).

Second, and more important, the regulations specifically allowed for exceptions to the long-standing requirement that all foreign exchange receipts be sold to the Bank of China. Individuals receiving remittances from their relatives abroad, for example, were required to sell most of it to the Bank of China but were allowed to retain a portion. Chinese citizens returning from work or study abroad with foreign currency savings were no longer required to sell any foreign exchange to the Bank of China. By the mid-1980s individuals could open foreign exchange accounts at the Bank of China or other banks authorized to deal in foreign exchange. By the middle of 1990 individual hard currency accounts reached $3.8 billion, $2.8 billion of which was on deposit at the Bank of China (Xiao Qu).

But the most important exception to the previous practice of compelling the sale of all foreign exchange earnings to the Bank of China was a provision allowing enterprises to retain a share of their foreign exchange earnings (State Council 1980a, 120). This creation of import entitlements, which as discussed in the next section of this chapter could be resold, is common in the early phases of liberalization in developing countries that followed import substitution trade strategies (Krueger 1978, 44). Variants on this scheme were adopted in the 1950s in some of the socialist economies of Eastern Europe in their early reform efforts (Nuti and Sengupta; Plowiec, 356). A foreign exchange retention scheme was introduced in 1987–8 in the Soviet Union as part of its external sector reforms (IMF et al., 4).

As discussed in Chapter 2, in the prereform era Chinese enterprises had little incentive to export. They were paid in domestic currency for the goods delivered to foreign trade corporations. The price they received was the same regardless of whether the good was sold abroad or at home. And they gained no explicit claim to use any of the foreign exchange earned. Similarly, provincial and other local governments, which managed a large share of export-producing firms, as well as the major production ministries, had little or no economic incentive to encourage or require their subordinate firms to produce for export because none of the foreign exchange earnings accrued to these units. Local governments and ministries that sought import goods had to get their projects approved by the central planning apparatus, most usually the State Planning Commission.

Beginning in 1979 the central government gave up its monopoly on the control of foreign exchange by introducing a "foreign exchange retention system" (waihui liucheng zhidu) allowing both export-producing enterprises and their superordinate level of governmental administration to gain a claim to the use of a share of the foreign exchange earnings from exports of both goods and services. Although the term "retained foreign exchange" was used to describe these funds, it is important to note that the funds were actually held by the Bank of China and could be used only under certain conditions. Retentions thus initially entailed the right to use foreign exchange and did not constitute a foreign exchange allocation by the Bank of China.

To encourage incremental growth of exports, retentions for most commodity exports were allowed only from earnings above and beyond the level of exports achieved in 1978. However, as can be seen in Table 3.2, for certain new types of trade that were being introduced in 1979, such as compensation trade and processing and assembly of foreign-supplied parts and components, the retentions were a share of all earnings. The retention rates were structured to give stronger incentives to exploit the new trading opportuni-

Table 3.2. *Foreign exchange retention rates, 1979*

Category of export earnings	Rate
From commodities produced under ministerial management	20 percent of earnings above level of 1978[a]
From commodities produced under local management	40 percent of earnings above level of 1978[b]
Exports based on imports	15 percent of net earnings[c]
Fees from processing and assembly of foreign components	30 percent of all earnings
Medium and small-scale compensation trade	15 percent of net earnings[d]

[a]Retained foreign exchange was divided equally among the ministries responsible for production and distribution of the product, the locality (province, municipality, or county) where the enterprise was located, and the producing enterprise.
[b]Retained foreign exchange in this category was shared between the locality or county and the enterprise producing the export good.
[c]Net foreign exchange earnings equal total foreign exchange earnings from exports less foreign exchange spent for imported raw and processed materials, equipment, machinery, and so forth.
[d]Compensation trade involves the foreign supply of machinery and equipment in exchange for a specified quantity of goods produced with the equipment. Net foreign exchange earnings are the earnings from exports beyond those required to compensate the foreign party for supplying the machinery and equipment.
Source: State Council (1979b, 1,021–4).

ties created in 1979. For example, as shown in Table 3.2, the retention rate for incremental exports produced by firms under management of one of the ministries of the central government was only 20 percent of earnings over the level of exports achieved in 1978 while the rate for incremental exports produced by firms under local management was twice as high – 40 percent. Thus there was an extra incentive for provincially and other locally-led enterprises, and for provincial and local governments, to seek out new export markets via the newly sanctioned provincial and local trade corporations. However, earnings from ten export commodities (grain, steel products, coal, crude oil, refined petroleum products, cement, logs, pig iron, zinc, and edible vegetable oil) were excluded from the system (State Council 1979b, 1,022).

In addition, in 1979 the central government approved the expansion of a similar system for sharing in the foreign exchange earnings derived from nontrade sources of foreign exchange such as overseas Chinese remittances, various port fees paid by foreign vessels, earnings from foreign tourism and

Table 3.3. *Retained foreign exchange, 1979–88*

Year	Millions of $	Percentage of export earnings
1979	854	6.5
1980	1,579	9.0
1983	6,700	30.0
1980–6	46,700	
1988	18,510	44

Notes: Data for 1979 and 1980 are exclusive of retentions of nontrade foreign exchange earnings. These amounted to $1,192 million in the two-year period. The source does not break down this total into individual years.
The figure for 1983 is estimated based on the report that on average the retention rate was 30 percent of foreign exchange earned from exports and the export value of $22.32 billion reported by the Ministry of Foreign Economic Relations and Trade.
Sources: 1979, 1980: State Council (1982, 567).
1983: Sun Wenxiu (1989, 54).
1980–6: Song Hai (1988, 143).
1988: Sun Yong (1989); Sun Wenxiu (1989, 55).

friendship stores and so forth.[9] Retention rates ranged from 15 percent of the foreign exchange remitted for the construction and repair of houses of overseas and returned overseas Chinese to as high as 50 percent for some types of tourism earnings (State Council 1979c). In 1979 and 1980 a total of $1,192 million in nontrade foreign exchange income was retained to finance import expenditures of localities and central level ministries involved in tourism, overseas Chinese affairs, port development, and so forth (State Council 1982, 567).

Provincial and local governments and enterprises producing export goods gained control of a significant magnitude of foreign exchange in the first two years this system of sharing foreign exchange revenues was implemented. As shown in Table 3.3, retained foreign exchange was $854 million in 1979 and rose to $1,579 million in 1980. Although these amounts represented a relatively small share of total commodity export earnings, they provided substantial increases in the foreign exchange available to both enterprises and to local governments. At that time the center allocated provincial and local governments a total of only $500 million annually in foreign exchange, which they could expend largely at their own discretion (State Council 1982, 567). In subsequent years this program of sharing foreign exchange proceeds was adjusted repeatedly and, as a result, the magnitude of the funds retained expanded significantly.[10] In the early 1980s the State Council concluded special deals providing preferential retention rates to certain geographic regions and specific vertically organized production systems (Yin Ling, 27). Guangdong, Fujian, and Xinjiang fell in the former category while petroleum, machinery and electronics, military industry, and science and education were in the latter (Sun Wenxiu, 54). For petroleum and goods produced by the military system, the retention rate was 100 percent of the value of exports in excess of a specified level.

In 1982 the State Council overhauled the system in an effort to remedy problems that had occurred in the first few years. Instead of the various rates for different categories of export products shown in Table 3.2, the State Council fixed rates for each region that were equal to the share of total export revenues retained in the previous year. The new rates applied to most export earnings, regardless of source. However, the separate rate for income from processing was retained and raised[11] and a special rate of 50 percent for earnings from the export of machinery and electronics replaced the old system in which retentions were set at 30 percent of the planned level of exports (Yin Ling, 27). The provincial rates, which ranged from as low as 3 percent to as high as 25 percent, reflected the differential success various provinces had in promoting their exports after the reform of the foreign trade system began in 1979. Those that had been more successful in generating export earnings via the new forms of trade achieved a larger volume of retained foreign exchange. As a result their retentions as a share of exports were higher and under the modified rules these provinces earned higher retention rates that beginning in 1982 applied to the entire volume of their exports (with the exception of certain products still excluded from the program), not simply the amount over some defined base level. Whereas the average provincial retention rate was only 8 percent, the rapid growth of petroleum and military exports resulted in the average foreign exchange retention rate rising to about 30 percent of export earnings by 1983 (Sun Wenxiu, 54).

The state in 1985 raised the foreign exchange retention rates to a minimum of 25 percent a concession to those provinces that had been less successful in increasing their exports in the early 1980s. The rate for Guangdong and Fujian, however, was boosted to 30 percent. And the state permitted retention of one-fourth of the earnings from the export of the ten products previously excluded from the system, except for crude oil and refined products, where the rate was set at 3 percent.

In 1985 the State Council also approved more regional and sectoral preferences. Four autonomous regions – Inner Mongolia, Xinjiang, Guangxi, and Ningxia – and three provinces – Yunnan, Guizhou, and Qinghai – were allowed to retain half of their foreign exchange earnings rather than one-fourth, the more common rate at that time. Tibet continued to enjoy the 100 percent retention rate it had been awarded earlier. These special rates appear to have been a concession to the relatively less developed regions which had complained that China's opening to the outside world had skewed patterns of development to their disadvantage (Shirk, 60–4; Sullivan, 203–4). Because the total exports of these eight administrative areas in 1985 was only about $925 million, less than 4 percent of China's exports of goods, the concession was not very costly from the point of view of the central government (Ministry of Foreign Economic Relations and Trade 1986, 966). The state raised the retention rate applied to earnings from the export of machinery and electronic products to 65 percent.

By 1985 the state instituted a two-tier system in which above-plan exports were subject to a preferential retention rate. In addition to the basic retention rate which applied to exports up to the plan target, say 25 percent of foreign exchange earnings in most provinces, 70 percent of the above-plan amount could also be retained (Sun Wenxiu, 55). In 1988 the retention rate for earnings from above-plan exports increased to 80 percent (Yang Jianhua, 3).

By 1986 retention rates for foreign exchange income from trade ranged from 25 percent for most of the country to as high as 100 percent in the four special economic zones – Shenzhen, Zhuhai, Shantou, and Xiamen – and the four development zones – Hainan, Huangpu, Guangzhou, and Xijiang (Yang Xiong, 36–7). Where the basic rate of 25 percent was in force half the amount went to the enterprise and half to the level of government that managed the enterprise.

In 1987 the State Council expanded the system of preferential rates introduced earlier to stimulate exports produced in specified industrial sectors. The retention rates for earnings from the export of some categories of textile products, including garments, were boosted by either 5 or 7 percent, resulting in an average increase of 4 percent in the retention rate for the sector as a whole (State Planning Commission et al. 1987a). Rates for specified light industrial products were also increased by either 5 or 9 percentage points, resulting in an average increase of 4 percent in the retention rate for the sector as a whole (State Planning Commission et al. 1987b).

These adjustments, which took effect on January 1, 1987, were a precursor of a more far-reaching State Council decision taken in September 1987. This established a highly preferential retention rate of 70 percent for export earnings of enterprises in three industrial branches – light industry, arts and crafts, and garments. In exchange for being granted that preferential retention rate these sectors were also made responsible for their own profits and losses. That means that the state no longer provided fiscal subsidies to offset the domestic currency losses firms in these three sectors sustained on exports. To facilitate this prospect, the state granted these three sectors more authority than other sectors to spend their retained foreign exchange (Sun Wenxiu, 55). They were permitted to use retained funds to import necessary raw materials or to sell it in the foreign exchange adjustment centers (discussed further below), where they could convert their foreign exchange earnings into renminbi at a very favorable rate compared to the then prevailing official exchange rate. As set forth in the next section of this chapter, other exporting sectors faced much more severe limitations on their use of retained foreign exchange in this period.[12]

As a result of this proliferation of special preferential retention rates the volume and share of retained foreign exchange increased dramatically, both in absolute amount and as a share of total export earnings. For the seven years 1980–6 total retentions were $46.7 billion, an average of $6.67 billion per year, almost three times the average of retained foreign exchange in 1979–80. By the mid-1980s 42 percent of all foreign exchange was in the hands of the provinces and export producers, only 58 percent was controlled directly by the central government (Song Hai, 143). This placed huge quantities of foreign exchange beyond the immediate direct control of the central government. By 1988 retained foreign exchange totaled $18.5 billion, over 40 percent of China's total export earnings. This diminution in the monopoly control of foreign exchange earnings constituted a major step toward internal convertibility of the renminbi for trade transactions.

Foreign exchange trading rights

The value of retained foreign exchange was enhanced by the opening of "foreign exchange adjustment centers" (waihui tiaoji zhongxin) in which enterprises with retained export earnings and other authorized holders of convertible currencies could sell foreign exchange for domestic currency.[13] This enhanced export incentives for two reasons. First, there were some large scale commodity exporters who were unable to utilize all of their retained foreign exchange to purchase imports. Even under the more decentralized environment discussed at the outset of this chapter, these firms may have had little prospect for receiving the licenses required for the imports they desired. For those firms income in domestic currency, which is easier to spend, may have been preferred.

Second, the exchange rate in the adjustment or transaction centers was far more favorable for exporters, providing an additional incentive to sell goods on the international market. Although the rate has varied over time and space, it was generally in the range of 6 to 7 yuan per dollar in 1987 and averaged 6 yuan in 1988. Thus in 1988 the swap rate was two thirds more than the official exchange rate of 3.7 (Working Party 1988, 27). In effect introducing trading rights for retained foreign exchange constituted a de facto devaluation of the yuan.

These centers were an outgrowth of the system introduced in October 1980, shortly after the introduction of foreign exchange retention rights, in which some firms with surplus foreign exchange were allowed to sell it through the State Administration of Exchange Control (SAEC) or through the Bank of China (Ministry of Foreign Economic Relations and Trade 1987, 20). The nation's first foreign exchange trading room was established in the Guangzhou (Canton) branch of the Bank of China in 1980 (Vogel, 353). In Shanghai these transactions began in 1981 (Chen Weihua 1988b). It is not clear how the price of these early transactions was determined but it evidently was set by the state, because the buying and selling units were not allowed to deal directly with one another. In some markets in the early 1980s the government sought to set the price at the level of the internal settlement rate, 2.8 yuan per dollar.[14] Foreign-invested firms were excluded from participating in these markets. The annual transaction volume was quite modest, a few hundred million dollars, in the early 1980s.

The first formally sanctioned foreign exchange transaction, or swap center, opened in 1985 in the Shenzhen Special Economic Zone (Zhang and Wang). The Shanghai center opened the following year in November (Wang and Juhua). Initially the transaction volume appears to have been small. The main purpose of the centers was to solve the foreign exchange problems of joint ventures.[15] Indeed in Shanghai and elsewhere the centers initially were called the "foreign exchange adjustment centers for foreign invested enterprises."[16] The centers provided a swap market for those few ventures with excess foreign exchange earnings to sell to ventures that sold their output primarily on the domestic market and did not have sufficient hard currency income to provide to the foreign partners. The incentive for sellers of foreign exchange was to acquire domestic currency on more favorable terms than the official rate. That allowed them to purchase inputs needed from the domestic market at a lower cost, measured in terms of foreign exchange.

The main reason the volume of transactions in the foreign exchange adjustment centers increased slowly was the foreign exchange crisis of 1985–6. Beginning as early as the fourth quarter of 1984, the volume of imports, particularly consumer durables such as motor vehicles, color televisions, refrigerators, washing machines, and motorcycles, accelerated markedly while export growth stagnated at best. For 1984 as a whole, data compiled by the Ministry of Foreign Economic Relations and Trade showed that imports grew by almost 40 percent while exports grew only 10 percent. The trade deficit for the year as a whole was $1.1 billion, a sharp reversal from the surpluses enjoyed in the previous three consecutive years.

The situation worsened at an accelerating rate in the early part of 1985. Exports actually declined slightly in the first half of the year while imports shot up by more than 70 percent compared to the first half of 1984. The trade deficit in the first half of the year was three times that sustained for all of 1984. By the end of June, foreign exchange reserves controlled directly by the central government fell by more than one third compared with the level at the end of 1983.

In response to this hemorrhage of foreign exchange reserves, the central government took drastic measures both to reduce the overall trade deficit and to redirect the commodity composition of imports away from consumer durables and toward machinery, equipment, and other goods more directly relevant to meeting national economic development goals.

Among the earliest of these steps, the State Council on March 13, 1985 announced additional controls on the use of retained foreign exchange (State Council 1985d; Sun Wenxiu, 55). The text of this directive of the State Council is vague, so it is difficult to judge precisely how these new controls, which are referred to in the directive itself and in several other sources as "norms to control the use of retained foreign exchange" (liuoheng waihui shiyong de kongzhi zhibiao), actually worked or precisely when they went into effect (Fu Ziying 1989, 18; Shen Juren, 4; Song Hai, 144; Sun Wenxiu, 55; Yang Xiong, 37; Ying Ling, 30). But effectively the controls were used to freeze a large share of the foreign exchange that was nominally being "retained" by exporting enterprises, local governments, and to a lesser extent central ministries. The Director of the State General Administration of Exchange Control apparently was referring to this, the promulgation of additional legal sanctions for the violation of foreign exchange controls (State Administration of Exchange Control 1985) and perhaps other measures, when he disclosed toward the end of 1985 that in response to dwindling foreign exchange reserves the state in the second quarter had taken "appropriate measures" to cut down on unnecessary imports (Tang Gengyao 1985, 22).

One stimulus to impose these additional restrictions on the resale or the use of retained foreign exchange was the Hainan Island auto import scandal of 1984–5. In April 1983 the Party Central Committee and the State Council approved a plan calling for the accelerated development of Hainan, a large island off the coast of Guangdong Province. Among other things, this provided the island with enhanced authority to arrange its own imports, including motor vehicles (Vogel, 291). Because low-quality domestic vehicles were vastly overpriced on the domestic market, Hainan officials quickly discovered that they could reap vast profits by reselling these vehicles to units elsewhere in Guangdong and in other provinces that were not allowed to import vehicles. Local foreign exchange swap markets were part of this scheme because they allowed Hainan Island car sellers to convert their domestic currency earnings into foreign exchange which, in turn, would be used to finance even more imported vehicles (Vogel, 368). By the time central officials called a halt to this scheme in 1985, Hainan officials had spent more than one billion dollars in foreign exchange on vehicles and other consumer durables.

Despite the additional controls on the use of retained foreign exchange and other measures to curb imports and promote exports, China incurred a record deficit in its merchandise trade account in 1985. The freeze on the use of retained foreign exchange continued in 1986. By the end of the year the central government had blocked the expenditure of $19.1 billion of retained foreign exchange. These funds, in turn, were "borrowed" by the central government to finance centrally managed imports. For the years 1980–6 as a whole, almost one fifth of the imports of the central government were financed by spending the retained funds that had been earmarked for exporting enterprises and their supervising government agencies (Song Hai, 143).[17]

As these controls on the use of retained foreign exchange and other restrictions gradually were eased, the volume of foreign exchange transactions on the swap market grew substantially. Most importantly, domestic firms, except for private enterprises, gained greater access to the market. As was noted above, the light industry, arts and crafts, and garment sectors were provided enhanced access to the swap market in 1987. And in 1988 the state abolished the special controls on the use of retained foreign exchange that had been instituted in 1985 (State Council 1988, 387). The abolition of these controls was reflected in the opening of the Shanghai swap center to domestic firms on a trial basis in April 1988. In September 1988, after more than $500 million in transactions had been completed, the market celebrated its official opening (Chen Weihua 1988b; Wang Juhua).

The prohibition against individuals, as opposed to state and collective enterprises and other units, entering the foreign exchange market began to erode, at least at the margin. Beginning in 1987, overseas Chinese in Ningbo were allowed to convert their foreign exchange to domestic currency in the local swap center, at rates that increased their incentive to provide financial support to their family members and relatives living in China. In 1988 this practice was extended to foreign exchange centers in Shenzhen, Xiamen, Quanzhou, and Wuhan. And in the same year Chinese citizens were allowed to purchase dollars to pay the fees required to take the Graduate Record Exam and the Test of English as a Foreign Language in China (Liu Hong 1989b). In 1989 this also was allowed in Shanghai (Xinhua 1989a).

The volume of foreign exchange transactions and the number of markets grew dramatically in the latter part of the 1980s. By 1988 there were thirty-nine foreign exchange adjustment centers across China and the annual transaction volume was $6.264 billion, approximately $2 billion more than in 1987 (Reporter 1989a). In 1989 the number of markets expanded to about eighty and trading volume grew almost 40 percent to reach $8.566 billion (Wang Xiangwei 1990a; Zhang and Wang). By 1990 the transaction volume reached $13.2 billion (Ying Pu). Moreover, the great bulk of both the buying and selling volume was generated by domestic firms rather than joint ventures or wholly foreign-owned firms. Of the total turnover in 1988 foreign invested firms sold $662 million and purchased $220 million. In 1989 their trades on the buy and sell sides combined were $2.32 billion with sales of foreign exchange again roughly three times purchases (Qu Yingpu 1990a). The largest single foreign exchange market was in Shanghai, where the volume of transactions in 1988 reached $736 million. Transactions involving foreign-invested firms that year totaled $86 million, about one eighth of the overall volume (Shen Feiyue 1989b; Wang Juhua). In 1989 the transaction volume in Shanghai rose by three fourths to reach $1.29 billion (Xinhua 1990c).

Although the volume of transactions grew markedly in the late 1980s, it is difficult to know how to interpret the price at which foreign exchange changes hands in the foreign exchange adjustment centers. First, as already suggested, the government limits entry into the market several ways. Individuals generally are not permitted to buy foreign exchange except for very limited purposes. Purchases by enterprises and other units require preapproval of the intended use of the foreign exchange to be purchased. In most cases this means the would-be purchaser must have an import license to purchase a specific commodity before even registering with the local branch of the State Administration of Exchange Control as a buyer. The limits referred to in published materials seem rather elastic suggesting they do not restrict entry on the buying side of the market.[18] However, the regulations are subject to interpretation by the authorities in the foreign exchange market and the standards for approval appear to tighten in periods during which China experiences balance-of-payments problems.

An additional barrier to the entry of would-be buyers of foreign exchange appears to apply, at least sporadically, to joint-venture firms. As suggested above, they wish to sell domestic currency in order to acquire the foreign exchange they will remit abroad to provide a financial return to the foreign partner in a joint venture. The Chinese joint-venture regulations from the outset sought to encourage joint ventures to earn this foreign exchange by exporting. By 1986, in response to an expressed desire on the part of foreign-invested firms to have greater access to the domestic market, the State Council (1986b) promulgated a new regulation that allowed joint ventures to obtain access to foreign exchange for certain types of goods sold on the domestic market. These included sophisticated goods produced with advanced technology and goods classified as import substitutes. The logic was that if foreign exchange previously allocated to purchase these goods on international markets could be saved because sophisticated joint venture products obviated the need for imports why not allow joint ventures to have access to the foreign exchange so saved? In some swap markets, foreign-invested firms reportedly are not allowed to sell renminbi unless they can produce documentation demonstrating that their renminbi funds are derived from the sale of products that have been specifically registered and accepted by the relevant authorities as "import substitute products." In practice such documentation has been difficult to obtain because the relevant authorities may wish to preserve these markets for would-be Chinese producers. Because there is no data on the cumulative domestic currency holdings of joint-venture firms that they would choose to convert to foreign exchange if this requirement was not a constraining factor, it is difficult to judge how much demand for foreign currency is effectively suppressed.

A second factor that makes it difficult to interpret the swap market price is that at least until the late 1980s, the government did not allow supply and demand to determine freely the market price of foreign exchange. The price in each market was pegged daily by the swap center authorities and all transactions had to take place at the posted price. Not only did the state intervene by pegging the price, it also was a net purchaser of renminbi (seller of foreign exchange) in order to curtail the rise in the price of foreign exchange (Yan and Shen, 17). In Shanghai the local branch of the State Administration Exchange Control established an experimental stabilization fund in 1988 to finance interventions in the market designed to reduce fluctuations in the price of foreign exchange. But its small size, $3.5 million, was deemed insufficient to play an effective role (Liu Hong 1989a). Thus a larger fund was established in early 1989. In late 1987 the local authorities in Guangzhou also intervened in the market, but less directly. The municipal government enjoined firms known to have retained foreign exchange to sell it in the auction market in order to prevent a further fall in the value of the renminbi (Vogel, 389–90).

A third constraint that makes it difficult to interpret the significance of the swap market rate is that transactions on the swap market could not be used to establish open positions in foreign exchange holdings. Thus the market could not be used to speculate against the value of the domestic currency. Participants on the buy side are limited to those holding an approved import license. And once funds are purchased they must be used to finance imports within six months.[19] The state effectively foreclosed the possibility that a buyer of foreign exchange could resell at a profit later, after the price of foreign exchange rose.

By September 1988 Shanghai was said to be the first center where the price of foreign exchange was determined by supply and demand (Shen Feiyue, 1989b). The procedures used in this market to set the price of foreign exchange seem relatively transparent, reducing the likelihood of heavy-handed government intervention. The market is Walrasian in character – the daily market clearing price is established by an auction, which occurs before any transactions are allowed. Each day the market was open (Monday, Tuesday, Thursday, and Friday in the late 1980s), brokers and dealers registered the volume of foreign exchange they would be willing to buy or sell at the previous day's price.[20] If demand and supply were not in balance the price of foreign exchange would rise or fall by one one hundredth of a yuan every two minutes. Participants in the market could modify the quantities of foreign exchange they were prepared to buy or sell. Or additional buyers or sellers could enter the market at the new price. This procedure continued until demand and supply were equal. All orders were filled at that price and the market closed until the next trading day.

This procedure does not preclude intervention by the market authorities. For example, they could place orders to sell foreign exchange through one of the market's licensed brokers to stem a decline in the value of the domestic currency. Or they could "encourage" a local firm known to have significant retained foreign exchange to sell it on the market to achieve the same purpose. However, as compared to the earlier practice, in which the authorities simply fixed the price arbitrarily and then allowed transactions to occur only at that price, market forces appear to have become more important in the Shanghai swap market in the late 1980s.

A related indicator of the meaning of the swap market rates is the degree to which local markets have become more integrated horizontally over time. If individual markets in various cities remain separate they may be easier to manipulate than if there is a single large integrated national market. In the mid-1980s it was frequently said that firms were allowed to buy or sell foreign exchange only in their own local market, even if a more favorable price existed in a more distant swap market. Whether this was a result of central regulations or local government efforts to manipulate the market is not clear. But substantial intermarket price differentials existed, suggesting either the spread of information about these markets was very limited or that other constraints limited the arbitrage that would virtually eliminate intermarket price differentials for foreign exchange in a competitive situation.

By the latter part of the 1980s, two developments should have led to greater interregional market integration. First, the Chinese maintained that transactions were permitted across provinces, autonomous regions, and municipalities (Working Party 1988, 27). Second, beginning in 1988 the central government announced that as part of the foreign trade contract responsibility system (see Chapter 4), it would establish a national foreign exchange swap center in Beijing that would carry out arbitrage transactions to reduce the differences in the price of foreign exchange in different local markets (State Council 1988, 387; Sun Wenxiu, 55; Shen Juren, 4). That apparently reflected an attempt to provide a more level playing field for all provinces as they became responsible for meeting specific export targets under the new foreign trade contract system. The higher rates prevailing in some markets, such as Shenzhen and other special economic zones previously had given those regions an edge because they could export higher cost products and cover part or all of their domestic currency "losses" by selling the foreign exchange retained from these export earnings at a more favorable, i.e. more renminbi per dollar, rate (Wang Deyun; Yang Xiong).

Open publication of systematic information on swap market rates began in 1989 (Chinese Finance and Banking Society 1989, 148). Data on monthly high, low, and average rates in five markets, which were geographically widely separated, showed that intermarket differences in swap rates were significant in 1988. For example, in the first quarter when what must have been extraordinary official constraints held the value of the dollar to well under 2 yuan in Shanghai, the average rate in the Tianjin swap market was more than 3.5 times the Shanghai rate. In the remaining three quarters of the year the differential between the cities with the highest and lowest average monthly rates averaged about 7 percent and the highest intermarket spread, which occurred in September, was 14 percent. However, in the absence of comparable data for earlier years it is difficult to judge whether the market for foreign exchange was becoming more integrated in the closing years of the 1980s.

Despite the sources of ambiguity discussed above, it is useful to consider both the divergence between the official exchange rate and the auction rate and between the auction rate and the black market rate for foreign exchange as indicators of what the equilibrium exchange rate might be. First, the spread between the auction market rate and the official exchange rate narrowed significantly in 1989–90. In 1988 buyers of foreign exchange on the swap market paid an average of 6 yuan, a premium of two thirds over the official exchange rate. However, in late 1989 the official rate was devalued to 4.2 yuan per dollar and the swap market rate was 5.7 yuan (Xinhua 1989b). In late 1990, just after a further devaluation of the official rate to 5.2 yuan, the auction market rate was 5.3 yuan in Shanghai and from 5.5 to 5.7 in other cities (Wang Xiangwei 1990b). Thus the spread between the two rates had been reduced to 10 percent or less.

Analyzing the spread between the auction market rate and the black market price of foreign exchange is more problematic than the first spread, just discussed, for at least two reasons. First, the black market is a market for foreign currency rather than for foreign exchange deposits. Because foreign currency is used to purchase imports smuggled into China or to finance other illegal transactions, its price can be expected to vary with the effectiveness of enforcement of China's customs regulations and other laws. For example, one does not need an import license to buy foreign exchange on the black market. By contrast, the Bank of China is required, in principle, to check trade documents prior to authorizing a payment from a foreign exchange account to be sure that the goods conform to those originally specified in the license issued to the purchaser by the Ministry of Foreign Economic Relations and Trade. Because there is smuggling, both across the Taiwan straits and over the border with Hong Kong, of goods for which import is either banned or licenses issued for quite limited quantities and for which domestic prices are quite high, one would expect the black market price to be above the auction market price.

Second, by their very nature data on black market prices are problematic. Black market prices for foreign exchange appear in print infrequently but when one asks in China one can always get a quote on the current black market rate. However, one is never confident that the rate quoted is an actual price or the respondent's best guess of the prevailing price. Moreover, unless one has an opportunity to ask reasonably well-informed respondents quite regularly about the current rate, it is difficult to judge the time trend of the black market rate.

Despite these problems, it appears that the differential between the swap rate and the black market rate was relatively modest, particularly when compared to the differentials that prevailed in the Soviet Union in the late

1980s.[21] For example, in 1988 when the official rate was 3.7 yuan per dollar (see Appendix A), the swap market rate ranged from 5.7 in the early months of the year to 7 in the closing months. The rate was said to be above 7 in a small number of markets such as Zhuhai, and to have averaged 6 yuan for the year as a whole. The comparable black market rates were 7 and over 8.5 for the start and the end of the year, respectively, with peaks exceeding 10 yuan (Hu Keli, 12). Although no estimated average black market rate for 1988 was provided, these data suggest the margin between the black and swap market rates in 1988 was only about one fourth, a rather modest differential given the risks associated with the black market which, after all, was illegal.

The margin between the two rates declined further in 1989. By mid-December 1989, just after the devaluation of the official exchange rate to 4.2, the black market rate in Shanghai fell sharply from 6.5 to a range of between 5.4 and 5.5 (Chen Weihua 1989). That meant the premium over the official rate had shrunk considerably and that the black market rate was approaching the swap rate, which was 5.3 in Shanghai at the time. Given the apparent reduction in the gap between both the official rate and the swap market price and between the swap and black market prices for foreign exchange one might tentatively conclude that although the swap market rate is not necessarily an equilibrium rate that it has become an economically more meaningful rate. In short, initially a large excess demand for foreign exchange at the official rate led to a substantial premium in the swap market. And the limited volume of swap market transactions meant a significant demand for foreign exchange was satisfied only at a higher black market price. Devaluations of the official rate have reduced the excess demand flowing on to the swap market. And the growing volume of swap market prices has cut the remaining excess demand satisfied on the black market.

Exchange rate policy

Revisions in exchange rate policy complemented the relaxation of exchange control in the export promotion strategy adopted after reform began in the late 1970s. It was then evident that the decentralization of trade authority to localities and enterprises, in and of itself, could not be relied on to increase exports. The state had revalued the yuan steadily upward vis-à-vis the United States dollar after 1971, from 2.46 per dollar to 1.49 per dollar by the end of 1979 (see Appendix A). Because of relative price stability in China compared to the rest of the world the real appreciation of the exchange rate was less than the change in the nominal rate against the dollar.[22] But the yuan remained highly overvalued and, as discussed in Chapter 2, in the closing years of the 1970s most commodity exports incurred significant financial losses measured in domestic currency (see Table 2.1). For example, Beijing municipality in 1980 incurred losses on 357 of 559 categories of export products. The loss rate exceeded 70 percent for more than one hundred product categories and cumulative losses for the year were 900 million yuan (Liu Yaoyu, 112–13). Thus the greater the volume of exports the greater the losses measured in domestic currency (Wu and Chen, 36).

The losses on exports became a quite urgent matter for the central government because in 1980 the profits on imports, for the first time since the mid-1960s, were no longer sufficient to offset export losses.[23] Thus the necessary subsidies for money losing exports could no longer come from within the Ministry of Foreign Trade. In 1980 the Ministry required a separate 3.18 billion yuan appropriation from the state treasury to offset this loss on foreign trade transactions (Hu Changnuan, 496). These unanticipated financial losses appear to have contributed significantly to the state's budgetary deficit in 1980, which ran 4.75 billion yuan above the budgeted amount of 8 billion yuan (Wang Bingqian 1981, 29).

To reduce the domestic currency losses of foreign trade and provide greater incentives for exporters the state effectively cut the value of the yuan by almost half by introducing an internal settlement rate of 2.8 yuan to the dollar in trade transactions beginning January 1, 1981 (Hu Chuangnuan, 496; State Council 1980b). That devaluation was a major step not only because of its large magnitude but also because it marked a fundamental turning point in how the exchange rate was fixed by the state. As noted in Chapter 2, in the early 1950s the exchange rate was fixed in part on the basis of the relative prices of a basket of consumer goods in China and in major cities in the world. Many basic consumer goods in China were underpriced due to state subsidies, and this contributed to a substantial overvaluation of the yuan. This overvaluation persisted over the decades, as reflected in the data in Table 2.1.

The internal settlement rate, by contrast, was fixed on the basis of the cost of earning foreign exchange in world markets. The value 2.8 was selected because the average domestic cost of earning a dollar in international markets in 1979 (the most recent year for which data was available when the decision was taken by the State Council in July 1980) was 2.40 yuan. Excluding crude oil, which was vastly underpriced on the domestic market, the cost of earning a dollar was 2.65 yuan. The internal rate of 2.8 was derived by averaging these 2 cost figures and then adding a 10 percent margin to provide a profit incentive (Wang Dongmin, 21).

The exchange rate of 2.8 was to apply only to trade transactions. Because the rate applied to the foreign exchange transactions between the Bank of China, on the one hand, and foreign trade corporations and other Chinese units authorized to carry out trade transactions, on the other, Chinese sources referred to it as "an internal settlement rate" or "internal settlement price" – never as an exchange rate. This was part of a rather transparent strategy to deny that China was operating on what amounted to a dual exchange rate system in which one rate applied to trade and another rate applied to nontrade transactions.

Foreign exchange derived from nontrade transactions, most importantly foreign remittances and tourism expenditures, continued to be converted to yuan at the official rate. That meant foreign travelers in China converted their monies to foreign exchange certificates (which in turn were pegged at par with the yuan) at a far less favorable rate than did Chinese foreign trade corporations or other sellers of Chinese goods in world markets. Similarly, Chinese citizens who received remittances from abroad by bank transfer did not get the advantage of converting their hard currencies to renminbi at the substantially more favorable internal settlement rate. Although foreign tourists had little choice (except to the extent they availed themselves of an active black market for foreign exchange certificates and foreign currency) but to suffer from this effective dual rate, overseas Chinese drastically cut their remittances to their relatives living in China (Wu and Zhang, 10). Remittances fell from a normal level of $600 to $700 million annually in the late 1970s to $171 million in 1985 (Wu and Chen, 33; "China's Balance of Payments in 1982–86"). Overseas Chinese financial support for their mainland relatives probably did not diminish. They sought to escape the price discrimination of the dual rate by converting their hard currency to goods in Hong Kong and then taking these items with them when they visited (Wu and Chen, 73). And they increasingly took the risk of mailing foreign bank notes to their relatives who would then exchange them for yuan on flourishing black markets at a much more favorable rate (Wu and Zhang, 10).

The substantial devaluation of the yuan inherent in the adoption of the internal settlement rate initially reduced the import substitution character of the trade regime only marginally and had limited positive effect on resource allocation. There were two reasons for this. First, as in the case of the similar foreign trade conversion ratio introduced in Hungary in the mid-1960s, the rate was based on the average rather than the economically more appropriate marginal cost of earning foreign exchange (Balassa 1970, 15). Because the cost of incremental exports no doubt exceeded the average cost of all exports the internal rate was not high enough to cover the cost of additional exports and thus provided inadequate incentives to boost exports. Second, the domestic pricing of both imported goods and of export goods changed only modestly. In short, few users of imported goods paid higher domestic prices and few producers of export goods received more units of domestic currency for their exports, both of which normally would occur in the case of currency devaluation. Understanding the reason for this anomalous response requires a close look at how prices of traded goods were determined, beginning in 1981.

Pricing of traded goods

Because the basic principles of price formation for traded goods, which had been last revised in 1964, were not altered when the internal settlement rate was adopted, the domestic prices of most traded goods initially changed little as a result of the effective devaluation of the Chinese currency. On the import side the principle of setting prices at the same level as comparable domestically produced goods continued to apply to most imports. Thus a broad range of imports, particularly products judged closely related to either the national plan or the people's livelihood, were sold in China at prices unchanged by the adoption of the internal settlement rate. For example, although the foreign trade corporations responsible for the import of grain, cotton, sugar, chemical fertilizer, and insecticide had to pay the Bank of China more for the foreign exchange needed to purchase these goods on world markets, they transferred the products to relevant domestic units (the Ministry of Food in the case of wheat, the Ministry of Textile Industry in the case of cotton, and so forth) at uniformly established state domestic prices unaffected by the devaluation of the yuan. These ministries, in turn, sold the goods (cotton to textile factories under the ministry, flour to the permanent urban population), at prices that did not reflect any of the higher cost, measured in domestic currency, of purchasing the goods on international markets. The losses that the national foreign trade corporations incurred in this process were subsidized fully from the state budget (Hu Changnuan, 504).[24] Table 3.4 identifies the most important of these goods, most of which were sold at a financial loss even prior to 1981. The introduction of the new internal exchange rate roughly doubled those domestic currency subsidies beginning in 1981.[25] A broad range of other import products also were priced on the basis of comparable domestically produced goods. These included goods imported under the state plan paid for from centrally controlled sources of foreign exchange for which profits and losses were to be borne by the foreign trade corporations. And it also involved goods such as industrial raw materials and agricultural producer goods imported by localities and

Table 3.4. *Price subsidies for five imported commodities, 1978–87 (millions of yuan)*

Year	Total	Of which				
		Grain	Cotton	Sugar	Chemical fertilizer	Pesticides
1978	1,435	550	634	–	239	12
1979	2,290	1,176	563	–	512	39
1980	4,310	2,076	1,042	153	981	58
1981	8,826	4,221	2,068	607	1,886	44
1982	5,679	3,438	633	174	1,396	38
1983	5,868	–	–	–	–	–
1984	4,100	–	–	–	–	–
1985	1,759	–	–	–	–	–
1986	1,334	–	–	–	–	–
1987	1,767	–	–	–	–	–

Notes: Dash means figure not available
Sources: State Statistical Bureau (1989a, 673)

ministries using their own sources of foreign exchange, such as retained export earnings (Hu Changnuan, 504–5). As discussed in Chapter 2 in the section *Pricing of traded goods*, this was a principle widely applied to imported goods beginning in 1964.

Potentially, goods priced by converting the import cost in foreign exchange to domestic currency using the exchange rate might have increased in price as a result of the de facto devaluation of the yuan in trade transactions in 1981. As discussed in Chapter 2, roughly 20 percent of China's imports prior to 1981, including machinery and electrical apparatus imported from market economies, was priced on the basis of this principle.

However, because of the actual procedures adopted, prices of goods based on import cost generally did not rise and in some special cases they actually may have fallen. There were two reasons for this. First, as discussed in Chapter 2, the domestic prices of these commodities were determined by converting the import price, including cost, insurance and freight, into renminbi using an exchange rate that was a premium over the official rate. For example, at the end of 1980, the official yuan–dollar exchange rate was 1.53 and the premium was 80 percent. So imports priced on the basis of import cost faced an effective exchange rate of 2.75 yuan per dollar. Using an exchange rate of 2.8 rather than 2.75 had virtually no effect on the domestic prices of imported goods that were priced based on import cost.

Moreover, the prices of certain imports continued to be priced based on the official exchange rate, with a modest premium. For example, whole plants, machinery and electrical equipment imported from the West were subject to conversion from international to domestic prices at an exchange rate that was only a 10 percent premium over the official rate. For machinery and equipment from socialist states the premium was 30 percent. These were the prevailing rates when the premium system of converting import cost to domestic currency finally was abolished effective July 1, 1985 (Contemporary China Series Editorial Board, 230; State Bureau of Commodity Prices 1985a; State Council 1985b). These premia appear to have been introduced in 1981. Thus in 1981, when the average official exchange rate was 1.71 yuan per dollar, machinery, equipment, and whole plants imported from the West would have been subject to an exchange rate of 1.88, a substantial preference compared to the internal rate of 2.8.

The internal settlement rate of 2.8 probably only raised the domestic cost of goods that were imported on a decentralized basis in the early 1980s (Wu and Chen, 70). Those importers responsible for their own profits and losses, for example under the agency system in which the foreign trade corporations simply acted as the agent of the importer, presumably paid more for their imports than they would have under the old system.[26] Thus in 1981, when the internal rate was introduced it would have raised the prices of no more than one eighth of China's imports. By 1984, the last year the internal rate was used, the effective devaluation of the renminbi would have fed through to affect the domestic prices of about one third of China's imports.[27]

Similarly on the export side most producers of goods for the international market initially received no benefit from the devaluation of the yuan in trade transactions in 1981. Foreign trade corporations continued to handle a large though declining share of export transactions as the agency system, in which the corporations charged only a commission, was slow to take hold (World Bank 1988a, 102–3). Only export producers using the agency system would have benefited, in terms of yuan earnings, from the devaluation of the currency.

As a consequence of this insulation of many users of imports and most suppliers of exports from the effects of the de facto devaluation of the yuan, the introduction of the internal settlement rate did not significantly alleviate the deficit in foreign trade measured in domestic currency. Indeed, given the constraints on domestic pricing, the main effect of devaluation was to reduce profits on imports and reduce losses on exports. As in the case of Poland, which in 1959 introduced a special exchange rate based on the price of earning foreign exchange, the internal rate did affect the distribution of profits and losses among the foreign trade corporations (Plowiec, 342). However, if trade were initially balanced and there were no changes in the quantities of exports and imports in response to the change in the exchange rate, the domestic pricing constraints would mean that there would be no change in the domestic currency profitability of foreign trade in the aggregate. In reality the reduction in import profits was so extreme that there were actually losses on imports in 1981. This was due largely to the new internal settlement rate and to a much lesser extent to a modest increase of 3.5 percent in the international prices of import goods (Chen Ying, 48; Ministry of Foreign Economic Relations and Trade 1989, 357). The roughly 9 billion yuan in losses in 1981 shown in Table 3.4, for import commodities for which domestic pricing was unchanged as a result of the introduction of the internal settlement price, accounted for about 80 percent of total import losses that year (Zheng Jianjing, 32). But losses on imports were very widespread. By 1983 China incurred losses on seventeen of its twenty-two most important imported commodities (Ma and Sun, 307).

Not surprisingly the adoption of the internal exchange rate changed exporting from a loss-making to a profitable activity for foreign trade corporations, at least temporarily. Profits on exports in 1981 were at an all-time historic high of more than 8 billion yuan (Wu and Chen, 37; Xiang Yin, 18).

Although export transactions in the aggregate were temporarily profitable, the numbers above make clear this was more than offset by the occurrence, for the first time ever, of losses on imports. With the cushion of import profits removed China continued to experience net financial losses on foreign trade, measured in domestic currency, of about 2 billion yuan (Wu and Chen, 37). Moreover exports moved back into the loss column within a year or two. For the years 1981–3 roughly 55 percent of the financial losses on external transactions was incurred on imports, the balance on exports (Xiang Yin, 15–16).

The internal settlement rate not only failed to resolve the problem of domestic currency losses on foreign trade. It also does not appear to have boosted the rate of growth on China's exports. In the four years the internal settlement rate was used, 1981–4, China's exports grew from $20.9 to $24.4 billion – a much lower rate of expansion than in the years just prior to 1981 (Ministry of Foreign Economic Relations and Trade 1989, 353). One reason appears to be that the devaluation of the yuan was insufficient to provide most producers with an incentive to export via the agency system. In Shanghai, for example, two thirds of all exports continued to require subsidies even at the more favorable exchange rate prevailing beginning in 1981. Because these subsidies were not available for exports via the agency system, decentralized exports grew moderately. Moreover, for China as a whole the number of export products requiring subsidies remained large and grew rapidly. The number of money-losing export commodities expanded from 1,038 in 1982 to 1,783 in 1983 (Ma and Sun, 307).

In short, the internal exchange rate failed to meet either of its two objectives. Domestic currency losses on foreign trade transactions continued unabated in the early 1980s. Indeed losses, which totaled 19.6 billion yuan in the four years 1980–3, were not only substantially greater than in the earlier period of losses during the late 1950s and early 1960s, but more than offset the entire cumulative trade profits of 1953–79 (Ma and Sun, 307). And export growth was below expectations as well.

The final blow to the internal exchange rate system introduced in 1981 came from the international community. The Chinese were keenly aware, as a result of the annual consultation between the International Monetary Fund and the People's Bank of China, that the sustained use of a dual exchange rate system was in violation of IMF standards. According to the Fund, which "suggested that China return to a unitary exchange rate," a dual exchange rate is allowed only to deal with short-term, balance-of-payments problems (Wu and Chen, 70).

In addition to this pressure from the International Monetary Fund, the dual exchange rate became an issue in trade complaints brought against China in the United States, one of China's largest export markets in the first half of the 1980s. American firms faced with competition from Chinese-produced goods argued that the introduction of the internal settlement rate was the equivalent of an export subsidy, grounds for bringing an anti-dumping proceeding against Chinese imports.

The existence of a multiple exchange rate system that could have made exports cheaper and imports more expensive was an issue in two important formal complaints brought to the United States Department of Commerce and the International Trade Commission. The first was an antidumping proceeding brought against the importers of Chinese menthol. In their response to that case, which was filed prior to but heard after the introduction of the internal settlement rate, the Chinese denied that multiple exchange rates were used to subsidize Chinese domestic producers (Stoltenberg, 44). The Department of Commerce ruled that Chinese menthol was sold at less than fair market value. However, they also said that the imports had not caused or threatened material injury to the U.S. producer. Thus in that case no action was taken against the import of Chinese menthol into the U.S. market.

The second case, brought by the American Association of Textile Manufacturers in 1983, was far more serious. The Association specifically charged that the internal exchange rate subsidized Chinese exports, including textiles. Ultimately the Association withdrew its complaint after it was assured by the executive branch that new curbs on Chinese textile sales in the U.S. market would be introduced. By the time the new U.S. textile quotas for China were announced, the Chinese government already had decided to abandon the internal exchange rate system. The official exchange rate, in any case, had depreciated steadily after 1980, eroding whatever advantage the internal rate initially had given to Chinese exporters. The average rate in 1984 was 2.33 yuan, and by the end of 1984, the official exchange rate had moved to 2.80 yuan to the dollar, paving the way for the reintroduction of a unitary exchange rate beginning in 1985.

Reform of the pricing of traded goods and of the exchange rate in the early 1980s reduced the import substitution character of China's foreign trade regime only marginally. The center had decentralized trade authority and reduced its monopoly control over the allocation of foreign exchange earnings from both trade and nontrade transactions. It also had devalued the yuan via the introduction of the internal settlement rate. Although the share of import users who had to bear the rising cost of imports increased, the continued pricing of most imports on the principle of equality with the prices of comparable domestic goods provided significant insulation of domestic producers from international competition. Similarly, few export producers initially benefited from the de facto devaluation of the domestic currency.

Reform accelerates

The state liberalized pricing of traded goods at a more rapid rate after the early 1980s, resulting in a significant erosion of the import substitution character of the trade regime. The greatest change was for imported goods where the use of the agent system expanded rapidly in the mid-1980s. Goods imported under the agent system were subject to "foreign trade agent price formation" (waimao daili zuojia). That meant the import price times the exchange rate formed the basis of the domestic price. To this was added customs taxes, product taxes or value added taxes, bank charges, and the handling fee of the agent. The share of import goods whose domestic prices were based on the import cost rose from about 20 percent in 1984 to 80 percent in 1986 (Chen Jiaqin, 54).[28] By 1986 pricing according to the principle of comparable domestic products was limited to a list of twenty-eight commodity categories which comprised only 20 percent of the value of imports.[29] Traditional pricing applied only to the share of imports of these goods that fell under the central foreign exchange plan. When these commodities were imported outside the plan or were paid for from local sources of foreign exchange, the domestic price was based on the cost of imports. All other products were to be priced based on the cost of imports (State Bureau of Commodity Prices, Ministry of Foreign Economic Relations and Trade, and Ministry of Finance, 1986).

This reform in the domestic pricing of imported commodities was not simply a minor accounting change. Rather it was a substantial erosion of the airlock system that traditionally had insulated China from the world economy. The shift to pricing based on import cost required users of imported goods to pay higher domestic prices and made them more sensitive to the world prices of goods they used.

Predictably, various units sought preferential treatment to avoid the higher prices they would be forced to pay under this new regulation because certain commodities not on the list escaped pricing based on import cost after 1986.[30] There is ample precedent for this type of lobbying as in late 1970s and early 1980s when the textile industry successfully refused to pay more for domestic cotton following the state's decision to raise the price paid to cotton growers in 1978, 1979, and 1980. Although the cotton textile industry was among the most profitable in China, it did not have to absorb the 30 percent increase in the price of raw cotton. Rather, the Ministry of Finance was forced to provide a subsidy so that the price of cotton sold to the factories of the textile industry could go unchanged (Lardy 1989, 304).

However, in the second half of the 1980s sector after sector was forced to pay substantially more for imported goods. For example, the center in January 1988 informed the textile industry that it would no longer subsidize the domestic sale of imported wool, chemical fiber, and chemical industry monomers. Citing rising costs following the July 1986 devaluation of the renminbi, the imposition of value-added taxes on imports of chemical fiber and wool beginning in April 1987, and rising world prices, the center told the Ministry of Textile Industry that the financial burden of distributing imports at unchanged prices had become intolerable. Thus the Ministry of Textile Industry was forced to impose the agent pricing system for these commodities, meaning that the domestic prices of these imported goods would henceforth be based on the import price converted to domestic currency at the official exchange rate (State Bureau of Commodity Prices, State Council, et al. 1988).

Similarly, the State Council and the State Bureau of Commodity Prices announced in 1989 that most steel and nonferrous metals imported within the scope of the foreign trade plan and paid for with central foreign exchange resources would be subject to pricing based on import cost beginning on

November 1, 1989 (State Bureau of Commodity Prices Foreign Price Office 1989, 162). That decision removed two of the most important categories of import commodities from the list of twenty-eight categories of import goods priced on traditional principles.[31] The effect of this decision became clear at the end of 1989 when the renminbi was devalued by more than 20 percent. Companies with foreign steel on order reportedly tried to cancel their contracts on the grounds that the devaluation would raise the price above that of domestic steel (Qin Xiaoli). Under the system prevailing prior to November 1989, users of imported steel products would have been insulated from the effects of a devaluation of the renminbi.

By the end of 1989 the number of imported commodities the central government continued to subsidize so that they could be sold at the same price as comparable domestic goods had been reduced to fourteen. And effective April 30, 1990 the list was further reduced to eight commodities.[32] In some cases of the twenty commodities stricken from the list between 1986 and early 1990 the government adjusted the prices of domestically produced goods so that the gap between the international and the domestic price was eliminated or at least greatly reduced. Thus the imports of these twenty commodities are no longer explicitly subsidized by the central government and international and domestic prices for these goods have been brought into closer alignment.

By mid-1990 the State Bureau of Commodity Prices estimated that the domestic prices of 90 percent of all of China's imports were based on the import price.[33] That was a dramatic change from as recently as 1984 when only 43 percent of imports were priced based on the basis of import cost (Contemporary China Series Editorial Board, 230; State Bureau of Commodity Prices Foreign Price Office 1989, 162).

The pace of change, however, was slower for export goods where traditional pricing arrangements had insulated domestic producers from international prices for decades. The slower evolution of the domestic pricing arrangements for export goods becomes clear from an examination of the export planning procedures that prevailed after the first decade of reform.

In the late 1980s export products were divided into three categories. The most highly controlled first category included twenty-one goods for which export volumes were specified in the mandatory portion of the foreign trade plan and for which the volume of exports could not be increased or lowered without the explicit authorization of the State Council. The head offices of the specialized foreign trade companies were responsible for implementing the plan for sixteen of these products. Responsibility for plan implementation was divided between the head offices of the foreign trade corporations and their provincial branch offices for the five remaining products.[34] Category one products included crude oil, refined petroleum products, coal, tungsten, antimony, tea, tobacco, rice, corn, beans, bean products, cotton yarn and gray goods, cotton-synthetic yarns and gray goods, raw silk and cloth, and so forth (Zhou Chuanru, 11). These twenty-one commodities accounted for about 25–30 percent of the value of China's exports in 1988 (Ministry of Foreign Economic Relations and Trade 1989, 372–450).[35]

The value of exports of category two products, which were subject to guidance planning, was also specified in the plan in order to ensure a "balance between domestic and international uses" (Li Lanqing 1988b, 12). Only specifically authorized export companies could handle these goods. Because a list of the ninety-one products falling into category two has not been openly published, it is not possible to measure the share of exports subject to guidance planning by adding up the volume of exports of these commodities. But, according to information supplied by the Chinese authorities to the General Agreement on Tariffs and Trade, guidance plan exports accounted for only 15 percent of China's exports in 1988 (Working Party 1988, 21).

Category three export goods, which were managed in a decentralized fashion outside the plan, accounted for 55 percent of total exports. But even these commodities could be exported only by enterprises that had been vested with export rights (Zhou Chuanru, 12).

Category one exports specified in the foreign trade plan, for the most part, appear to have been subject to traditional pricing. The specialized national foreign trade corporations and their provincial branch offices continued to purchase planned quantities of these export goods from domestic producers at the same state-fixed price as comparable goods sold on the domestic market. However, even domestic firms producing category one export goods were not fully insulated from world prices. First, even if the nominal price of the goods for export was fixed, firms undoubtedly sought to bargain over the other terms and conditions specified in the contracts they signed with foreign trade corporations. Foreign trade corporations were also in a position to supply certain scarce materials and inputs at favorable prices in order to assure timely delivery of export goods that were most desirable, even when they were specified in the mandatory export plan. Second, producers also could initiate above-plan exports for which they would receive a price that, over time, was increasingly related to the world market price for that commodity. It is not clear the extent to which producers of exports covered under the guidance plan were required to deliver their goods to export companies at ex-factory prices. But they too could export above-plan quantities of their products for which pricing was more flexible.

Decentralized exports should have been the least insulated from world market prices. Producers of these goods were not compelled to deliver them to foreign trade corporations, either national or provincial, at state fixed prices. In principle, these firms could hire a foreign trade corporation to act as their agent. Under this system they would pay a modest commission to the corporation for handling the international transaction and they would receive a price based on the international market conditions. But, at the end of the 1980s less than 10 percent of China's export products, presumably largely category three goods, were exported under the agency system.[36]

The slow spread of the agency system for exports, however, does not mean that producers of category three export goods were insulated from world market prices. Pricing of most of category three exports, as well as above-plan exports of goods in categories one and two, followed neither the pure agency system nor the traditional pure procurement system.

However, over time two factors brought domestic goods prices closer to international prices. First, producers bargained with their customary foreign trade corporations seeking the most favorable price and other terms. Information initially was distributed very asymmetrically. In many cases, producers knew little about international market conditions for their products. Foreign trade corporations deliberately withheld market information from export producers in order to maintain their power to exploit those firms by paying them low prices for their goods (Yang Peixin 1988a, 28). Even for goods that could be sold internationally at a relatively high profit, foreign trade companies initially offered prices only marginally above the state-fixed ex-factory prices. But over time, as producers learned more about the international demand for their goods, they sought to capture these profits by demanding a higher price from the foreign trade corporations. And they sought to pay lower commissions and fees to the corporations for handling their export goods.

Second, as the expansion in the number of foreign trade corporations eroded the monopoly powers of the old national trade corporations, producers could offer their goods to more than one potential exporter. Competition between trading corporations, of course, was also a major source of information for producers about international market conditions for their goods. This process tended to move the domestic prices of category three exports and above-plan categories one and two exports closer to world market prices. Thus the price received by the producer reflected both the firm's knowledge about international market conditions and the degree of competition among foreign trade corporations that could handle the transaction. As competition among foreign trade corporations increased over the decade as a result of their expanding numbers, the influence of international prices on the domestic prices of exported goods rose. Export producers were particularly assiduous in bargaining for higher domestic prices following devaluations of the renminbi.

Other export promotion measures

In addition to the policies already discussed in this chapter, China adopted several other export promotion measures that are commonly observed in the early stages of trade liberalization in developing countries. These included special programs of enhanced export credits; preferential interest rates on domestic currency loans to firms producing for export; subsidized domestic transport, storage, and insurance of export goods (Li Yang, 21) and the development of manufacturing facilities devoted exclusively to export production. The magnitude and significance of these programs, except for export credits, is not known. The lack of information on these programs presumably is related to China's effort, beginning in 1986, to become a contracting party to the General Agreement on Tariffs and Trade. All of these export promotion measures appear to be in violation of the GATT Code on Subsidies and Countervailing Duties (1979).

Export credits

The origins of China's program of export credits are not clear. Indeed, the World Bank's most exhaustive study of China's foreign trade system reported that "there seems to be no specific facility in China to finance the production and sale of exports" (World Bank 1988a, 177). The periodic Chinese publications that report on the quantities of domestic credit extended to Chinese firms do not break out export credits as a specific item.

Yet sporadic news accounts divulge information on export credits extended by the Bank of China. The role of the Bank of China, traditionally the sole bank authorized to deal in foreign exchange and international payments, suggests there was a specific export credit facility available to exporters above and beyond the regular credits they received from specialized banks such as the Industrial and Commercial Bank of China.[37] Some export credits, such as the two billion yuan earmarked for the development of exports from machinery and electronics equipment industries during the Seventh Five–Year plan (1986–90) were clearly provided to promote exports in certain priority sectors (Zheng Tuobin, 4). But what portion of export credits are so designated to achieve export targets embedded in various plans is impossible to determine from openly published materials.

However, there is no doubt that the magnitude of export credits grew rapidly and was relatively large by the end of the 1980s. Domestic currency loans outstanding to export-oriented firms and trade corporations totaled 100.8 and 120 billion yuan in 1988 and 1989, respectively, a substantial increase over 1984 when the figure stood at 40 billion yuan (Xinhua 1990a; Zhang Gang, 63). These funds were particularly important in 1989 and the early part of 1990 because domestic monetary policy was tightened to reduce inflationary pressure. These large export credits, equal to more than half the value of exports in the late 1980s, helped to insulate export-producing firms, at least in part, from the domestic credit crunch at the end of the decade. That may explain in part the continued robust growth of exports in a period when domestic economic performance was anemic compared to most of the decade of the 1980s.

Another type of export promotion policy that appears to have been of significance in the 1980s was the expanded development of "export commodity production bases and specialized industrial export factories" (Fu Zhongxin, 6). The origins of this system can be traced to the early 1960s when China was just beginning, in the wake of the split with the Soviet Union, to redirect its exports to market economies. The development of export commodity production bases involves targeting certain industries to become major sources of exports. The best example in the 1980s was machinery and electronic products, a sector in which the state has made a strong push since 1985 to promote exports (Ren Kan). In that year the State Council endorsed a specific decision calling for vastly increased exports of machinery and electronic goods. Although the document approving this plan is not available, the effects of the decision are apparent in many actions. Already noted above in this chapter is the special preferential rate for the retention of foreign exchange earned in this sector. In addition the state provided loans at preferential interest rates, special bonuses to firms that exported, an exemption from paying import duties on needed imports of materials and components and "the establishment of an export production system for machinery and electronic exports" (Ni Yijin, 307–9). For several years in the second half of the 1980s the entire program to promote machinery and electronic exports was under the direction of a special State Council Office for the Management of Machinery and Electronic Exports.

Other ad hoc policies to promote exports in specific sectors also existed. In the mid-1980s, for example, the state provided special enterprise "technical reform funds" (jishu gaizao jijin) to promote exports of light industrial and textile products produced in coastal regions. Neither the magnitude of the funds the state provided nor the duration of this program is known. The program was structured to provide domestic currency funds equal to 40 percent of the value of exports over and above the level achieved in 1985 (Zheng Tuobin, 4). The incentive was thus similar to the special foreign exchange retention rates provided to specific sectors. But the funds were provided in domestic currency and used to upgrade and renovate capital equipment.

Summary

The decade of the 1980s was one of far-reaching reform of China's foreign trade system. Much of the traditional structure was profoundly changed. The old reliance on a handful of foreign trade corporations acting on behalf of the Ministry of Foreign Trade was transformed. Literally thousands of trading companies were authorized to carry out trade transactions. Equally important, the relaxation of the system of stringent exchange control provided access to sources of foreign exchange that did not exist in the prereform era. What began as a modest system of foreign exchange entitlements for exporters steadily widened as the center provided greater and greater incentives for exporters. With some setbacks, such as the foreign exchange crisis that began in 1984, controls over the use of import entitlements gradually were relaxed. The opening of formal swap markets in foreign exchange toward the end of the decade provided an innovative mechanism, short of internal convertibility of the domestic currency, for the reallocation of foreign exchange to meet the demands of a diverse group of importers. Unable to get an official allocation of foreign exchange at the official exchange rate, buyers in these markets were willing to pay a higher marketlike rate to acquire imported goods for which they could obtain an import license. This was an important step, because by the end of the decade about one fifth of all foreign exchange earnings were reallocated via the swap market to importers willing to pay a marketlike price for foreign exchange. For this class of importers, the airlock that traditionally separated world and domestic prices had vanished.

The mirror image of this emergence of decentralized trading, which proceeded particularly rapidly on the import side, was a shrinkage of the traditional foreign trade plan. Increasingly, the state used a system of import and export licenses to regulate the commodity composition of imports and exports, rather than specifying import and export products in great detail in physical terms in the foreign trade plan.

Finally, and perhaps most importantly, the Chinese began to adopt a more realistic exchange rate policy and reformed the pricing of traded goods. The value of the domestic currency in trade transactions was cut almost in half near the outset of reform and this was followed by further significant devaluations in 1985, 1986, 1989, and 1990. Although progress was initially slow, by the end of the decade the domestic prices of almost all imports were based on world market prices. With a few exceptions, imports were no longer available to privileged users at far below world prices. And a growing share of exporters was able to bargain to receive domestic currency prices that more closely approximated world prices.

Thus the reforms of the 1980s transformed the structure of the foreign trade and foreign exchange control systems. But what effect did the changes in the underlying economic incentives have on the observed patterns of trade? Did the actual choices of import and export goods become economically more rational as the extreme import substitution bias of the traditional foreign trade system began to erode? It is to this question that I turn in the next chapter.

4

The efficiency of China's foreign trade

Evaluating the economic consequences of the reforms described in Chapter 3 is difficult. In principle the foreign trade reforms in place by the end of the 1980s should have led to a significant improvement in the efficiency of China's foreign trade. Reforms of the pricing of traded goods have almost certainly greatly reduced the wide and variable gaps separating domestic prices from those prevailing in international markets. Combined with the persistent move toward a more realistically valued official exchange rate and the substantially increased use of auction markets to allocate foreign exchange, a growing share of importers and exporters face prices that more clearly reflect real opportunity costs rather than arbitrary prices set decades ago. Thus one would expect the efficiency of China's trade to rise considerably. Seeing precisely why this should be the case is made clearer by examining how distortions in the domestic market in the early to mid-1980s made it difficult to raise the efficacy of foreign trade by introducing a more decentralized trading system. Inefficiencies stemmed from several sources.

Export planning

Although the decentralization of foreign trade decision-making described in Chapter 3 drastically reduced the share of China's exports subject to mandatory planning (zhiling xing jihua), that process was gradual. As late as 1986–7, more than 70 percent of all exports still fell within the mandatory plan (Wu and Zhang).[1] The planning process appears to have identified these exports without adequate consideration of relative real costs. In the initial stages of the export planning process the State Planning Commission and the Ministry of Foreign Economic Relations and Trade compiled a list of export products based on suggestions from various bureaus supervising industrial enterprises. In addition to specifying quantities of various goods, the plan included an estimate of the cost, in terms of domestic currency, of earning foreign exchange. This plan then was submitted to the Ministry of Finance, which approved, among other targets, a figure for the average cost of earning foreign exchange. The Ministry of Foreign Economic Relations and Trade then set cost targets for earning foreign exchange in major product categories and for various corporations (Wu and Zhang). Because these targets were ultimately the rates at which exporters, typically foreign trade corporations, could convert foreign exchange earnings to domestic currency, they were effectively commodity specific exchange rates. Moreover, within each foreign trade corporation cross subsidies further expanded the degree to which effective exchange rates were differentiated across products.

Four factors undermined the economic rationality of export planning in the first half of the 1980s. First, because the character of domestic price formation was only partially reformed, Chinese measures of the cost of earning foreign exchange may have been economically misleading. As discussed later in this section, a strategy of minimizing the domestic currency cost of earning foreign exchange might have made little economic sense.

Second, the provision of commodity specific exchange rates, via highly differentiated rates of subsidy to different categories of export goods, tended to make the financial returns the same for all export goods. Thus in the initial process of identifying export goods the incentive to select comparative advantage (i.e. relatively low cost) products was undermined since if a nominated high-cost product was included in the approved plan an extra subsidy in the form of a more favorable exchange rate would also be approved. That reduced the incentive to select comparative advantage goods for export at any given time, thus reducing the efficiency of exports (Yang Jianhua, 5). It also eroded the incentive to hold down the cost of manufacturing export goods or to shift over time from higher cost to lower cost exports. When production costs of an export good rose sharply the competitive position of the good in the international market would not necessarily be eroded. Rather, it was more likely that the Ministry of Foreign Economic Relations and Trade would assign the good a more favorable exchange rate so that the producing firm's domestic currency receipts would rise by enough to cover its increased production costs. This process appears to have been the principal reason that the cost of earning a dollar of foreign exchange in the 1980s tended to rise even more rapidly than domestic prices. For example, in the five-year period of 1982–6, whereas the retail price index rose 20.3 percent, the cost of earning foreign exchange rose by 40 percent (Zhou Xiaochuan 1990a, 6).

Third, the pressure to fulfill export targets, specified in terms of foreign exchange, limited the relevance of the specified levels of domestic currency expenditure per unit of export earnings. Faced with a choice of failing to fulfill the export target or exceeding their domestic cost target, exporters invariably incurred higher costs in order to meet their target for export earnings. In short, "mandatory plan export commodities must be exported regardless of the cost of earning foreign exchange" (Wu and Zhang). When this occurred the previously approved cost levels were then adjusted upward, leaving the government with a higher than anticipated financial loss on exports. Until the late 1980s these export losses were borne entirely by the central government. As discussed later in this chapter, the resulting burgeoning subsidies for exports became a highly contentious issue in intergovernmental finance in the 1980s.

Fourth, the negotiation for commodity specific exchange rates meant that export planning remained highly bureaucratic. The opportunity for decentralized export decision-making was reduced when such a large share of exports required subsidies to be saleable on the world market and the subsidies had to be negotiated on an item-by-item basis. It is for this reason the agency system was so slow to take hold, particularly for exports (Lu Jinhao, 44).

These sources of economic inefficiency stemming from export planning in the first half of the 1980s were reinforced by the overvaluation of the exchange rate. The judgment that the domestic currency was overvalued is based on two factors. First, as was shown in Table 2.1, the average financial cost of earning foreign exchange in the 1980s was higher than its price. Second, excess demand for foreign exchange had led to increased controls on the use of retained foreign exchange in early 1985, as discussed in Chapter 3. The volume of foreign exchange transactions through the parallel foreign exchange market was very modest and the center reasserted the traditional virtual monopoly it had on the allocation of foreign exchange. The overvalued exchange rate undermined the incentive for decentralized exporting and provided implicit subsidies of imports.

The best evidence on the degree to which the distortions discussed above militated against the introduction of a decentralized trading system in the first half of the 1980s is provided in Table 4.1. These data show the financial profits earned or the financial losses sustained on export transactions in eighteen industries in 1983. They are derived from China's input–output table which includes data on the value of exports measured both in domestic prices and in terms of international prices, converted into domestic prices at the official exchange rate.[2] As explained in Chapter 2, a financial loss on an export transaction occurs when the domestic currency earnings from the sale of the good internationally are less than the domestic currency earnings from the sale of the same good on the domestic market. These financial losses are offset by subsidies. On the other hand, a financial profit is recorded when the

Table 4.1. *Financial profits and losses on exports by sector, 1983*

Industry	Profit or loss (million yuan)	Profit or loss (%)
Ferrous metal	−.006	−1.7
Nonferrous metal	−.166	−11.8
Electric power	−	−
Coal and coking coal	.071	10.4
Petroleum	4.904	56.9
Heavy chemical	−.859	−53.4
Light chemical	−1.352	−91.3
Heavy machinery	−2.872	−47.9
Light machinery	−1.268	−81.2
Building materials	.062	+8.6
Heavy forestry	−.020	−13.8
Light forestry	−.046	−28.2
Food Products	−1.580	−41.5
Textile	−2.007	−29.4
Tailoring and leather	−.535	−15.2
Papermaking, cultural and educational goods	−1.210	−50.9
Other	−.512	−45.5
Agriculture	−1.667	−17.2

Note: Financial profit (loss) is the difference between the domestic currency earnings received by the exporter (calculated by converting the foreign exchange earnings to domestic currency using the internal settlement rate) and the domestic FOB (free on board) price of the same goods. The FOB price is the sum of the ex-factory price (the price the producer would receive for delivery of the goods to the domestic distribution system) plus the cost of moving the goods to a Chinese port. That price would fall short of the price paid by the final domestic user since that would include markups to cover distribution costs, taxes, and profits at the wholesale and retail levels. The FOB price is the appropriate price for calculating the profitability of foreign trade since it is a measure of the opportunity cost of goods sold on the international market. Percentage of profit or loss is the absolute profit or loss expressed as a percent of the foreign exchange earnings (as recorded by the Chinese Customs Administration) converted to yuan at the official exchange rate.
Source: State Statistical Bureau National Economic Balance Statistics Department (1985, 7).

earnings from the sale of a good internationally exceed those from the sale of the same good on the domestic market.

Given the only partially reformed character of China's price system in the first half of the 1980s there clearly is no necessary relationship between these financial profits and losses and real or economic profits and losses. For example, an export may be financially profitable largely or even only because certain inputs into the production process are priced below real economic costs. In the extreme, such exports may be financially profitable even though the value added of these products measured at international prices is negative, thus reducing the value of the exporting country's gross national product (McKinnon 1990a). Alternatively an export may incur financial losses but real economic gains if some of the inputs used in the production process are overpriced.

Three striking facts emerge from Table 4.1. First, financial losses in domestic currency were sustained on exports in fifteen of seventeen sectors.[3] Only exports of products from the petroleum, coal and coking coal, and the building materials industries were profitable in terms of domestic currency.

Second, aggregate financial losses were a staggering 14.1 billion yuan, fully 3 percent of China's 1983 national income (State Statistical Bureau 1984, 29). Export losses were equal to one third of the value of exports, measured in domestic currency.[4]

The subsidy of exports in 1983, of course, is not surprising. It was inevitable given the overvalued exchange rate. Sellers of goods in international markets inevitably had losses when they converted their dollar earnings to domestic currency at the internal rate of 2.8 yuan per dollar when the average cost of earning that dollar was in excess of 3 yuan.

Third and most important, even on the highly aggregated basis of Table 4.1, rates of profit and loss varied widely across product categories. Losses ran from about 2 percent for ferrous metal products to over 90 percent for exports of light chemical products. That means that in order to earn 1 yuan from the sale of light chemical products on the world market producers in the industry had to give up 1.9 yuan in domestic market sales. In other words, the subsidies provided to the industry approached the domestic value of foreign exchange earnings. At the other extreme, profit rates ranged up to 57 percent in the case of petroleum.

That range of financial profits and losses can also be expressed in terms of the average de facto exchange rates prevailing in different industries. The subsidies provided in light chemicals were the equivalent of an exchange rate of 5.34 yuan per dollar – a rate almost twice as favorable to exporters as the internal settlement rate of 2.8 prevailing in 1983. On the other hand, the petroleum industry could break even on its external transactions even with an exchange rate as low as 1.59 yuan per dollar.

It is important to note that the magnitude of required export subsidies would have been substantially smaller had the domestic currency been less overvalued. Indeed, a uniform subsidy rate across all sectors would be the equivalent to a devaluation of the yuan. However, even with a uniform subsidy or a more reasonable exchange rate, the data underlying Table 4.1 would show rates of financial return on different export categories that varied enormously. At the overvalued internal settlement rate the rate of profit from the export of petroleum approached 60 percent – that is, every 100 yuan spent in acquiring petroleum products for export generated about 160 yuan in income for the exporter. A more reasonable exchange rate would reduce the magnitude of losses and the rates of losses in fifteen sectors but would raise the profit rate on petroleum, coal, and building materials exports. The huge range from the highest profit to the greatest loss rate would not change appreciably.

The existence of widely varying implicit product-by-product exchange rates is important for two reasons. First, it underlines the difficulty of introducing decentralized decision-making in foreign trade in a partially reformed domestic economy. In a decentralized environment those engaged in trade could be expected to respond to financial incentives. Exporters, for example, would have little information on the real economic costs of their products and even when they did would have no incentive to take these into account in making trade decisions. In short, the economic environment was ill-suited to the push for decentralized exporting that was the centerpiece of the major foreign trade reform document promulgated by the State Council in 1984.

Second, widely varying product-specific exchange rates signal the potential for significant misallocation of resources even under the largely unreformed trade system of the early and mid-1980s when most exports still fell within the scope of the mandatory export plan. The likelihood is that China was exporting products that contained or embodied widely varying quantities of domestic resources for each dollar of foreign exchange earnings. Under these conditions, shifting the composition of exports could raise the efficiency of China's foreign trade. The problem is that without domestic prices that reflected domestic resource cost, it was difficult for Chinese planners to know the optimal mix of either exports or imports. Was China an exceptionally low-cost producer of petroleum and petroleum products, coal and coking coal, and building materials (the three categories of exports showing significant financial profits)? Were these products so abundant on the domestic market that comparative advantage dictated their export? And were products by the light chemical sector so expensive and thus relatively more scarce on the domestic market that they were less attractive (i.e. lower profit) exports?

Addressing this issue requires a more detailed analysis of relative Chinese and world prices.

Domestic and world price structures

In an open economy with competitive markets one would expect to find that domestic prices for a broad range of goods, generally referred to as tradeable goods, would be closely related to world market prices. In the absence of tariffs, quotas or other quantitative restrictions there would be a tendency for domestic and world prices of tradeable goods to be equalized. If the domestic price of a good, for example, was relatively low, world demand for the good would lead to increased exports, a reduction in domestic supply, and thus an increase in the domestic price level. On the other hand, domestic goods with relatively high prices would be subject to competitive pressures from increased imports. If domestic producers did not lower their prices to meet the foreign competition, imports might satisfy all domestic demand and force the local producers out of business. Transport costs and other market imperfections, as well as exogenous shocks that move markets away from equilibrium, of course, complicate the description above. In developing countries pursuing import substitution strategies, there are a variety of distortions that cause systematic divergences between world and domestic prices. Thus in the real world price equalization is only a tendency and will not be realized in every period.

As discussed in Chapter 2, China's prices were largely cut off from the influence of world prices by the mid-1950s. Although trade volume was significant at that time, the domestic pricing of traded goods largely insulated China from fluctuations in world prices. That insulation was increased beginning in 1963 when a larger share of imports was priced by reference to prices of comparable domestic goods.

Given the infrequency of adjustments to domestic prices it is quite likely that the disparities in China's domestic price structure relative to the world price structure increased over time. It is well known that relative scarcities of various goods change significantly during the process of industrialization. That should lead to major changes in relative prices. The output of manufactured products that are relatively scarce in the initial stages of industrialization tends to rise most rapidly as industrial output expands. The relative prices of these goods typically fall substantially over time (Gerschenkron, 47).

Distortions in China's price structure arise from several distinct sources. First, the prices of most manufactured goods were set in the early to mid-1950s and were rarely if ever adjusted over the ensuing decades. Because the pace of industrial development in China over this period was the most rapid of any country in the world, static industrial prices almost certainly led to price distortions greater than one would anticipate based on the relative price changes that occurred during the historically much slower pace of industrialization of the now advanced industrial countries.

Second, the prices of many manufactures in China were established at relatively high levels. Particularly for products not previously produced in China pricing procedures adopted in the 1950s led to an upward bias. Firms were allowed to set prices for new products on the basis of the relatively high costs incurred during the stage of trial manufacture. But later, as production levels rose and costs fell due to economies of scale and the mastery of new production technologies, the firms frequently did not have to reduce their prices or did so only with a considerable lag (Field, Lardy, and Emerson, 7).

Third, in addition to the distortions in the prices of manufactured goods discussed above, the Chinese in the 1950s established relatively low prices for most basic raw materials and energy sources. The rationale for relatively low prices for coal, electricity, and so forth was that the great majority of these products satisfied interindustry demands and charging higher prices would simply raise the costs and reduce the profits on final goods. For example, if the relative price of coal was higher that would raise costs and reduce profits both for goods, such as steel, which used coal as an input in the production process, and for services, such as rail transportation, which relied heavily on coal for fuel. Although in theory such a policy would not have affected aggregate profits it was deemed undesirable because the primitive fiscal system meant the state relied almost entirely on the profits of state enterprises to finance government expenditures. It was thought these revenues would be most readily mobilized if profits were concentrated in enterprises producing predominantly final goods rather than intermediate goods or raw materials.

The initial underpricing of basic raw materials and energy sources was compounded over time. In contrast to manufactured goods, the cost of extracting most raw materials and energy sources rose over time as more easily exploited deposits were exhausted. Moreover, the prospects for containing rising costs with technological innovations were far more limited in raw materials exploitation than in manufacturing. Thus for example, the cost of producing coal rose steadily from 9.00 yuan per ton in 1952 to 17.78 yuan per ton in 1979 (Xu, Chen, and Liang, 164). Because the price received by producers was adjusted upward only in 1965 and 1979 and even then by proportionately less than the increase in production costs, profits in the industry were squeezed. By 1980 the industry could not even cover its operating costs even though its capital was provided largely interest free. Thus the industry became dependent on government subsidies for its survival.

The discovery of large-scale, easily exploited petroleum reserves in the late 1950s and early 1960s initially made it seem that oil would be an exception. Production costs throughout the period from 1957 to 1975 averaged almost two thirds less than the level of the early 1950s (Hu Chuangnuan, 292) and the state lowered the wellhead price of crude by about 20 percent, from 130 to 103 yuan per ton, in 1971 (Zheng Jifang, 25). However, the cost of producing crude oil rose after the mid-1970s while the price for crude remained unchanged. In the 1975–85 decade production costs for crude rose by 90 percent, an annual rate of 7.5 percent (Zheng Jifang, 26). After the mid-1980s one major field after another fell into the red. The wellhead price of crude was raised belatedly in January 1988, but the increase was only 10 yuan per ton, less than 10 percent (State Commodity Price Bureau Heavy Industrial Products Price Office, 145). At that price even the Daqing field, China's largest and one of the lowest cost producers, was expected to run a deficit in 1989 for the first time because of a tripling of production costs in the previous decade (Chen Weihua, 1988a). Thus the state raised the wellhead price of crude to 137 yuan per ton in 1989 and then to 167 yuan per ton in 1990 (Ye Dongfeng, 36).

These distortions are readily apparent in the date in Table 4.2, which compares relative Chinese domestic and world prices in the mid-1980s for a number of traded commodities. These data were compiled by Chinese researchers on the basis of carefully specified comparable commodities. There are few comparisons of the prices of industrial machinery or consumer durable goods, presumably because of the difficulties of measuring and adjusting for differences in product quality for these nonhomogeneous goods.

Despite the limitations in the sample of goods shown in Table 4.2, it bears out some of the observations offered above. When converted from domestic to international prices at the then prevailing internal settlement rate of 2.8 yuan per dollar, the prices of coal, crude oil and heavy fuel oil were far below the world level. But refined petroleum products, such as gasoline, were priced much closer to world levels, reflecting the Chinese practice of structuring prices so profits were generated disproportionately in final goods. The pattern is similar within the metallurgical category. Raw materials were underpriced by significant margins. Coking coal and iron ore were priced at about one third and 60 to 90 percent of the world price, respectively. And relative prices of intermediate products were low, but as one moves through the steel-making process relative prices began to rise. The price of pig iron was under half the world price and crude steel in ingot or billet form was about 40 to 60 percent of the world price. Finished steel products such as sheet steel, I beams, and steel channel were priced at about three fifths to three quarters of the world price. Finally, specialized products such as stainless steel plate were more than twice the world level.

In short, the data on relative Chinese prices in Table 4.2 appear not to reflect relative costs of production nor relative scarcities of various products

Table 4.2. *Relative Chinese and world prices, 1984*

Category and product	State-fixed price (international price = 100)
Agricultural products	74.6
Cereals	87.6
rice	61.3
wheat	121.9
corn	77.8
Edible vegetable oil and oilseeds	111.23
soybean oil	156.8
peanut oil	92.7
rapeseed oil	127.4
Industrial crops	72.0
cotton	72.9
jute	74.6
Meat, eggs, and leather	52.1
Light and textile industry products	79.0
Cotton piece goods	76.3
Cotton yarn	51.1
Raw silk	26.4
Polyester filament	208.6
Polyamide fiber filament	197.0
Newsprint	64.9
Chemical products	109.9
Inorganic products	108.5
sulfuric acid	159.7
caustic soda	76.2
soda ash	79.4
sodium nitrate	175.1
potassium sulfate	56.7
ammonium nitrate	103.5
potassium chloride	76.1
sulfur	114.2
Organic products	134.7
Synthetic materials	109.7
Energy	24.5
Coal	24.3
Coking coal	32.0
Crude oil	17.3
Gasoline	93.5
Diesel fuel	48.7
Fuel oil	12.9
Building materials	33.2
Plate glass	41.7
Cement	32.2

Table 4.2. *(cont.)*

Category and product	State-fixed price (international price = 100)
Metallurgical products	53.4
Iron ore	60–90
Pig iron	43.6
Steel ingot	61.1
Steel billets	38.1
Carbon steel	61.4
Sheet steel	74.0
I beams	61.5
Steel channel	75.4
Stainless steel plate	208.6
Nonferrous metals	87.8

Notes: The original source provides commodity specifications for each product category and the nature of the prices being compared. Chinese domestic prices are ex-factory for manufactured goods and ex-mine for coal and other mineral products. For agricultural goods Chinese prices are a weighted average of quota and overquota purchase prices received by producers. Chinese prices were converted to dollars at the internal settlement rate of 2.8 yuan per dollar to make the comparisons with international prices, all of which are quoted in U.S. dollars.
Source: Ma Hong and Sun Shangqing (1988, 374–91).

in China, but the arbitrary character of state-fixed domestic prices. Thus these prices could not be used to select rationally China's import and export goods. Nor could the efficiency of China's foreign trade be judged by measuring the financial profitability of import and export transactions.

Beginning in 1983 the official creation of parallel open markets for producer goods provides the first indication of the relative scarcity of many industrial products in China (Byrd; Wu and Zhao). Because purchasers of these goods generally used them to produce overquota output that was not subject to state price control, the market prices of these commodities should reflect the marginal value of these goods to their purchasers. Thus these market prices provide a better measure of the scarcity or opportunity cost of these products than do state fixed prices.

Table 4.3 provides a comparison of state and market prices for selected industrial goods and energy sources. The data in this table strongly suggest that the high "profits" recorded for exports in the petroleum, coal, and building materials sectors stem from the underpricing of these goods on the domestic market rather than from a comparative advantage in the production of those goods. That is particularly apparent in the energy sector. The state-

Table 4.3. *State-fixed and market prices for selected industrial goods, 1985–6*

Product	State-fixed price	Market price	Premium (%)
Coal (yuan/ton)	38.6	91	136
Crude oil (yuan/ton)	100	545	495
Diesel fuel (yuan/ton)	330	700	112
Fuel oil (yuan/ton)	65	460	607
Cement (yuan/ton)	62	210	239
Plate glass (yuan/m²)	2	6	200

Note: Market price observations are from "representative markets" in late 1985 and the first part of 1986.
Source: Ma Hong and Sun Shangqing (1988, 393–96).

set price for crude oil, for example, was less than one fifth of the world level. That was the price paid for crude that was allocated by the plan to priority users. But in the mid-1980s, the price paid by those who either did not receive a state allocation or found this allocation insufficient, was more than five times that of the state-fixed price. Thus, the market price of crude oil was roughly equal to the world price. Similarly, the state-fixed price of diesel fuel was just under half the world price. But the market price of diesel was just over twice the state-set price. In short, the market prices of crude, diesel, and fuel oil were all close to the world market price (Ma and Sun, 307).

What does this imply for the "profitability" of exports in the petroleum sector? If exporters of petroleum had to pay the domestic opportunity cost for crude oil their export "profits" would have been nil. Financial profits were created by providing crude oil to exporters at a small fraction of the world price. Access at these low prices was assured because crude oil remained one of the commodities subject to mandatory export planning (World Bank 1988a, 106). That meant crude oil and refined petroleum products were delivered to the relevant foreign trade corporation at the ex-factory price.

In the face of growing energy shortages at home, exports of crude oil and of refined products actually accelerated remarkably after 1983 (Lieberthal and Oksenberg, 262–3). As a means of covering growing financial losses in the petroleum industry, the state introduced a contract system that allowed the sale of incremental crude oil output either on the world market or on the internal market as so-called high-price oil (Zheng Jifang, 25). As a result, crude oil exports, which had been on a plateau of from 13 to 15 million metric tons annually since the late 1970s, shot up to 22 million metric tons in

1984 and reached a peak of 30 million metric tons in 1985 (State Statistical Bureau 1985, 502; 1987, 598). Exports of refined petroleum products also reached a peak in 1985 although the proportionate increase over the average level of exports in the earlier years of the decade was less.

Although the contract system for the distribution of oil was designed in part to provide additional revenues to oil fields to offset rising production costs, this did not occur at the Daqing oil field, China's largest. The state purchased all of the output, including over-quota production of Daqing, denying it an opportunity to market even as much as half a percent of its output. Marketing remained squarely in the hands of the China National Chemical Industry Import and Export Corporation (Sinochem), which controlled almost all of China's petroleum exports, and the China Petroleum Corporation (Sinopec), which was responsible for both the refining of crude oil and the domestic distribution of petroleum products.[5]

Despite the obvious reason for the high profitability of petroleum exports the Chinese press trumpeted the profitability of Sinochem (Xie Songxin 1986). The Corporation was praised both for its number one rank among all foreign trade corporations as an exporter and praised for the "profits" earned through its international transactions.

The situation was similar for exports of coal and of building materials, which were monopolized by the China National Metals and Minerals Import and Export Corporation. Table 4.3 shows that coal and key building materials sold on the domestic market at roughly two and a half and three times the state-fixed prices, respectively. The high profitability of exports in these sectors was simply a function of the artificially low state prices for these products. Like Sinochem, if the Metals and Minerals Import and Export Corporation had to pay the domestic opportunity cost of these materials, exports would not have been financially profitable.

The data on the profits and losses of exports and imports discussed above are for 1983 and the domestic price data are for a year or two later. These data tend to support the view that in the mid-1980s bureaucratic pressures resulted in trade decisions that sometimes overlooked well known distortions in China's domestic price structure. Exports of petroleum accelerated because this served dominant bureaucratic, not economic, interests. The Ministry of Finance supported petroleum exports because that tended to hold down the cost of earning foreign exchange and thus the need for more export subsidies. Sinochem and perhaps the Ministry of Petroleum Industry also stood to gain from the high profits that external sales generated.[6] But the domestic economy suffered because widespread energy shortages in the 1980s reduced the rate of capacity utilization of machinery and equipment in many sectors and limited the development of the petrochemical industry and transportation.[7]

Light industry spokesmen argued against the strategy of increased oil exports on the grounds of economic efficiency. Adopting an explicit comparative advantage framework, they argued that the value of the products they could sell internationally if less oil were exported and the energy made available to enterprises producing light industrial goods would exceed the income gained from selling oil directly on the international market (Ma and Sung, 307). Other authors criticized the oil export strategy on similar economic grounds (Wu and Chen, 225; Zhang Weiying, 188; Zhang Wenzhong, 47).

Some authors recognized that the influence of distorted domestic prices was not confined to the direct sale of petroleum and petroleum products. The export of energy intensive products also appeared financially profitable but only because energy was underpriced on the domestic market. In at least a few cases the value added of energy-intensive export products measured at international prices was negative, the possibility raised by McKinnon (1990a) in his discussion of the problems of trade liberalization in reforming socialist and formerly socialist economies (Ye and Xu, 15).

But not until the international price of oil collapsed in 1986–8 did the growth of petroleum exports level off. As late as 1988, when the average price the Chinese received for crude oil was less than one fourth the peak level of 1984, the volume of such exports was still almost one fifth above the 1984 level and off only 10 percent from 1985, the peak year of crude oil exports. The domestic criticism of petroleum exports continued into the late 1980s with the China International Engineering Consulting Corporation, an influential body advising the State Planning Commission, taking a very public position for slashing oil exports (Xie Songxing).

Ultimately, judging the economic rationality of petroleum exports is an empirical question that lies beyond the scope of this volume. Unfortunately, Chinese critics of petroleum exports have not openly published the detailed methodology and the data supporting their assertion that the efficiency of Chinese trade would have been higher if oil exports had been lower and the supplies of energy to producers of light industrial export goods increased. But their general analytical framework for addressing this issue, a comparison of the real resource costs of earning foreign exchange via alternative exports, was conceptually correct. Moreover, in my extensive reading of Chinese periodicals that address issues of the efficiency of foreign trade, I have never found any rebuttal of the views of the critics of the economic rationality of petroleum exports.

Table 4.4. *Financial profits and losses on imports by sector, 1983*

Industry	Profit or loss (–) (million yuan)	Profit or loss (%)
Ferrous metal	−.515	−5.2
Nonferrous metal	−.275	−5.8
Electric power	−.018	−16.4
Coal and coking coal	−.100	−61.7
Petroleum	.021	23.1
Heavy chemical	.184	2.1
Light chemical	.109	15.5
Heavy machinery	.935	8.6
Light machinery	.611	22.0
Building materials	−.463	−53.8
Heavy forestry	−.227	−11.4
Light forestry	−.004	−9.9
Food products	.989	50.6
Textile	1.563	36.8
Tailoring and leather	−.036	−31.3
Papermaking, cultural, and educational goods	.040	2.2
Other	.231	21.2
Agriculture	−2.637	−26.5

Note: Financial profit (loss) is the difference between the earnings from the sale of imported goods on the domestic market and the cost of imports, where the latter is the world price converted to yuan at the internal exchange rate of 2.8 yuan to the dollar (the rate importers paid the Bank of China to acquire foreign exchange for trade transactions). Percentage of profit or loss is the absolute profit or loss expressed as a percentage of import cost.
Source: State Statistical Bureau National Economic Balance of Statistics Department (1985, 7).

Imports

The distortions discussed at the outset of this chapter are also reflected in the magnitude of financial profits and losses on various import products in 1983. Table 4.4 shows these data, again organized along branch of industry lines. Like exports, financial profitability varied widely. Nine sectors incurred losses ranging from 5 to over 60 percent of import costs. Profits in the remaining sectors were as high as 50 percent. In terms of effective exchange rates the importers of coal and coking coal implicitly were provided foreign exchange at rate of 1.07 yuan per dollar, a rate more than one and a half times more favorable for importers than the then prevailing internal exchange rate of 2.8.

Again these financial profits and losses largely reflect a combination of

Chinese import pricing policy and the nature of the Chinese domestic price structure rather than real economic gains or losses from import transactions. In 1983 most imported goods were sold at the same price as comparable domestic goods. Losses on imported coal and coking coal were inevitable given that imported coal fell within the mandatory plan and was sold at the same price as domestically produced coal that was subject to state allocation, about one fourth the world level. Losses also were predictable in the building materials category where domestic prices were also set artificially low. Similarly, significant losses for agricultural products, which were underpriced on the domestic market, and high profits on processed food products, which tend to be overpriced on the domestic market, were predictable.

The overall magnitude of import losses, of course, would have been substantially greater if the cost of imports had been measured at an exchange rate that reflected the marginal cost of acquiring foreign exchange. Even more sectors would show financial losses and in the few sectors still showing financial gains profits would be reduced. But the variability in the implicit exchange rates across sectors would not be significantly reduced from that shown in Table 4.4.

The variability of exchange rates across product categories is a measure of the degree to which the state-directed trade pattern implicitly redistributed resources across sectors. Some imports, mostly raw materials for heavy industry, were sold at a loss on the domestic market, providing significant subsidies to end users. Other imports were sold at significant financial profits. The latter suggests a considerable degree of protection for some domestic producers. They were insulated from foreign competition because imports were marked up to at least the level of prices of comparable domestic goods rather than being sold at the world market price.

That pattern of subsidies and protection is characteristic of the import substitution trade regime. It reflects a considerable degree of government intervention in determining the pattern of imports. As in the case of exports it suggests the difficulties of decentralizing trade decision-making – and signals the potential for resource misallocation as well. It is likely to be accompanied, for example, by a significant state-directed flow of resources into protected sectors in order to expand production. But the goods in question could be produced at a lower real resource cost on the world market. A parallel misallocation arises for goods sold below the world price. Underpricing of certain imports may create excess demand requiring continued government intervention to allocate available supplies. Over time potential domestic producers, which might be able to produce the good with a lower level of real resources, are discouraged from entering into production by the availability of subsidized imports. Resource misallocation in this case occurs because the goods could be produced at a lower real resource cost on the domestic market.

Foreign trade contract system

What is the evidence that China's pattern of trade evolved in an economically more rational fashion after the mid-1980s? Did the reforms discussed in Chapter 3 have a cumulative positive effect over time? This is a difficult question to answer.

Clearly the share of trade transactions made on a decentralized basis grew significantly after the mid-1980s. To the extent these trade revisions were made on the basis of prices reflecting opportunity costs, one would expect the composition of trade to evolve in an economically more rational way. In addition, it is possible that trade decisions made by central administrative authorities could have been made increasingly on the basis of parallel market prices more accurately reflecting opportunity costs rather than state-fixed prices. That too would improve the efficiency of China's trade.

Although such an empirical study is not possible two types of indirect evidence bearing on these issues is available. First is the issue of whether commodity specific exchange rates persist. Because at the time this study was written the Chinese had not yet released input–output tables for years after 1983, we do not know whether the variation in implicit exchange rates persists after 1983. My tentative conclusion is that the range of commodity specific exchange rates must have been compressed because of the far-reaching reform of traded goods pricing discussed in Chapter 3.

However, variability was not eliminated and differentials in the financial cost of earning one dollar of foreign exchange persisted. The ranking of export sectors, from high to low cost, in the late 1980s was light industry, handicrafts, native products and domestic animals, machinery products, medicines, food products, textile products, metals (gold, silver, copper, iron, and tin), and chemical industry products including petroleum. The largest loss sectors in absolute terms were native products and domestic animals, light industry, food products, and textiles. Generally speaking, exports of fuel and mineral products and raw materials remained highly profitable whereas exports of finished industrial products as well as agricultural and subsidiary products incurred domestic currency losses (Li Chengxun, 90). Unfortunately, the specific implicit exchange rates prevailing in these various sectors in the late 1980s is not known. However, as late as 1988 foreign trade corporations, which still handled a large volume of exports, were using above-average returns from relatively lower cost export products to subsidize financial losses on products with above-average costs (Zhao Shengting 1988, 45).

Second, one can examine the discussion among those interested in foreign trade to judge the degree to which reforms after the mid-1980s focused on the financial or the real consequences of trade decisions. My judgment is that there was widespread confusion in China over the economic significance of the financial losses on foreign trade transactions. As discussed in Chapter 3, some argued that the profits and taxes collected in earlier stages of manufacture more than covered the losses incurred on the export of final goods and thus justified budgetary subsidies for exports.

Several arguments against the view that export subsidies were "false losses" and thus of little concern appear ultimately to have been more powerful. First, in the absence of reliable data on production costs planners could never be sure whether price subsidies simply offset domestic price distortions, facilitating trade based on underlying comparative advantage, or whether they reflected resource misallocation. Some tried to sidestep this problem, advocating subsidies only for which losses were "rational" (Wu and Chen, 50). The underlying problem was that price distortions made it impossible to identify the economically rational pattern of trade (Wang Zhenzhong, 42; Zhang Weiying, 188; Zhong Pengrong, 58; Zhou Jianming, 31). Thus there was no way of identifying the products for which export subsidies would be economically justifiable.

Second, rebating of indirect taxes on exported goods did not significantly diminish the magnitude of export subsidies. This meant that the decentralized export decision-making process envisaged by the 1984 foreign trade reform decision could not be fully realized.

Third, at least some key bureaucracies believed the distinction between economic losses and financial losses was irrelevant. Financial losses were all that mattered to the Ministry of Finance, the bureaucracy that had to come up with the funds to subsidize loss-making export enterprises. The Ministry had strongly supported earlier measures restricting exports of products that sustained losses in excess of 70 percent. And they appear to have supported a similar measure in 1984 prohibiting the inclusion in the export plan of any product with a foreign exchange cost in excess of 5 yuan per dollar of foreign exchange earnings (Zhu and Bao, 46).[8]

The problem of foreign trade losses actually became more acute for the Ministry of Finance in the mid-1980s as the use of a system of fiscal contracting with provincial governments became widespread. These contracts typically required each provincial government to remit to the center a fixed amount or a fixed share of the revenues assigned to provincial and local governments for collection. These amounts or shares usually were fixed for a three-year period and allowed local governments to retain all or a high share of revenues collected above some basic quota amount. These systems were applied initially to a few provinces on an experimental basis but were popularized in 1985 to include all provinces (Oksenberg and Tong; World Bank 1988b, 440–3). The flow of funds this system provided to the center was critical because the revenues collected directly by the central government covered only a fraction of their own fiscal expenditures.

This system of intragovernmental finance ultimately was incompatible with a foreign trade system in which the central government assumed full responsibility for losses on foreign trade, using only ad hoc rules like the 5 yuan per dollar limit on the cost of earning foreign exchange. From the point of view of the Ministry of Finance, the foreign trade sector comprised a massive leakage to its carefully constructed contract system to cover government finance. In effect the provinces had an incentive to increase their export of relatively costly goods because the center was obligated to provide additional subsidies to cover the losses. The subsidies were particularly onerous for the Ministry because they were difficult to budget. Thus while the center collected some revenues from the localities through the contract on finance, simultaneously they were giving back a significant portion of these funds in unanticipated export subsidies.

Discovering the magnitude of these foreign trade subsidies, particularly on the export side, is quite difficult. Since China expressed an interest in the mid-1980s in becoming a contracting party to the General Agreement on Tariffs and Trade, data on export subsidies have been closely held within China and only rarely appear in printed materials available to foreigners. The GATT Code on Subsidies and Countervailing Duties (1979) strongly discourages subsidies on export goods and authorizes countermeasures, such as countervailing duties, when subsidized goods are shown to cause an injury to the domestic industry of the country in which such goods are sold.

Although there is no systematic data on export losses, they appear to have risen sharply in the mid-1980s despite the devaluation of the yuan during these years (see Appendix A) and the rebate of billions of yuan of indirect taxes paid on export goods, discussed in Chapter 3. Financial losses on exports, which ran 5.2 billion yuan in 1983 fell dramatically in 1984 to only 30 million yuan because the cost of earning a dollar of foreign exchange fell from 3.02 to 2.79 yuan (Ren Long, 22). That decline in the cost of earning foreign exchange appears to be the result of the new prohibition on exports costing more than 5 yuan per dollar and a dramatic jump in the sale of crude oil on world markets, one of China's cheapest exports.[9]

However, with the considerable softening of the world oil market after 1984, the average domestic currency cost of exports rose sharply despite further increases in the quantity of oil exports. Although the value of the yuan fell throughout this period, increasing export earnings measured in domestic currency, losses per unit of foreign exchange remained high (see Table 2.1).

Given the rapidly rising volume of foreign trade, foreign trade losses rose in the second half of the 1980s. Exports did not require domestic currency subsidies in 1985 but import subsidies exceeded 5 billion yuan (Wu and Chen, 224). In 1986 losses on exports alone exceeded 7 billion yuan (Wang Yiqian, 259).[10] Losses on imports were placed at 12 billion yuan (Jing Ji, 38). By 1987 central government budgetary subsidies of foreign trade exceeded 20 billion yuan (Xiao Xiru, 25).[11] The data in Table 2.1 show that the gap between the cost of earning foreign exchange and the official exchange rate rose sharply in 1988 presumably leading to even higher export subsidies.

In the face of growing domestic currency losses in foreign trade transactions in the late 1980s, the central government instituted a system of foreign trade contracting (State Council 1988, 385–94). Under the system, all provincial level units of government administration[12] and national foreign trade corporations entered into foreign trade contracts with the state. The contracts specified three targets: the quantity of export earnings, expressed in terms of foreign exchange; the quantity of foreign exchange to be remitted to the central government; and the level of profits and losses in foreign trade transactions, measured in domestic currency. The latter target specified the maximum amount of domestic currency subsidy the central government would provide and made the contracting party responsible for all losses in excess of the contracted amount while allowing them to retain any surplus if losses were reduced below the plan level (State Council 1988, 386).

The center designed the contracts to provide local governments and national trade corporations increased incentives to export. The key feature allowed contract holders to retain a large share of the foreign exchange they earned that was above the basic contractual amount. In 1987, when the system was applied on a limited basis, the retention rate for over-quota earnings of foreign exchange was 70 percent (Lu Libin, 20). It was raised to 80 percent in 1988 (Fu Ziying 1989, 17). The incentive was enhanced by three additional measures. First, the central government pledged that the basic contractual amount would not be ratcheted up annually but would remain unchanged for three years. Moreover, the central government abolished the system of quota controls for retained funds that, as discussed in

Chapter 3, effectively had frozen a large share of retained foreign exchange (Fu Ziying 1989, 18; Shen Juren, 4; Sun Wenxiu, 55).[13]

Third, and closely related to the second, the government appears to have further liberalized controls on how retained foreign exchange could be spent (State Council 1988, 386). The regulations stipulated that 40 percent of the retained funds could be held in a foreign exchange account, literally "ready foreign exchange" (xian waihui). Presumably these funds were on deposit at the Bank of China or other financial institution authorized to deal in foreign exchange and could be drawn against with few constraints. The balance was only an entitlement, literally "retained foreign exchange credited to an account" (jizhang waihui liucheng), not a foreign exchange account. There are no published materials that I have seen that allow me to judge the degree to which this system provided readier access to retained foreign exchange. But clearly the intent was to overcome the apparently widespread skepticism among exporters that they would be able to actually spend the foreign exchange they were allocated under the retention system.

The foreign trade contract system was implemented for national foreign trade corporations in 1987, and in 1988 the State Council extended it to provincial level administrative units. In each case the contractual targets were set at the actual levels of the prior year (Lu Libin, 21). For example, in Shanghai, the contract called for the remission of $1.5 billion annually for three years beginning in 1988, roughly half of the foreign exchange generated by the export of goods produced in the municipality and the amount actually remitted in 1987.

It should be noted that these procedures for establishing the three contractual targets effectively built in the differentiated rates for the retention of foreign exchange that existed across regions. But highly varied marginal retention rates were reduced by requiring all regions and most industrial branches to remit a uniform 20 percent of foreign exchange earnings above the contractual amount to the center. One exception was the machinery and electronics sector, which was allowed to retain its privileged 100 percent rate of retention for overquota foreign exchange earnings. Another was the special economic zones that held on to their 100 percent rate of retention until 1989 when they were forced to follow the national pattern and remit 20 percent of their above-quota foreign exchange earnings to the central government (Sun Wenxiu, 55). Administratively, that was a considerable simplification because just prior to the institution of the new system there were eighteen separate rates of retention of foreign exchange that applied to different regions and branches of industry (Wu Zesong, 10). More importantly, the tendency toward the unification of the marginal retention rates reduced one of the most obvious economic distortions in the foreign trade system. A reduction in the disparity in the marginal rates lessened the prospect for inefficiency that arose from the export of higher cost products from regions that had more favorable retention rates.

The contracts between the Ministry of Foreign Economic Relations and Trade on the one hand and provincial-level governments and national foreign trade corporations on the other formed the basis for contracting between the latter units and the export-producing enterprises under their jurisdiction (Fu Ziying 1989). A variety of approaches were used in contracting with lower levels. Some provinces, for example, signed contracts with all of their lower-level administrative units whereas others signed contracts with each of the vertically organized producing systems (Wu Zesong, 11; Xu and Zhu, 25, 6).

Summary

On the basis of the evidence reviewed thus far it is not possible to give a definitive answer to the question of whether the efficiency of China's foreign trade increased as a result of the foreign trade and exchange reforms discussed in Chapter 3. However, the evidence analyzed in this chapter shows that large distortions impeded a more rational choice of traded goods. Most revealing, in my judgment, is that the central government, as it sought to sustain the rapid growth of exports necessary to generate the foreign exchange needed to finance imports, was increasingly preoccupied with the task of controlling financial losses. Ad hoc rules proliferated in an attempt to control the magnitude of financial losses. By the end of the decade, the contract system in foreign trade was adopted as a stop-gap measure. The underlying problem was that the decentralization of foreign trade had run ahead of the pace of domestic economic reform.

5

Integrated versus partial reforms

Reform of the foreign trade and exchange system by the end of the 1980s outpaced reforms of the domestic economy. Additional adjustments of the foreign trade system might marginally improve the rationality of some trade decisions. But further improvements in the efficiency of the external sector were largely dependent on additional internal reform measures. More far-reaching domestic price reforms appeared necessary to assure the economic rationality of decentralized export decisions. Among the most important prices in need of further adjustment was the official exchange rate, which was still somewhat overvalued at the end of the decade. Second, more developed factor markets were required to facilitate the reallocation of labor and capital in response to the new opportunities created by the opening of China to the world economy. In the 1980s the entrepreneurial sector of the economy, defined later in this chapter, had responded to these new opportunities. But the state-owned sector seemed handicapped by the legacy of centralized planning. Third, greater opening was critically dependent on both further domestic financial reform and more sophisticated aggregate demand management that would lead to greater macroeconomic stability.

This conundrum of balancing internal and external reforms was confounded by the conservative leadership, which seemingly consolidated its political power in the wake of the tragic slaughter of Chinese students and other protesters in Tiananmen Square in Beijing in June of 1989. Although Li Peng sought to project an image of continuity in China's policy of opening to the external world, neither he nor his conservative behind-the-scenes supporters seemed to appreciate sufficiently that this depended far more on further domestic economic reforms than it did on designating, with great fanfare, a new development zone in the Pudong district of Shanghai or making further adjustments in the legal structure of joint ventures in order to attract additional foreign investment.[1]

The constraining effect of the domestic economic system on the foreign trade system at the end of the 1980s is best introduced by examining further the economics of the foreign trade contract system.

The future of the foreign trade contract system

In many respects the contract responsibility management system adopted for foreign trade in 1987–8 appears to have been the product of bureaucratic compromise that ill served the goal of raising the efficiency of China's foreign trade system. It was not part of a package integrating reform in the foreign trade sector with reform of other aspects of the domestic economy, such as pricing. Rather, it reflected compromise among competing ministerial interests and a judgment of what was feasible given distortions in the structure of domestic prices (Li Lanqing 1988b, 10). It thus was a setback for those who in 1986 had advocated an integrated approach to economic reform that addressed issues of pricing, taxation, finance, and banking, as well as foreign trade (Zhou Xiaochuan 1988a, 16).

The major flaw was that the contract system was designed not to improve the efficiency of foreign trade but to stem the magnitude of foreign trade financial losses. The contract system, in effect, was an attempt by the central government to insulate itself from the rising demands for foreign trade subsidies, particularly for exports (Jiao and Zhou, 60; Qiu Jie, 11). These demands had accelerated rapidly in the mid-1980s, especially in 1986, so that the central leadership was ready to try out the contract system in 1987 as a means of limiting the demands of the national foreign trade corporations for more subsidies (Zhou Xiaochuan 1988a, 15). The expansion of the contract system to the whole nation in 1988 was an attempt to impose a hard budget constraint on the foreign trade transactions of provincial governments.

Capping export subsidies was seen as particularly crucial because of the system of fiscal contracting that was widespread by the mid-1980s. The center designed fiscal contracts to ensure a reliable flow of revenues to the center while providing sufficient funds to finance local needs. The problem quickly becomes one of leakage through the foreign trade sector. Prior to the contract system in foreign trade, the center had a virtually open-ended commitment to cover foreign trade losses of provincial and local governments (Xue Muqiao, 4; Zhong Pengrong, 57). While local governments dutifully fulfilled their contracts to remit fiscal revenues to the center on the one hand, on the other hand they exported ever higher cost products on the international market. That triggered larger central government subsidies on the trade account, undermining the fiscal contracts. Foreign trade contracting was grasped by the center as a means of plugging this growing leak of domestic financial resources.

Given the semireformed character of the Chinese price system, contracting could not be expected to contribute to more rational trade decisions. The system provided substantially enhanced incentives to export products that had artificially low domestic prices and to import products that carried relatively high domestic prices. These transactions would add to the financial profitability of local trade transactions and assist in meeting the terms of the trade contracts. But because the prices on which such profit-seeking transactions were based frequently diverged significantly from underlying economic values, these trade decisions could easily reduce rather than increase real economic welfare.

In this respect, China's experience may be consistent with that of other socialist economies studied by Murrell (1990). He found that the pattern of trade in the 1970s and early 1980s of what he calls the orthodox centrally planned economies – Czechoslovakia, East Germany, and the Soviet Union – was economically rational. In particular, he argues that the trade of these three countries was largely consistent with their underlying resource endowments. They tended to export products that required relatively large amounts of resources of which they had relatively large endowments and to import products that embodied relatively large amounts of resources of which they had relatively small endowments. In short, their patterns of trade were consistent with the basic neoclassical model of trade (Murrell, 169, 193).

However, the trade patterns of the two reformed socialist economies – Hungary and Yugoslavia – appeared to be economically irrational (Murrell, 193). Because these two economies were much more decentralized than the other socialist countries in Eastern Europe in the 1970s and early 1980s, Murrell concluded that market socialist reforms do not improve the rationality of trade decisions. Because China's reforms in the first decade most closely resemble those of Hungary, similar forces could lead to somewhat inefficient trade there as well.

A second flaw of the contract system was that it failed to increase the autonomy of some enterprises in foreign trade. That had been a key goal of the 1984 foreign trade reform initiative, but one that was difficult to follow through for reasons discussed in earlier chapters. The continued overvaluation of the domestic currency and the limited reform of the domestic price system, for example, made it difficult for some enterprises to expand significantly their truly decentralized exports. Rather than being responsible for their own profits and losses on export sales and using foreign trade corporations simply as an agent, these enterprises continued to sell their products to foreign trade corporations at prices more closely tied to domestic than internationl prices. The linking of domestic and international prices envisaged in the 1984 foreign trade reform thus developed only gradually on the export side.

The corollary of the relative lack of autonomy of enterprises in exporting was that the contract system actually enhanced the powers of local governments and made some enterprises even more subservient to them. It was provincial governments that signed the foreign trade contracts with the center and were responsible for their fulfillment. That gave them power over the allocation of export subsidies and greater control over the foreign exchange that was retained locally (Zhang Jiren). As discussed in Chapter 3, for example, when the most common foreign exchange retention ratio was 25 percent, regulations called for the even split of this between the local government supervising the enterprise and the producing enterprise itself. Beginning in 1988, when the contracts placed the control of these funds under local governments, there were increasing complaints that exporting firms never received their share of foreign exchange. Rather it all too frequently was siphoned off by local governments to finance their own list of preferred imports (Song Gongping, 52–53; Vogel, 390; Zhang Jiren, 21). That led to proposals that contracts be signed directly with enterprises producing export goods, in effect cutting out local governments (Tong and Hua; 11; Yang Xiong). Similarly, enterprises frequently did not receive the rebates of domestic taxes on export goods. These too were intercepted and pocketed by local governments.[2] All of these actions undermined the economic incentive for decentralized exporting.

Moreover, in the economic environment of the late 1980s, it is not clear that foreign trade contracting met the central government's limited fiscal goals. At a meeting in early February 1988, provincial governors criticized various features of the contract system (Li Lanqing 1988b, 10; Zou Siyi, 14). Among the demands aired apparently was that the central government agree to maintain the real value of the exchange rate during the initial three-year period the foreign trade contracts were to last. The governors were prescient in recognizing that domestic inflation could make the fulfillment of their contracts nearly impossible. Rising domestic prices, given a fixed exchange rate and a fixed fund for export subsidies, would hurt their exports without providing them with any commensurate reduction in the required quantity of exports or the required amount of foreign exchange to be remitted to the central government. But the People's Bank of China apparently adamantly refused to accept any limitations on its free hand in pegging the exchange rate. One alternative proposal was to recalculate the magnitude of the subsidies provided by the center on an annual basis, in light of the actual cost of earning foreign exchange in the previous year. But that also was rejected by the central government because it would have reopened annually the negotiation on the magnitude of foreign trade subsidies to be provided to each province (Zou Siyi, 15).

As Chinese prices began to rise in 1988 and 1989 it became increasingly difficult for local governments to fulfill their foreign trade contracts.[3] Part of the burden of the rising cost of earning foreign exchange was met by selling increased amounts of retained foreign exchange on local swap markets. This was particularly important in 1988 when the spread between the official exchange rate and the swap rate was relatively large, approximately 2.3 yuan, a premium of almost two thirds over the official rate.[4] However, that frequently meant that local governments, in their efforts to acquire more domestic currency to subsidize exports, sold the foreign exchange that should have accrued to enterprises, undermining the incentive for exporting by firms whose goods could be sold on the international market at a profit (Wang Shaoxi, 7). In addition some sources indicate that the central government had to raise domestic currency subsidies of exports beyond the initially contracted level in order to offset a portion of the growing losses of localities on foreign trade (Jiao and Zhou, 60; Liu Yun, 2–3).

However, by 1989–90, as a result of further devaluations of the official exchange rate and domestic financial tightening, selling retained foreign exchange earnings yielded less domestic revenue. The reasons was that the supply of foreign exchange on the market increased. As firms found it more difficult to borrow money from the domestic banking system, they sold more retained foreign exchange in order to acquire the domestic currency they needed for working capital to finance their inventories and so forth. The market value of the dollar fell steadily after mid-1989. In the last quarter of 1988 through late June of 1989 the average swap market exchange rate in Shanghai was 6.7 to 6.7 yuan per dollar (Chinese Finance and Banking Society 1989, 148; Frank Shen). The rate subsequently fell, reaching a low of about 5.4 yuan by mid-December (Chen Weihua 1989). Thus as their income from the sale of foreign exchange shrank, local governments found themselves forced to curtail other local fiscal expenditures in favor of subsidizing exports so they could meet their foreign trade contracts (Wang Shaoxi, 6).

These shortcomings and problems of administering the foreign trade contract responsibility system led to a debate among specialists on the future of the foreign trade contract system. Three alternative perspectives emerged in these discussions. The most conservative proposal called for the virtual restoration of the trading powers of the national foreign trade corporations (Wang Shaoxi, 7). These proposals did not necessarily specifically call for the abolition of the system of foreign trade contracting. But their recommendations to "change the phenomenon of excessive dispersion in the managment of foreign trade" and "to strengthen planning of imports and exports" made clear that they envisioned a substantial rollback of the decentralization of foreign trade that had occurred in the 1980s (Liu and Bao, 12). Those supporting this alternative also called for strengthened exchange control, in part through changes in the foreign exchange retention system. These revisions would both increase the central government's share of foreign exchange income and increase the central management of local foreign exchange expenditures. Some formulations were even more extreme calling for the outright abolition of the foreign exchange retention system (Yin Ling, 29).

At the other end of the spectrum were those who sought to expand further the rights of enterprises to pursue foreign business free from interference by either the central foreign trade administration or local governments. The heart of this proposal was to eliminate all state planning of exports, permitting firms to make exporting decisions based on a comparison of domestic and world market conditions (Chen, Feng, and Yang). On the financial side, they advocated an expansion of the role of the swap markets for foreign exchange and the elimination of direct allocation of foreign exchange by the central government (Yin Ling, 29). Although these proposals did not usually use the word convertibility, they clearly envisioned rapid movement toward this by allocating all foreign exchange through a market in which the price would be determined by supply and demand (Lin, Cai, and Shen, 31). Some proposed achieving this by expanding the share of retained foreign exchange, usually by allocating most or all of it to exporting enterprises rather than to local governments. The enterprises themselves would be responsible for their own profits and losses, ending the complex system of subsidies that prevailed, particularly for exports, in the 1980s.

One variant on this was a proposal for a system of taxation of foreign exchange earnings (Fu Ziying 1988; Wang Deyun, 38–9; Zhang Jiren, 21–2). At first glance, this would appear to be only a modest change from the system prevailing in the late 1980s. Of course enterprises received domestic currency, calculated at the official exchange rate, in exchange for the foreign exchange they remitted whereas they would receive no domestic currency for the foreign exchange given up under a tax system. Adjusting for this difference one could, however, calculate a tax rate that would be the equivalent of the retention rate it replaced. According to its proponents, taxation of foreign exchange earnings would differ from the foreign exchange retention system in several ways. First, it would constitute a substantial relaxation of exchange control as compared to the retention scheme. Enterprises, in effect, would be allowed to open their own foreign exchange accounts rather than surrendering all foreign exchange and receiving only a use right for a share of those earnings.

Second, a foreign exchange tax would be established by legislation passed by the National People's Congress and changes in the established tax rate would require new legislative action. By contrast, the retention ratios were established by administrative decree. Although the average rate moved up almost continuously in the 1980s, it could be reduced by administrative fiat at any time. Embedding the rate in law would provide exporters with some protection from an arbitrary reduction in the share of the foreign exchange earnings they were allowed to use. Presumably it would also make it more difficult for the central government to freeze the use of the funds, as had occurred in 1985–7.

Third, exporters would have more rapid access to their foreign exchange under the proposed system of taxing foreign exchange earnings. Under the retention system in use in the 1980s, use rights were credited to enterprise accounts with a considerable delay, long after the foreign exchange earnings actually were collected by the Bank of China. Firms producing goods for export reportedly waited at least one hundred days after the delivery of export goods to get access to retained foreign exchange (Zhang Jiren, 21). Under the proposed tax on foreign exchange earnings, exporting enterprises would have access to their funds immediately after the foreign purchaser made payment on China's export goods.

Finally, taxation of foreign exchange earnings was viewed as part of a reform that would make enterprises financially independent, eliminating the system of domestic currency subsidies of exports and imports.

In addition to these proposals for a return to the system of centralized foreign trade planning and foreign exchange control on the one hand, and more rapid movement toward convertibility on the other, proposals for minor tinkering with the existing system were common. By and large this perspective viewed the system of contracting for foreign trade as part of a broader system of contracting that had been extended to an increasing number of sectors of the economy in the 1980s. In part because the contract responsibility system initiated in agriculture in the early 1980s was so successful, there was a tendency to regard contracting as a panacea. As mentioned above, it was widely applied in intergovernmental fiscal relations. And it became a key element of industrial reform in the guise of the "enterprise contract responsibility system." Those who have pushed these contracting schemes appear to resist abandoning or even substantially modifying them in one sector for fear that would call into question the viability of contracting schemes in other sectors. Some even go a step further, calling for more explicit coordination of contracts in various spheres (Yang Peixin 1988b).

A common fault, to varying degrees, with each of these alternatives is that they pay insufficient attention to the broader economic environment in which foreign trade is conducted. As we have already seen, when reform of the external sector outpaces domestic economic reform the gains from increased trade fall below their potential. Providing increased incentives for decentralized exporting, for example, may not be the most appropriate policy when many domestic prices are still somewhat insulated from world prices. The evidence from the decade of the 1980s is that decentralizing foreign trade under these conditions led to extensive ad hoc government interventions. Licensing, for example, was expanded to a number of products that were so underpriced on the domestic market that decentralized exporting would have created endemic domestic shortages.

Domestic price reform

In addition to the expanded scope of export licensing and other ad hoc government measures, other indicators also point to the need for further domestic price reform. The partial reform of domestic prices created substantial rents or excess profits, which stimulated illegal transactions. A substantial portion of these excess profits arose in foreign trade, particularly in the allocation of import and export licenses. Because of differentials that sometimes existed between domestic and world prices, the right to buy or sell a product internationally could be extremely valuable. Because licenses were allocated bureaucratically rather than auctioned to the highest bidder, their allocation frequently bestowed substantial rents. These rents could be realized either by carrying out the approved but highly profitable trade transaction or through the resale of the license on the secondary market. Technically, the latter was illegal because licenses were not transferable. Potential legal sanctions appear to have had little restraining effect on the market for licenses, largely because of the profits that could be realized from these transactions. An export license for a single shipment of 10,000 tons of pig iron from Tianjin reportedly sold for from 100,000 yuan to 200,000 yuan in the late 1980s, implying that economic rents for the right to export pig iron were from 10 to 20 yuan per ton.[5] Resales of licenses, even to foreign businessmen in China, were widespread (Li, Meng, and Liu, 29).

In 1988 officials from the Ministry of Foreign Economic Relations and

Trade said that the ministry would introduce a bidding system for export quotas for some goods (Reporter 1988). That would allow the government to capture the rents implicit in these licenses, presumably drastically reducing the economic incentive for reselling the licenses in the market. However, more than two years later there was very little evidence that auctions were in use. Instead, export licensing procedures were tightened up to make the transfer of licenses more difficult (Yuan Zhou).

Another indicator of the critical need for further price reform was the simultaneous import and export of a single homogeneous product. Price controls may make the international sale of a product more attractive to the producer than the sale of the good on the domestic market. The artificial domestic shortage that price control creates then leads domestic users of the good to purchase the good on the international market. In effect, the international market was used to circumvent the distortion caused by irrational domestic prices. The losses to China are not necessarily simply the extra transaction costs. In some cases foreign firms are able to capture huge financial profits simply because domestic firms are prevented from buying and selling among themselves at free prices. In one example, the Number Three Printing and Drying Plant exported lining cloth. The foreign purchaser then turned around and resold the product, at twice the price, to a domestic user of lining cloth in China. Ironically, the plant's original plan called for delivery of this product directly to the end user in China but they diverted the product to the export market, where profits were higher (Chen and Wei, 6)!

Other examples of products that simultaneously are bought and sold internationally in large quantities because of domestic price distortions include petroleum coke, scrap steel, nickel ingot, sugar, animal hides, caustic soda ash (Chen and Wei, 6; Meng Zijun et al.).

Exchange rate policy

One key price in need of further adjustment at the end of the first decade of reform in 1987–8 was the price of foreign exchange. From 1980 through the middle of 1986 the government significantly reduced the overvaluation of the domestic currency. The largest single step was the introduction of the internal exchange rate cutting the value of the yuan by almost half, in 1981. That step was important not only because of its relatively large size but particularly because it was the first time the official exchange rate was set on the basis of the principle that the rate should cover the cost of earning foreign exchange.[6]

Although the internal settlement rate was abandoned at the end of 1984 the active use of exchange rate policy to serve China's foreign trade needs was not. The state steadily devalued the exchange rate during 1985 and the first half of 1986 from 2.80 to 3.20 yuan to the dollar. Then, in response in part to advice from the International Monetary Fund, the Bank of China on July 5, 1986 announced a 15.8 percent devaluation of the renminbi against all foreign currencies.[7] That was the single largest devaluation of the yuan since the introduction of the internal settlement rate in 1981. The yuan–dollar exchange rate then stood at about 3.7, so that its nominal value against the dollar was well under half compared to 1980.

The extent of decline in the value of the domestic currency against the currencies of other major trading partners varied. The depreciation against the yen was even greater, reflecting the fall in the value of the dollar against the yen in the first half of the 1980s. The depreciation of the yuan against the British pound and the Hong Kong dollar was significantly less whereas against the deutsche mark the yuan depreciated almost as much as against the dollar (Wu and Chen, 140–1). Given the relative importance of China's trade with Japan, Hong Kong, the United States, West Germany, and so on, one can estimate that China's nominal trade-weighted exchange rate fell by fully half between 1980 and July 1986. This trade-weighted exchange rate is usually referred to as the effective exchange rate.

Of course, if the prices of China's export goods rose over this period relative to import goods, due to higher domestic than world price inflation, some portion of the nominal devaluation of the yuan discussed above would be required to offset those price trends. This adjustment of the nominal effective exchange rate to account for differential inflation leads to the real effective exchange rate. In fact, the ratio of China's export to import prices was virtually unchanged during this period (Ministry of Foreign Economic Relations and Trade 1989, 357).[8] Thus we can conclude that China's real effective exchange rate in mid-1986 had fallen by half compared with 1980. It fell even further over the ensuing year because the nominal rate remained pegged to the dollar while the dollar depreciated against the yen, the deutsche mark, and other world currencies.

However, the real effective exchange rate actually fell, i.e. the renminbi appreciated in value until late 1989. That was an inevitable result of two trends. First, the relative prices of China's export goods rose because of rising domestic price inflation, particularly in 1988 and 1989. Second, the nominal value of the renminbi vis-à-vis the U.S. dollar was unchanged until late December 1989 while in the late 1980s the dollar was actually appreciating vis-à-vis several other major world currencies, particularly the Japanese yen. Thus the nominal effective exchange rate of the renminbi was appreciating slightly; that is, fewer units of Chinese currency were required to purchase foreign currency. And adjusting for changes in relative prices, the real effective exchange rate was rising somewhat more rapidly. That meant that the real domestic currency earnings received by Chinese exporters were falling and the real domestic currency price of imports was falling.

Trends in the real exchange rate have been shown to be closely related to the sustainability of trade liberalization programs. A real devaluation makes it more likely that an initial liberalization will achieve success and a further real devaluation during liberalization is associated with the survival of the initial program whereas a subsequent appreciation is usually associated with a collapse of the initial program (Michaely, Papageoriou, and Choksi, 215–19). The causation seems clear enough. A real devaluation is crucial for stimulating the growth of exports that, in turn, facilitates the liberalization program. Particularly when the degree of protection of import competing industries is reduced as part of a trade liberalization package, the expansion of exports is helpful in avoiding balance of payments pressures that would otherwise tend to undermine the liberalization program.

Fortunately, the appreciation of China's real exchange rate was halted on December 15, 1989, when the Bank of China announced a further devaluation of 21.2 percent in the value of the renminbi vis-à-vis the dollar, the first change in the official exchange rate in three and one-half years. That brought the official exchange rate to 4.7 yuan per dollar (Xinhua 1989b). A further devaluation of about 9.6 percent on November 17, 1990 moved the official exchange rate to 5.2 yuan per dollar (Xinhua 1990b). These changes offset the real appreciation of the renminbi that had occurred after mid-1986.

It is not entirely clear why China's policy of moving toward a more reasonable exchange rate stalled out between mid-1986 and the end of 1989. After moving steadily to devalue the domestic currency in real terms between the late 1970s and 1986, why should the government subsequently have allowed the real effective exchange rate to appreciate, at least through the end of 1989? Three factors appear most relevant.

First, many Chinese analysts argued that the policy of devaluation in the first half of the 1980s had failed and that further devaluations could not be expected to improve the trade balance (Wu Jingquan; Zhao Shengting). Various attempts to calculate the price elasticity of demand for imports and price elasticity of supply of exports were made. Some of these purported to show that the elasticities were relatively low so that devaluation could not be expected to increase exports relative to imports and so would actually worsen rather than improve the trade balance (Zhu and Lu). The problem, of course, was that the slow pace of reform in the domestic pricing of traded goods substantially inhibited the effect of exchange rate changes. As discussed in Chapter 3, in the early part of the 1980s only a small portion of imported goods was priced on the basis of import cost so a devaluation did not increase the average domestic price of imports very much and thus could not be expected to reduce the demand for imports significantly. Similarly, the limited use of the agency system for exports meant that few producers could be expected to increase the supply of export goods in response to a devaluation of the domestic currency.

However, in the absence of this constraint on the domestic prices of traded goods on an a priori basis one would expect a devaluation to improve China's trade balance significantly; that is, stimulate exports relative to imports. This is because despite the rapid growth of the absolute level of Chinese exports in the 1980s, China remained a relatively small exporter, supplying less than 1.5 percent of world exports (Ministry of Foreign Economic Relations and Trade, 1989, 358). Thus, the demand for China's exports should have been elastic and the volume of exports constrained more by China's ability to increase their supply rather than by the world's limited demand. The rapid growth of exports from the entrepreneurial sector of the domestic economy (analyzed in the section of this chapter, *Contrasting regional trade performance*), where changes in the exchange rate had a more direct effect on export earnings measured in domestic currency, shows that the response of some domestic firms was quite elastic. But the slow pace of reform of pricing of traded goods and other rigidities inhibited this response on the part of state-owned firms.

In short, the appropriate conclusion from the experience of the first half of the decade should have been to accelerate the pace of domestic reform to enhance the effectiveness of the exchange rate as a policy tool rather than to fix the nominal exchange rate vis-à-vis the dollar and allow a de facto appreciation of the real effective exchange rate. Indeed, some writers did draw this conclusion, arguing that to be effective, exchange rate policy needed to be coordinated with other domestic reforms, such as domestic pricing and a further shrinkage of the share of command plan imports and exports (Zhao Shengting 1987).

Moreover, some domestic reforms seem to have been based on this conclusion. As discussed in Chapter 3, in the mid-1980s and after, the share of imported goods priced domestically on the basis of import cost rose dramatically and, as reflected in Table 3.4, the magnitude of import subsidies for the most important of these imports fell significantly. Thus domestic consumers were less insulated from rising world prices for these commodities. And although many export producers were not in a position to take advantage of the agent system, the proliferation of foreign trade corporations allowed them to bargain for better prices for goods they provided for export. Particularly in the wake of domestic currency devaluations they sought to gain higher domestic prices from foreign trade corporations.

A second reason that the government abandoned its policy of moving toward a more realistic exchange rate after mid-1986 was the fear that devaluation would contribute to domestic price inflation (Zhou Xiaochuan 1988a, 16; Zou Siyi, 15). There is little question that under competitive conditions in a market economy devaluation would either raise the domestic price of imports directly, when imports were priced based on import cost. Or, if the government subsidized imports to prevent a rise in their domestic prices, under Chinese conditions it would raise prices indirectly because it would increase the already large government fiscal deficit, a portion of which was financed by printing money. Moreover, there would be second-round effects because if the prices of imported inputs rose that would raise the prices of domestic goods directly or require increased subsidies which would raise domestic prices indirectly by the mechanism just mentioned.

But judging the magnitude of this effect, particularly under a system of exchange control, is more difficult. Chinese policy was based on the view that the ratio of imports to gross national product, frequently referred to as the trade ratio, was relatively high so that the effect of devaluation on the domestic price level, ceteris paribus, would be substantial. Following the World Bank's (1985, 7) analysis of the openness of the Chinese economy, Chinese writers also began to argue that their nation's trade ratio had increased rapidly in the 1980s (Chen Gongyan, 69). Others took the argument a step further pointing out that the relatively high ratio of imports to national income meant that devaluation would have a significant effect on domestic prices (Cao Wushu, 28). For example, a unit of the State Planning Commission argued that each 1 percent devaluation would raise the overall price level by .28 percent because the trade ratio was 28 percent (State Planning Commission Economic Adjustment Bureau, 23).

As I point out in Appendix B, Chinese as well as World Bank procedures for calculating the degree of openness of the Chinese economy in the 1980s were seriously flawed. The use of the official exchange rate led to an undervaluation of China's gross national product measured in dollars so that the trade ratio was overstated. The degree of overstatement is difficult to judge but could quite easily be a factor of three or more. Thus the trade ratio in 1987, for example, would be about 10 percent rather than the 28 percent advanced by the State Planning Commission and other influential Chinese economists (Chen Gongyan, 69).[9]

Chinese economists overstated the effect of devaluation on domestic prices not only by exaggerating the openness of their economy but also by implicitly assuming in much of their analysis that the official exchange rate reflected an equilibrium between demand and supply for foreign exchange. But, as previously discussed, the renminbi remained overvalued throughout the 1980s and a formidable array of exchange controls was required to allocate limited supplies of foreign exchange in the face of excess demand. The disequilibrium in the foreign exchange market was reflected in the value attached to import licenses for some scarce commodities. As analyzed by Krueger (1978, 145–7), a devaluation under these circumstances would likely reduce the value of import licenses but not change the final price of the imported good on the domestic market. In short, the final price of scarce imported commodities may be determined by supply and demand on the domestic market. An overvalued currency means that imports will be relatively cheap, creating windfall profits or rents to those who control the supply of imports. When the quantity of imports is rationed by a licensing system in which licenses are allocated bureaucratically, instead of being auctioned to the highest bidder, most if not all of these rents will accrue to the license holders. When the domestic currency is devalued the importer must pay more units of domestic currency to purchase the goods abroad and the economic rent or premium attached to the license is reduced or, in Krueger's terminology, "absorbed." But the final, or scarcity, price of the good on the domestic market is unchanged. Thus devaluation would have no effect on the prices for this category of imports. However, such a devaluation might still be desirable because it would reduce the rent-seeking activity associated with import licensing.

Chinese writers implicitly overestimated the effect of devaluation on the domestic prices of exported goods as well. If the exchange rate reflects an underlying equilibrium in the supply and demand for foreign exchange, a devaluation would normally be expected to raise the domestic prices of exported goods. For most of its exported goods, China is a relatively small supplier to the world market, so one can assume, at least as a first approximation, that the world market price would not be influenced by the quantity of Chinese exports. A devaluation of the yuan would thus raise the domestic currency earnings from exporting, initially leaving the earnings from domestic market sales unchanged. Producers would soon shift more of their sales to the world market, a process that would continue until the resulting shortage on the domestic market raised the domestic price sufficiently to equalize earnings from international and domestic market sales. Thus devaluation would raise the domestic prices of export goods.

This would not fully apply in China, however, where the domestic currency was overvalued and, as we have seen, many exports required domestic currency subsidies. Recall that these subsidies compensated producers for the difference between what they would have received from selling the product domestically and their actual domestic currency earnings from selling the product internationally. A devaluaton in this case would simply raise the domestic currency earnings from selling the product internationally and reduce, by the same amount, the subsidies received. Thus, the exporter would receive more funds from the Bank of China when it converted dollar earnings to domestic currency and would receive fewer funds from domestic subsidies allocated through the Ministry of Finance. But for those exports that still required subsidies, even after the devaluation, there would be no incentive for increased exports, no emerging shortage of those goods on the domestic market, and thus no tendency toward open inflation (or toward repressed inflation if the domestic prices of the export goods were fixed by the state).

Therefore, the fear articulated by many Chinese writers that devaluation would contribute to inflation seems misplaced on two grounds. First, the ratio of the sum of imports and exports relative to the overall size of the economy was far lower than conventional calculations indicated. Thus even if a devaluation led to a proportionately equal change in the domestic prices of traded goods, the effect on the overall price ratio would be much less than many Chinese writers assume. For example, a 40 percent devaluation would raise domestic prices by approximately 10 percent if the trade ratio was 25 percent (and we ignore so-called second-round effects). If the trade ratio was really 10 percent the same large devaluation, in the first instance, would raise domestic prices by only 4 percent.

Second, given China's extensive system of exchange controls, devaluation would be expected to have little or no effect on domestic prices of a broad range of traded goods. This is particularly true on the export side where a large share of goods continued to be subsidized, at least until the late 1980s.

In addition to the beliefs that it would be ineffective and contribute to domestic inflation, competing bureaucratic interests constituted a third obstacle to the adoption of a more realistic exchange rate. The major central bureaucracies concerned with foreign trade reform had sharply divided interests on the exchange rate issue (Zhou Xiaochuan 1988a, 16). The Ministry of Foreign Economic Relations and Trade appears to have supported the policy of continuing to move toward a more reasonable exchange rate. Such a course would assist them in promoting exports and holding down the pace of expansion of imports and would lead to a less unfavorable trade balance.

Over the long run it might also pave the way for reducing the magnitude of foreign trade subsidies that the ministry had to seek from the Ministry of Finance.

Opposing them most obviously were the People's Bank of China and the bureaucracy responsible for price administration, notably the State Bureau of Commodity Prices. The State Planning Commission also appears to have been skeptical about the efficacy of devaluation. The terrain was depressingly familiar. Recall (see Chapter 2) that the People's Bank of China had fought off a proposed devaluation of the official exchange rate in 1963–4. The objections of the bank in the early 1980s to devaluation led to the adoption of an "internal settlement rate" as a thinly disguised alternative to a major devaluation of the official exchange rate (see Chapter 3). And we have it on the authority of a senior official of the Bank of China that the major devaluation of June 1986 was undertaken only after the IMF in May 1986 offered its "opinions" with regard to "problems with China's exchange rate" (Wu and Chen, 239–42). The State Bureau of Commodity Prices opposed devaluation because of its fear it would contribute to domestic price inflation.

As this stalemate continued and it became more and more difficult for foreign trade enterprises to fulfill their trade plans, particularly on the export side, two compromise measures were adopted in 1987 and 1988 (Zhou Xiaochuan 1988a, 16–17).

One step was to increase the authority of enterprises to import needed raw materials from abroad in order to increase their export earnings. As discussed later in this chapter, this was a core part of the coastal development strategy promoted by Zhao Ziyang beginning in early 1988.

A second compromise step, discussed in Chapter 3, was to allow the retention of more foreign exchange. This was proposed by the State Council Foreign Trade System Reform Small Group to the 1987 annual late summer conclave of senior officials at the seaside resort town of Baidaihe, where it received party approval (Li Lanqing 1988b, 15). Allowing exporters to convert a larger share of their foreign exchange earnings to domestic currency at a higher rate was the equivalent of a devaluation of the currency but allowed the People's Bank of China the fig leaf of an unchanged official exchange rate.[10]

Even so, the People's Bank tried to prevent the freeing up of controls in the foreign exchange adjustment centers, a development they feared would lead to a substantial fall in the value of the yuan. They advanced research they claimed supported their view that it was necessary to continue to control the price of foreign exchange in the swap markets. It took a further "investigation by leading central comrades" to determine the merit of the

Bank's refusal to go along with the change that had already been endorsed by the leadership of the Chinese Communist Party. According to Li Lanqing (1988b, 15), then a vice-minister of the Ministry of Foreign Economic Relations and Trade, this group ultimately rejected the bank's position, largely on the basis of the experience in the Shenzhen special economic zone, where the relatively unregulated swap market had not led to a "loss of control" (Li Lanqing 1988b, 15). However, the final State Council document, approved at the end of February 1988, was somewhat ambivalent, to say the least. As was so often the case in reform proposals of the 1980s, the document contained language that appeared to support diametrically opposing perspectives. The price of foreign exchange in the swap market was to "fluctuate based on supply and demand." However, in the very next sentence the State Administration of Exchange Control was authorized to "stipulate a ceiling price" (State Council 1988, 388).

This virtual paralysis on exchange rate policy from mid-1986 until the end of 1989 was not simply a standoff between the trade and banking bureaucracies. It also involved the interests of virtually all of China's production ministries through the rents that the overvalued exchange rate bestowed on the users of imported goods and the implicit taxes levied on export producers. It is important to recognize that these rents persisted in the late 1980s, even after the widespread adoption of the principle of agency pricing for imports. When imported goods were sold domestically based on the import price, the overvalued domestic currency made them available for a lower price than would have been the case at an equilibrium price of foreign exchange. One estimate for 1988 was that the overvalued exchange rate bestowed rents in excess of 93 billion yuan (Hu Keli, 12). That is the equivalent of about 7 percent of China's 1988 gross national product (State Statistical Bureau 1989a, 28).

This estimate is based on the assumption that the average price of 6 yuan per dollar prevailing in China's foreign exchange swap markets in 1988 represented an equilibrium exchange rate.[11] But most importers paid only 3.72 yuan per dollar, that is, the official exchange rate. Of course those importers purchasing foreign exchange on the swap market or using their own retained foreign exchange to finance imports paid the opportunity cost of foreign exchange, either explicitly or implicitly. Other users of imports received a subsidy of about 2.3 yuan per dollar's worth of imports, the difference between the swap market price and the official exchange rate. The estimated rent is simply the product of this 2.3 yuan subsidy and the value of imports not financed through retained foreign exchange, whether it was the importer's own or purchased on the market.[12]

In most economies with a single exchange rate, the corollary of the subsidy on imports is the tax on exports. To the extent exporters receive the official rather than the swap market rate, there is a tax on exports equivalent to the subsidy on imports. In 1988 this would have been 2.3 yuan per dollar's worth of export goods. In reality, some exporters received additional subsidies to cover a portion of or all of their domestic currency losses. However, the magnitude of subsidies to exports in 1988, probably something on the order of 7 billion yuan, appears to have offset only a very small portion of the tax imposed on exporters as a result of the over-valuation of the domestic currency.[13]

Without more detailed research based on material not yet available to foreign scholars, one can only conjecture about the distribution among various sectors of the economic rents and implicit taxes inherent in China's overvalued official exchange rate. Based on the largest import comodities, as measured by value, the key beneficiaries were the domestic users of chemicals, complete sets of equipment and technology, and steel. These three categories comprised two thirds of China's total imports in 1988. The chief bearers of the burden on the other hand, were the largest export suppliers – producers of crude oil, garments, and cotton piece goods. These three categories comprised one fourth of China's total exports in 1988 (Ministry of Foreign Economic Relations and Trade 1989, 372, 451).

Factor markets

In addition to price and exchange rate reform, China must further develop domestic markets for capital and labor if it is to gain greater economic advantage from participation in the world economy. As discussed in Chapter 1 many studies have shown that the marginal productivity of factors of production is higher in export-oriented than in nonexport-oriented industries. Thus, expanding exports contributes more to the growth of aggregate output than simply the change in the volume of exports (Feder, 59). This is all the more likely to be true in China, where exports were still a relatively small share of domestic output in the 1980s (see Appendix B).

Yet in the decade of the 1980s, Chinese reforms did little to develop the labor markets necessary to facilitate the reallocation of workers to higher productivity uses. Particularly in the state-owned sector, most workers continued to be assigned permanent jobs when they finished their educations. Workers had no right to quit or leave their assigned jobs and enterprises had no right to dismiss redundant labor (World Bank 1988b, 72). Furthermore, workers were dependent on their work units for their housing, medical care, retirement pensions, and a range of other benefits (Walder, 59–84).

As a result of this multifaceted dependency of workers on their work units, the share of the Chinese workforce changing jobs in a specified time period was extremely low not just in comparison to market economies but also compared to other socialist economies. In 1988, out of a total state-sector labor force exceeding 99 million, less than 850,000 workers left their jobs for reasons other than death or retirement.[14] Thus the turnover rate in 1988 was an astonishingly low 0.8 percent. The comparable figure for the Soviet Union, for example, was 17–20 percent (Granick). Mobility in China was also extremely low for scientific and engineering manpower, a part of the labor force particularly important for fostering technical change.

Increasing the mobility of the labor force in the state-owned sector requires a series of far-reaching reforms, most of which have barely begun. The system of initial job assignment for school leavers should be phased out and replaced with a system of genuine labor markets. That means abandoning the system of fixed wage scales that has prevailed in the state sector since the 1950s and introducing a system in which wages are determined by supply and demand. Similarly, urban housing should be marketed rather than being allocated through work units. That would remove one of the main impediments to the present system in which changing jobs automatically deprives a worker of his or her current housing. Finally, a retirement system based on contributions to a national social security type fund should replace the current arrangements in which payments to retirees are a current expenditure of the enterprise from which the worker has retired. The existing system discourages mobility because a worker's retirement income is heavily dependent on continuous employment at a single firm.

None of these steps – a market for labor with competitively determined wages, a market for housing, and a nationally based, actuarially sound system of income for retired workers – will be easily accomplished. But all are necessary to make possible the more efficient use of China's labor, particularly relatively scarce technical and managerial personnel.

Capital markets were also relatively underdeveloped and poorly suited to allocating investment resources to activities with the highest rates of return. Superficially there was a significant change in the first decade of reform in the sources of investment finance. Under other circumstances, these changes might have signaled the development of capital markets that would allocate investment resources more efficiently. On the eve of reform in 1978 enterprises still paid most of their profits directly into the state budget. And in return, fully two thirds of all investment in fixed assets in state-owned enterprises, including the category of projects known as "technical modernization and transformation investment," was financed by noninterest-bearing state budgetary grants (State Statistical Bureau 1985, 416–50). By 1988 the situation had changed drastically. In the state-owned sector of the economy, budgetary grants financed less than 15 percent of investment in fixed assets. The two largest sources of investment funds were funds internal to the enterprises, both retained earnings and depreciation funds, and bank loans, which supplied 40.5 and 24.2 percent of all investment funds, respectively. Foreign direct investment and foreign loans used for investment but not channeled through the budget financed an additional 9 percent of fixed investment (State Statistical Bureau 1989a, 478).

This change in the sources of finance was less important than it seemed. Investment decisions in the socialist sector were subject to a formidable array of administrative controls, the potential profitability of investment projects appeared to receive scant attention, and the incremental benefits or costs of investments did not clearly flow to the specific enterprise undertaking the project (World Bank 1988b, 69–71).

Chinese banks, for example, did not gather sufficient information or have sufficient staff expertise to evaluate the financial returns and risks of projects they financed. This capability probably would have been irrelevant in any case because much bank lending was done at the behest of local government authorities. Moreover, interest rates on such loans were fixed bureaucratically, so that changes in lending rates played little role in the equilibration of the supply and demand for loanable funds. And in the later half of the 1980s, when domestic inflation accelerated and the interest rate charged on borrowed funds was adjusted infrequently and by amounts that were too small, the real rate of interest on borrowed funds was negative. Finally, a growing portion of bank lending to state enterprises represented payments arrears; that is, the rollover of previous loans that enterprises could not repay. In short, with extraordinarily low (or even negative) borrowing costs and repayments of principal effectively subject to negotiation, the difference between government grants and bank loans as sources of investment finance were more apparent than real.

Even the extensive use of internal funds to finance investments is of less significance than it might be under other circumstances. Most important, "enterprises remain tightly restricted in the alternative uses to which their savings can be put" (World Bank 1988b, 71). As the World Bank has noted, for the mid-1980s the main anomaly in the structure of interest rates was the low rate paid on enterprise time deposits and on treasury bonds held by enterprises. The low rates provided inadequate incentives to hold deposits or bonds. To assure a "market" for government bonds, enterprises were assigned mandatory purchase quotas. This anomalous interest rate structure actually worsened as inflation rose in 1987–8. The low interest rates on enterprise deposits "reinforce the tendencies of Chinese enterprises to limit horizontal flows of funds and to use all available resources for sometimes not so profitable internal investments" (World Bank 1988b, 264).[15]

Additions to inventories of raw materials and intermediate goods were among the most common of those internal investments. Low rates of return on short-term financial instruments made it rational for firms to hold inventories that were far larger than the quantity that would be rational in a market economy in which the costs of holding such inventories would include the real opportunity cost of short-term capital. The tendency of firms in planned economies to hold excess inventories to counter so-called supply uncertainties is well-established, so a high ratio of inventories to output is not a new phenomenon in China. But it does appear as if the ratio of inventories to output of state firms rose to even higher levels in the 1980s. A more rational interest rate structure would help to reverse this tendency. Firms would place more of their liquid assets in short-term financial assets rather than inventories of raw materials and intermediate goods and thus increase the efficiency of resource use.

Markets for land in urban areas were the most rigid of all (World Bank 1988b, 74–5). There was no open market for land, meaning the limited reallocations that did occur depended on a highly bureaucratic process. Moreover, most state enterprises paid no land rent or other charges for the land they occupied, encouraging widespread hoarding and waste of land. As a result, successful enterprises were discouraged from seeking additional land for expansion through regular channels. And informal mechanisms that developed to get around the constraints of the official system were highly imperfect.

One consequence of these restrictions on factor mobility was that it was difficult for state-owned enterprises to respond to opportunities created by the increased openness of the economy to foreign trade. David Ricardo showed in the nineteenth century that nations could gain from trade simply by exchanging commodities, without any reallocation of factors of production within each country to increase the output of exported goods. Changes in each country's production structure, however, add significantly to the gains from trade, particularly when one shifts one's attention from Ricardo's static framework, which assumes no growth in output, to a dynamic framework.

Table 5.1. *Guangdong exports, 1978–90 (millions of $)*

		Of which		
Year	Total exports	Conventional exports	Processing and compensation trade exports	Exports of foreign-invested firms
1978	1,388	1,386	1	–
1980	2,195	2,106	89	–
1985	2,953	2,450	281	221
1987	5,444	4,531	303	611
1988	7,484	5,879	403	1,202
1989	8,168	5,250	613	2,277
1990	10,370	6,090	670	3,610

Notes: Foreign-invested firms include equity and contractual joint ventures as well as wholly foreign-owned firms. These data, except for 1978, are exclusive of exports produced on Hainan Island, which was delimited as a separate province in 1988. Hainan's exports in 1988 were $286 million (Ministry of Foreign Economic Relations and Trade 1989, 371). Date for 1990 are estimated based on exports through the end of November 1990.
Sources: Guangdong Statistical Bureau (1989, 331; 1990, 377); *Guangdong tongji yuebao* (Guangdong Statistical Monthly), no. 11, pt. 3, p. 8.

Contrasting regional trade performance

Many of the problems of domestic price distortions and underdeveloped factor markets discussed above can be illuminated through a comparison of different provincial level units in China in exploiting the opportunities presented by China's opening to the outside world. What accounts for the remarkable success of Guangdong Province in exporting as compared to the more sluggish performance of Liaoning and Shanghai, traditionally China's largest exporting provinces?

Guangdong's exports scored stunning advances in the 1980s, particularly in the second half of the decade. As shown in Table 5.1, the province's exports stood at only $1.4 billion in 1978. Exports rose to $2.9 billion by 1985 and exceeded $10 billion by 1990. Exports more than tripled between 1985 and 1990, a pace far exceeding the increase in exports for China as a whole. In the process, Guangdong in 1986 surpassed other leading exporting regions, such as Liaoning and Shanghai, to become China's largest exporter.

Exports from Shanghai, by contrast, grew relatively slowly over the same period. Exports in 1990, $5.32 billion, were less than twice the level of 1978 (Chu Lanfen; Shanghai Municipal Statistical Bureau, 351). In 1978 Shanghai's exports were twice those of Guangdong. By 1990 their relative positions were reversed and Guangdong's exports were twice those of Shanghai. The slow growth of Shanghai's exports in part was due to the opening of more cities to foreign trade, particularly along the Yangtse River, in the first decade of reform. Goods from east and central China that previously had been shipped through China's largest port increasingly were shipped abroad directly and these were no longer reflected in the municipality's export statistics. If we confine our attention to the international sales of goods actually produced in the city, Shanghai's dominant role as a supplier of Chinese exports in the 1970s and earlier is reduced somewhat. But on this measure the decline in the role of the city as an exporter in the decade of the 1980s was even more substantial. Between 1981 and 1988 exports of goods actually produced in the city rose by less than 7 percent. Because China's total exports rose by 115 percent during those years, Shanghai's share of China's exports in 1988 plunged by half compared to 1981 to comprise under 7 percent of total exports.[16]

One immediately wants to know to what extent Guangdong's success can be attributed to either locational advantages or to special privileges dispensed by Beijing. Does its proximity to Hong Kong and the rapid development of exports produced either by foreign invested firms in the province or through the new forms of trade, such as export processing or compensation trade discussed in Chapter 3, explain Guangdong's performance? In short, is Guangdong's success the result of geographic location or to other more fundamental characteristic of the province's economy? As Table 5.1 shows, export processing and exports from foreign-invested firms in Guangdong grew remarkably in the latter half of the 1980s, rising to 35 percent of total provincial exports by 1990. However, conventional exports also grew quite rapidly. Indeed, until the pace faltered in 1989, the growth of Guangdong's conventional exports almost matched the growth of China's total exports.[17] Thus, exports from foreign-invested firms, export processing, and compensation trade have boosted the export performance of the province significantly. But if conventional exports had not more than quadrupled between 1978 and 1990, Guangdong would be a second-tier exporter rather than number one. In short, the special privileges accorded to Shenzhen and other special economic zones and proximity to Hong Kong contributed to but can not fully explain Guangdong's success as an exporter.

In large measure, Guangdong's success in expanding its exports appears to be due to features of its economic structure that allowed it to respond more rapidly to the emerging opportunities of the 1980s. These characteristics allowed Guangdong to exploit its proximity to Hong Kong. Without these aspects of Guangdong's economy proximity to Hong Kong likely would have meant very little. Three features appear particularly relevant.

First, the structure of industrial output in Guangdong was more congruent with China's underlying comparative advantage in labor-intensive light industrial products.

The ability to respond flexibly to new opportunities presented by China's opening to the world market is particularly evident in Guangdong's rapidly rising production and export of labor-intensive products such as shoes, garments, cotton piece goods, silk piece goods, plastic articles, toys, and tools. Exports of each of these products at least tripled between 1985 and 1988, and Guangdong accounted for a rising share of national exports of several of these goods. For example, by 1988 Guangdong's toy exports accounted for about half of national exports of toys, cotton knitwear about one fifth, plastic articles about one fourth, and so on (Guangdong Statistical Bureau 1989, 337; Ministry of Foreign Economic Relations and Trade 1989, 378–450).

As a result the structure of Guangdong's exports changed remarkably during the decade. The province since the 1950s had been a major supplier of vegetables, live pigs, and other agricultural products to neighboring Hong Kong. As recently as 1985, fully one third of the province's exports remained agricultural products, about twice the national share.[18] Because of the rapidly rising share of light industrial goods in its exports, by 1988 the share of agriculture in Guangdong's exports had fallen to under one fourth. That trend reflects the relative importance of light manufacturing in the province. In 1988, for example, 70 percent of the province's manufacturing output originated in light industry, whereas in Shanghai the share was only 55 percent. Moreover, the share of light industry in Guangdong's industrial output was rising sharply throughout the decade, whereas in Shanghai the share rose only slightly. In short, Guangdong's product mix was initially more oriented toward light industrial goods in which China had a comparative advantage and the province was able to shift the composition of its industrial output even more in that direction over the decade of the 1980s. That, in turn, allowed the province to shift its mix of export products much more rapidly than Shanghai.

Indeed, it was in large part the dynamic growth of exports of garments, toys, footware, and other light industrial goods from Guangdong and Fujian that accounted for the rising share of manufactures and declining share of primary products in China's exports in the latter half of the 1980s (World Bank 1990a, 80-1). The share of primary products in China's total exports, which averaged just over 50 percent in 1980–5 fell to under one third by the late 1980s (Ministry of Foreign Economic Relations and Trade 1989, 351; State Statistical Bureau 1990b, 642).

The second feature of Guangdong's industry, closely related to the first, that gave it an advantage in exporting was its far more flexible industrial structure, compared to Shanghai. This is reflected in the relatively small average size of its firms and the relatively smaller share of output produced in state-owned firms. In 1988, the value of industrial output in Guangdong and Shanghai was also identical. But Guangdong had more than twice as many firms and a much smaller share of these firms were state-owned. In Guangdong more than three quarters of all firms were what I refer to as entrepreneurial firms: urban collective, township and village, private, and joint-venture firms that in many ways operated in a more marketlike environment than state-owned firms.

Entrepreneurial firms generally paid something closer to the real value for their capital, both fixed and working, rather than borrowing from the specialized state banks at subsidized interest rates. They were particularly dependent on funds borrowed on informal credit markets and on retained earnings (World Bank 1990a, 15). They purchased the bulk of their inputs on relatively free markets rather than receiving materials allocated by the government at fixed prices. They paid their workers wages based on their profitability rather than following the pattern of fixed wage scales used by state firms. And they sold most of their output at market prices rather than delivering it to the state-run commerical network at a fixed price (Byrd and Lin). Most of these firms were sponsored by local state governments or at least depended on their implicit support (Byrd and Lin). Despite this dependence, these entrepreneurial firms appear to operate in a much more marketlike environment than large state-owned firms.

In Guangdong in 1988, entrepreneurial firms produced 60 percent of all manufactured goods, whereas in Shanghai their share was barely one third (Guangdong Statistical Bureau 1989, 139; Shanghai Municipal Statistical Bureau 130). Of particular note is the relatively large share of output in Guangdong produced by private and rural enterprises. By contrast, a larger share of nonstate output in Shanghai was produced in larger urban collective firms over which the municipality could exercise relatively more authority.

Liaoning, whose exports also faltered once the price of oil softened in the mid-1980s, was in these respects similar to Shanghai. It was one of the most industrialized and the most urbanized of China's provinces and its industrial structure was even more strongly skewed toward heavy industry than Shanghai's. The communists inherited a major heavy industrial base built up by the Japanese in Manchuria during the 1930s and they continued to push the development of producer goods industries there after 1949, particularly in the First Plan. In the mid-1980s, fully two thirds of manufactured goods in the province originated in heavy indsutry. Moreover, like Shanghai, about two thirds of its manufactured goods originated in state-owned plants. Output of village and township enterprises was extremely low, under 5 percent of manufacturing output in the province. Its export structure was highly skewed with about three quarters of exports originating in heavy industry. Perhaps not surprisingly the value of the province's exports in 1988 was less than it had been in 1980, a period of time during which China's exports as a whole almost tripled (Liaoning Economic and Statistical Yearbook Editorial Committee, 449, 467, 568).

Guangdong's entrepreneurial firms appear to have played a major role in the national expansion of exports by nonstate firms. Exports from the province's foreign-invested firms (Table 5.1) accounted for fully half of all China's joint-venture exports in 1988 (Ministry of Foreign Economic Relations and Trade 1989, 54). Guangdong's township and village enterprises also produced $2.015 billion in export goods in 1989, a disproportionately large share of national exports originating in that sector (Zhang Zuoqian, 25). Nationally this sector was very dynamic (Zweig). Their exports rose from $5 billion in 1987 to an estimated $12.5 billion in 1990, increasing the township and village enterprise share of China's exports from one seventh to more than one fifth (Wang and Che, 60; Wang Jian, 37; Xinhua 1990d).

The dynamic nature of township and village enterprises is evident even in Shanghai. In 1988 these firms produced $1.135 billion in export goods – over one third of the export goods produced in the municipality – and almost twice the $599 million in exports the previous year (Reporter 1989b). That figure is enormously revealing of the dismal export performance of state-owned firms in the municipality. It means that the exports of Shanghai's state enterprises probably fell by about one third in the decade of the 1980s. The modest growth of the exports produced in the city was possible only because the explosive growth of township and village enterprise exports more than offset the collapse of exports of state-run firms.

Also, Guangdong appears to have been less handicapped than Shanghai by the increasing regional fragmentation of China's economy in the 1980s. As decentralization of resource allocation power proceeded in the 1980s, the skewed structure of Chinese domestic prices encouraged regions that had traditionally supplied tobacco, cotton, animal hides and other agricultural goods to Shanghai to develop their own processing industries. The structure of prices guaranteed that disproportionately more profits were generated in processing than in raising the crops or the animal husbandry products. Revenue sharing systems and decentralized investment authority introduced in the early 1980s provided the fiscal incentive and the economic possibility for regions that had previously transferred their agricultural raw materials to other provinces to construct their own processing plants and capture more revenues locally (Chen and Wei). This conflict between producing and processing regions led to a series of what were called commodity wars in the 1980s. The most widely publicized were the "wool war," the "leaf tobacco war," and the "silkworm cocoon war."

Some Chinese writers used the analogy of feudalism, in which local feudal lords established trade barriers, either to prevent the outflow of locally produced agricultural products and raw materials so that more goods would be processed locally or to increase their market power so as to be able to charge higher prices to outside buyers, to explain developments in the latter half of the 1980s. In either case, the objective of these local leaders was to generate more fiscal revenues which, under the prevailing system of fiscal contracting, could be retained for local use (Shi Fu).

The trend toward regional fragmentation, however, was not limited to agricultural raw materials. Because of the inconvertibility of the domestic currency, producers of industrial inputs and semiprocessed goods were reluctant to supply factories in other regions that were producing final goods for export. The retained foreign exchange accrued entirely to the exporting firm and the local government supervising its affairs. A supplier firm from the same region would undoubtedly bargain with the local government to gain a claim to some of the foreign exchange. But a supplier firm in one province would have no status to present such a claim to another provincial government. Price distortions, which resulted in most industrial profits being generated in the final stage of production, had always constituted a disincentive for transactions between firms that did not share the same supervising entity, whether a ministry or a local industrial bureau. But the opening of the economy to external trade in the 1980s exacerbated this problem because of the inconvertibility of the domestic currency.

Increasing regional fragmentation appears to have had a differential effect on Guangdong and Shanghai. Light industry in both provinces was heavily dependent on raw materials originating in farming rather than industry.[19] They both depended much more on animal hides, tobacco, raw cotton, and so forth than they did on chemical fibers, plastics, and so forth. As reform got underway in the late 1970s, the central government reduced significantly its role in assuring the interregional transfer of many of these raw materials. A larger and larger share of these came under the control of provincial and local governments (Wong). But Guangdong could rely on its vast and productive agricultural hinterland, whereas the municipality of Shanghai depended primarily on goods transferred from the neighboring provinces of Jiangsu and Zhejiang and, to a lesser extent, provinces farther up the Yangtse River, such as Hubei and Hunan. In the late 1970s, the flows of agricultural raw materials to the city fell by one third resulting in significant unutilized capacity in many industries and depressed industrial growth (Zhou Xiqiao, 30).[20] That almost certainly adversely affected Shanghai's export performance as well.

The central government initially sought to alleviate this problem by various administrative measures to restrict the development of new processing plants in raw-material producing regions. Many of these new facilities, in the view of the center, were too small to exploit fully economies of scale and they competed with existing factories for raw materials, lowering the rate of capacity utilization, thus reducing economic productivity.

Most of these measures were ineffective and the proliferation of, for example, cotton textile mills in traditional cotton-producing regions, such as Shandong and Hebei, continued for much of the decade, further reducing the flow of raw materials to traditional textile industry centers such as Shanghai.

This led ultimately to the adoption of what was referred to in China as the strategy of coastal development (Zhao Ziyang 1988). This strategy sought to utilize foreign trade to overcome two domestic obstacles to China's increased participation in the world economy – the overvalued exchange rate and the semireformed character of domestic prices. The underpricing of agricultural products, for example, had made it increasingly difficult for major urban manufacturing cities such as Shanghai and Tianjin to acquire sufficient raw materials. Thus, one key feature of the coastal development strategy was to ease limitations on the import of raw materials. That would allow the industries in major urban coastal manufacturing centers to develop without increased reliance on raw materials from inland regions.

Furthermore, the easing of restrictions on raw materials imports, in theory could help overcome the obstacle to exporting that was imposed by an overvalued exchange rate. Coastal exporters receive an inappropriately low number of units of domestic currency for each dollar's worth of exports. But if they can import raw materials duty free, the same overvalued exchange rate works in their favor. The implicit subsidy of imported inputs offsets part of the implicit tax on exports. It is for this reason that allowing duty-free imports of raw materials and intermediate goods is viewed as a partial offset to the distortions caused by an overvalued domestic currency (World Bank 1988a, 44).

Politically, the coastal development strategy was responsive to the demands of coastal regions, such as Shanghai, to have more assured sources of supply of raw materials. And intellectually it was justified by what was referred to in China as "the great international circle." This was essentially an argument, based on the theory of comparative advantage, that China should exploit its relatively abundant factor of production, labor. There had been considerable debate among Chinese economists since the early 1980s on export-oriented development. Reportedly, Zhao's attention was drawn to this discussion and the "great international circle" formulation by a policy memo written by Wang Jian, a staff member in the State Planning Commission.

The coastal development strategy received considerable attention in the Chinese press in the early months of 1988, largely because Zhao, then general secretary of the party, personally promoted it. However, there are few details known about precisely what additional authority or resources were made available to coastal areas. The light industry, arts and crafts, and garment sectors had already received authorization to make extensive use of imported raw materials in 1987. This was to have been financed by their increased retained foreign exchange revenues. The 1987 reform, recall, provided them with a preferred retention rate of 70 percent of the foreign exchange they earned. More broadly, all sectors were already eligible to exploit the provisions of the export processing program introduced in the late 1970s, which was discussed in Chapter 2. And in August 1987 the State Council had approved a plan for rebating all import tariffs on raw materials and equipment that were imported and then used to produce exports (Sun Wenxiu, 56).

In principle, freer access to imported raw material should have been an important impetus to improved allocative efficiency since the exemption from import duties would allow producers in coastal regions to escape the vagaries of domestic pricing by relying on raw materials purchased at world prices.

In practice it is difficult to judge the results of the program. In Shanghai it seems to have failed, at least in the 1980s. Imports did not begin to make up for the decline in centrally allocated raw materials. For example, the planned supply of domestic raw cotton allocated by the state fell by almost half, from 324,100 tons in 1986 to 173,500 tons in 1988. And the actual amount supplied fell below the planned level by an increasing margin over time. In 1986 the city received 98.9 percent of promised supplies but this slipped to 83.7 percent and 72 percent in the succeeding two years. Thus actual deliveries of raw cotton in 1988 were more than 60 percent below the level of 1986. As a result, the city's textile industry operated substantially below capacity throughout this period.

This situation does not appear to have been ameliorated by the adoption of the coastal development strategy in 1988. Imports were far from sufficient to replace decreased domestic supplies of raw cotton. In 1988, for example, Shanghai imported cotton worth only $18.89 million (Rong, Zhong, and Dai). That would have been sufficient to purchase only about 11,000 tons of cotton, a tiny fraction of the raw material shortfall faced by the cotton textile industry in Shanghai.[21] As a result, in that year Shanghai's exports of textiles, cotton cloth, and printed cotton cloth all fell sharply.[22] In the first two months of 1989, 60 percent of the city's textile production capacity was idle because of a shortage of raw cotton (Rong, Zhong, and Dai).

The foreign exchange provisions of the coastal development strategy appear to be the key reason Shanghai could not easily use imports to acquire sufficient raw materials. As discussed above, the handicap that the overvalued exchange rate imposes on a firm's exports will be partially offset by the right to import duty-free inputs at the same exchange rate. However, under Zhao's coastal development strategy locally retained foreign exchange was to be the main source of financing substantially increased quantities of imported raw materials (Zhao Ziyang 1988, 20). Thus Shanghai's imports of raw cotton were financed not with officially supplied, underpriced foreign exchange but with the retained foreign exchange of the municipality and local firms. Because this foreign exchange could be sold on the swap market, its opportunity cost in 1988 was not 3.7 yuan per dollar but 6 yuan per dollar. Thus there was no implicit subsidy of imported inputs to offset the tax on exports that was implicitly imposed by the overvalued exchange rate.

Finally, Shanghai appears to have been a victim of China's largely unreformed national tax structure. From the 1950s on the central government was heavily dependent on the remission by Shanghai of taxes and enterprise profits generated in the city, China's largest industrial center. Remissions typically accounted for 80 percent or more of local fiscal revenues, leaving the city with a paucity of resources to modernize its aging industrial facilities (Lardy 1978, 161–4). Although the fiscal burden on the municipality was reduced somewhat in the 1980s, it was still substantial. In the mid-1980s (1983–7) the municipality's fiscal expenditures grew from 1.9 billion yuan to 5.0 billion yuan. But fiscal revenues grew from 15.4 billion yuan to 16.5 billion yuan. Although the percent of local fiscal revenues remitted fell from 87.6 percent in 1983 to 69.6 percent in 1987, the vast majority of the city's fiscal revenues averaging in excess of thirteen billion yuan per annum were remitted to Beijing to finance central government expenditures (Ministry of Finance General Planning Department 1989, 53, 89). The state reduced the burden to a fixed annual sum of 10.5 billion yuan beginning in 1988 (Chen and Gong, 477).

Guangdong Province was treated far more generously. In the mid-1980s it was able to spend most of its fiscal revenues. Its quota of tax revenues to be remitted to the center was reduced from 1.0 billion yuan in 1980–2 to 772 million yuan in 1986–90 (World Bank 1988b, 442). The actual amount remitted appears to have been somewhat higher, about one billion yuan by the late 1980s.[23] And in 1991 Ye Xuanping, the provicial governor, was quoted as saying that the province had agreed to increase its remittances to 1.3 billion yuan to help the center cope with a burgeoning fiscal deficit.[24]

A comparative analysis of the fiscal capacity of Guangdong and Shanghai lies well beyond the scope of this volume.[25] But there seems little doubt that the relative fiscal burden imposed by the central government on Shanghai was far greater than that imposed on Guangdong (White). The consequent shortage of resources for modernization and investment in Shanghai must have been a factor contributing to both the city's relatively slow growth in the 1980s and its modest export performance.

In short, Shanghai's participation in the world economy in the 1980s was handicapped by basic structural features of its economy and China's domestic fiscal system that limited domestic economic reforms had done little to change. The city's fiscal position was perilous, providing insufficient funding to upgrade the deteriorating infrastructure of the municipality (White, 47–58). Manufacturing remained predominantly state-run and turned out disproportionately heavy industrial goods not readily saleable on international markets. Exports of the municipality's state enterprises actually fell sharply in the 1980s. The growth of the city's labor force was limited by centrally mandated restrictions on labor migration and much of the city's large existing labor force was tied to state factories and could not easily shift into entrepreneurial firms. The city's township enterprises were successful exporters. But they produced only one fifth of the city's manufactured goods, so their success was sufficient only to offset the decline of state exports. Finally, the expansion of that portion of state-owned industry that should have been best able to exploit newly opening international markets – the textile, garment, and other light industries – was handicapped by regional fragmentation of markets for raw materials. That fragmentation, in turn, was the result of domestic price distortions and the inconvertibility of the domestic currency that provided every incentive for raw material producing regions to develop their own processing industries rather than supply raw materials to traditional manufacturers in Shanghai. Yet, as will be explained below, further progress toward making the renminbi a convertible currency depended critically on further domestic economic reform.

In the decade of the 1980s, China substantially relaxed its system of exchange control. As discussed in Chapter 3, by the end of the decade a large share of total export earnings was either sold on the swap market or used to finance imports that fell outside the scope of the state plan and which were regulated primarily by a system of licenses. In either case, this meant that the user of these imported goods was paying a market price for foreign exchange, either explicitly or implicitly. Moreover, the relatively small spread in 1990 both between the official exchange and the swap market rate and between the swap market rate and the black market rate indicated that the degree of disequilibrium in these markets had shrunk over the latter years of the 1980s. The disequilibrium was certainly substantially less than in similar markets in the Soviet Union. Indeed, the spread between the official and swap market rates in China was far less than the spread between the official and the auction market rates for the zloty in the months prior to Poland's introduction of internal convertibility of the zloty in trade transactions in early 1990.[26]

Financial reform and aggregate demand management

The seeming convergence of the swap and official exchange rates did not mean that China was necessarily within striking distance of making the renminbi an internally convertible currency for trade transactions. Convertibility of the currency depended critically on further domestic financial reform that imposed more stringent credit constraints on Chinese enterprises. In the closing months of 1988 and through most of 1989, Chinese firms faced a temporary constraint on their ability to borrow domestic funds because of the austerity policy imposed by the government starting in the late fall of 1988. Although the growth of credit to enterprises was curtailed for a period, this was achieved without significant reform of the underlying domestic financial system. The state controlled bank lending mainly by administrative fiat while the underlying excess demand for credit remained.

Two key reforms were lacking. First, the state did not rely sufficiently on interest rate policy to curtail the demand for credit. Credit was controlled by lending quotas that were imposed on banks. The State Planning Commission and China's central bank, the People's Bank of China, determined the allowable increase in total bank credit in a given time period. That increase was then allocated among the Industrial and Commercial Bank, China's largest bank, and other specialized banks, such as the Agricultural Bank of China and the Chinese People's Construction Bank. Each of these banks divided its allowable credit expansion quota among its branches in each province and independent municipality. Thus in 1988 and 1989 the price of credit, to those who did receive loans, remained relatively low because lending rates were raised substantially less than the increase in price inflation. For example, the state raised the lending rate on one-year working capital loans in the fall of 1988 by only around one percentage point, from 7.92 to 9.00 percent, a rather modest adjustment given the fact that the rate of inflation soared to 18 percent compared to 9 percent when the previous rate had been set in 1985 (State Statistical Bureau 1987, 647; 1990a, 38; World Bank 1990, 28). The lending rate was raised further to 11.34 percent in 1989 and then reduced to 10.08 percent in 1990 (World Bank 1990c, 28, 119). Thus in 1988 and much of 1989 the real rate of interest on one-year working capital loans was negative. Not until the closing months of 1989 was the real interest rate positive.

Second, state firms did not bear the full cost of borrowing funds, so higher interest rates would not necessarily have reduced their demand for borrowed funds. There were two reasons for this. First, the real costs of borrowing were reduced by allowing firms to repay interest and principle from pretax income. Loan amortization was a deductible expense. In 1988, for example, enterprises used about 25 billion yuan in pretax profits to repay loans, substantially cutting their tax payments to the state treasury (Wang Bingqian 1989). Second, in most years in the 1980s, between one third and one fourth of state-owned enterprises incurred financial losses that were covered by special budgetary subsidies.[27] For these firms interest and amortization of loans was paid with increased budgetary subsidies. As shown in Table 5.2, these subsidies soared from about 12.5 billion yuan in 1978 to 57.85 billion yuan in 1990. Losses absorbed more than one fifth of domestic fiscal revenue by the end of the decade, up sharply from the early reform years. Detailed time series data that show the distribution of enterprise losses among different sectors of the economy are not available to foreign researchers but the largest share appears to have been generated in the commercial sector.[28] Within industry the largest loss-making sectors were coal, petroleum, and machine building, accounting for well over 90 percent of the total (Zhang Yuan, 46).

The absence of financial discipline on Chinese enterprises makes it difficult to achieve internal convertibility of the domestic currency for trade transactions. As long as firms have access to domestic credit at a below equilibrium price, either because the interest rate is too low or because

Table 5.2. *Subsidies of losses of state-owned enterprises, 1978–91 (billions of yuan and as a percentage of government fiscal revenues)*

	Billions of yuan	Percentage of government fiscal revenues
1978	12.490	11.1
1979	8.606	7.5
1985	24.523	13.6
1986	32.478	14.7
1987	37.643	18.5
1988	44.646	17.6
1989	59.976	21.5
1990	57.850	18.8
1991	55.672	16.2

Notes: The figures for 1991 are the budgeted amounts. The data in column two are calculated on the basis of the Chinese definition of revenues, i.e. inclusive of funds that would be treated as financing items in Western fiscal systems (see Notes to Table 5.3). The figure for 1979 in the original source is given as 7.8 percent of "internal financial revenue." To make it comparable with entries for other years, it has been recalculated taking into account foreign borrowing that was channeled through the state budget in 1979.
Sources: Wang Bingqian (1989, 2; 1990, ix, xi–xii; 1991, 34–7); Ministry of Finance General Planning Department (1989, 16–17).

financial losses are covered by subsidies, the demand for foreign exchange to pay for imports will be excessive.

Under conditions of credit tightening, such as prevailed during much of 1989, the gap between the swap market rate and the official exchange rate narrowed. But as credit policy was eased, at first modestly in the final quarter of 1989 and then more broadly in 1990, one would expect, ceteris paribus, the gap between the market and swap rates would widen steadily. The absence of a growing spread may be due to the further devaluation of the official exchange rate in late 1989 and late 1990. Or it could have been due to more stringent bureaucratic constraints being posed on the entry of would-be buyers of foreign exchange into the swap market, a sign, though difficult to measure, of disequilibrium.

Macroeconomic stability

A second prerequisite for further external reform is greater macroeconomic stability. In the decade of the 1980s, China went through several periods of excess demand leading to domestic inflation that tended to undermine the opening of China to the world economy. Excess demand led to a deterioration in the trade account and to the imposition of more ad hoc controls on trade to prevent a depletion of China's foreign exchange reserves. In Chapter 3, I have already explained how the environment of excess demand in 1984–5 led to a rapid deterioration of China's trade account and thus to the reimposition of more stringent controls on the use of retained foreign exchange. In each period of excess aggregate demand the central government has resorted to ad hoc controls on imports that have undermined partially the liberalization of trade that had occurred in prior years. Ad hoc import controls have been combined with increased pressures to achieve higher export targets, reducing the scope for decentralized exporting.

Macroeconomic instability also has been reflected in domestic price inflation that undermined China's attempt to introduce a more realistic exchange rate. This was particularly evident between mid-1986 and late 1989 when rising domestic inflation combined with a fixed exchange rate led to an appreciation of China's real effective exchange rate.

Inflation was brought under control by 1990 through the use of restrictive monetary policy. But there has been no fundamental reform of the underlying system that periodically has led to excessive credit creation via lending to enterprises. Unless further financial reforms are introduced, the 1990s will almost certainly be marked by one or more periods of excessive monetary expansion based on unconstrained borrowing by state enterprises.

State budgetary policy also contributed to periods of excess demand and inflation as well. During the decade of the 1980s, the state budget was almost continuously in deficit, even on its inadequate accounting principles, which treat both domestic and foreign borrowing as regular tax revenues. The cumulative deficit from 1979 through 1990 was more than 80 billion yuan. And as reflected in Table 5.3, if the officially reported deficit is adjusted appropriately, the cumulative deficit was more than twice that amount. More significantly, the deficit rose sharply in two periods, contributing to macroeconomic instability. In the first, the deficit shot up to 20 billion yuan, more than 5 percent of gross national product, when reform was getting underway in 1979. The deficit was then reduced significantly over a period of years until it reached a low of less than 3 billion yuan, a small fraction of 1 percent of gross national product in 1985. The second surge occurred in 1986–9 as the deficit rose almost tenfold in absolute terms and reached almost 2 percent of national output. A major effort to bring the deficit under control appears to have achieved some success. As shown in Table 5.3 in 1990 the

Table 5.3. *State fiscal deficit, 1978–91 (billions of yuan and as a percentage of gross national product)*

Year	Officially reported deficit (surplus) (BY)	Financing items treated as tax revenue (BY)	Total (billions of yuan)	Deficit (surplus) % of GNP
1978	(1.017)	–	(1.017)	(.3)
1979	17.067	3.531	20.591	5.2
1980	12.750	1.443	14.193	3.1
1981	2.551	1.019	3.570	.7
1982	2.934	2.834	5.768	1.1
1983	4.346	3.694	8.040	1.4
1984	4.454	4.843	9.297	1.3
1985	(2.162)	5.029	2.867	(.3)
1986	7.055	8.809	15.864	1.6
1987	7.959	8.972	16.931	1.5
1988	7.855	19.403	27.258	1.9
1989	9.535	20.174	29.709	1.9
1990	15.043	16.916	31.959	1.8
1991	12.346	10.793	23.139	

Notes: The figures for 1991 are the budgeted amounts. Financing items include government bonds, treasury bills, construction bonds issued to finance key projects, and that portion of foreign borrowing that is allocated through the state budget. These items are measured on a net basis, i.e., new borrowing less loan repayments. *Sources:* Ministry of Finance General Planning Department (1989, 11–12, 48, 68–71); Wang Bingqian (1990, ix–x; 1991, 34–5); State Statistical Bureau (1989a, 28; 1990a, 28; 1991, 4)

deficit as a share of gross national product declined slightly and the budget figures for 1991 project a decline in the absolute size of the deficit.

Except for 1979 and 1980, Chinese deficits as a share of national output seem relatively small. Considerable public attention in the United States was given to the government's fiscal deficit in the second half of the 1980s. The U.S. deficit peaked at 3.2 percent of output in 1988. The Chinese deficit also was well below the Soviet deficit, which rose to 8–9 percent of national output by the end of the decade of the 1980s (IMF et al., 10).

However, the Chinese deficits reported in Table 5.3 are understated by an unknown amount. This is because tax revenues have been overstated by the practice of allowing money-losing state enterprises to pay some or all of their tax obligations using funds borrowed from the banking system. State enterprises are the source of about three fourths of fiscal revenues. To the extent they continue to pay taxes, loss-making enterprises essentially have become an intermediary between the treasury and the banking system, artificially reducing the deficit officially reported by the Minister of Finance.

In addition to adding to the deficit funds borrowed by enterprises from the banking system to pay taxes, the deficit should be adjusted to include enterprises' expenditures that in most countries would be included in public outlays rather than the spending of individual firms. This would include an array of social services, a substantial portion of the costs of housing in urban areas, and so forth. These outlays are treated as a current cost of Chinese firms. To the extent that these expenditures reduce profits that enterprises might otherwise submit to the government as tax revenues, or increase the magnitude of subsidies that enterprises receive from the budget, they should not be added to the deficit reported in Table 5.3 But an unknown share of these expenditures is financed from bank loans and thus not included in the officially reported budget deficit.

Ronald McKinnon (1982) has clearly laid out the reasons why a balance between government revenues and expenditures is a necessary condition for the full liberalization of foreign exchange. When, as in China in the 1980s, the sale of government bonds finances was only a portion of the fiscal deficit, government borrowing from the banking system becomes a source of inflation. Because this portion of government borrowing occurs at a zero or low nominal interest rate, it imposes a substantial tax on the banking system. As bank earnings are squeezed, banks must raise lending rates on other borrowers or suffer an erosion of their capital base. In the absence of capital controls these borrowers will borrow abroad, resulting in capital inflows that further increase the domestic monetary base, if the exchange rate is pegged, or lead to an inappropriate exchange rate appreciation, if the exchange rate is free to move. The result is that it is rational to continue to rely on exchange controls and to restrict international capital flows until government revenues and expenditures are balanced. Only then can restrictions on capital flows be removed and a flexible exchange rate introduced.

China and the world economy

The evidence from developing countries, discussed in Chapter 1, is that more open economies achieve economic performance that is superior to closed economies by just about every important economic measure. They grow more rapidly, achieve greater efficiency in the use of scarce resources, and achieve superior distributive outcomes as compared to inwardly-oriented economies that insulate domestic producers from the world economy.

However successful the more open strategy is when it is maintained in the long run, transitions from relatively closed toward more open trading systems by developing countries have collapsed or been partially reversed more often than they have succeeded (Michaely, Papageorgiou, and Choksi). The initial obstacles facing China seem at least as severe and probably more severe than those encountered by most developing countries that have attempted to modify significantly their earlier inwardly-oriented strategies. That judgment is based on several factors. Most obviously, China initially insulated its economy from the world economy more than most developing countries that attempted to shift toward more open strategies of economic development. This judgment is based not only on a comparison of the value of trade relative to the output of goods and services in these economies. Rather it is based primarily on the principles of pricing of traded goods and the initially dominant role of planning in determining imports and exports in China. It was not simply that the Chinese domestic currency was more overvalued than that of most developing countries pursuing a strategy of import substitution. Because most imports were priced on the basis of comparable domestic goods, with additional markups for higher quality when that was the case, Chinese domestic industries were provided an unusually high degree of protection. Users of imported machinery not available from domestic sources and priced on the bases of import cost received the implicit subsidy provided by an overvalued exchange rate. The insulation on the export side was even more complete because monopolistic trade corporations purchased export goods from domestic producers at the same price these firms would receive if the goods were sold on the domestic market.

These pricing principles and the Chinese practice of leaving the prices of many manufactured goods unchanged for decades meant the disparities between domestic and world prices in China in the late 1970s probably surpassed those prevailing in other developing countries that have sought to shift toward a more open development strategy.

Second, prior to the initiation of economic reforms in 1978 China lagged behind most developing countries in the development of markets for the allocation of labor and, to a lesser extent, capital and intermediate goods. In comparison with the Soviet Union and the more orthodox socialist economies of Eastern Europe, China's resource allocation system was somewhat decentralized even prior to the reform decade of the 1980s. But larger shares of capital goods, and particularly labor were subject to direct government allocation than in most developing countries undertaking trade liberalization.

Generally speaking, countries that have had longer and more stringent trade restrictions require a more radical transformation to liberalize their trade regimes (Michaely, Papageorgiou, and Choksi, 40). Thus, given China's initial conditions when its economic turn outward began in the late 1970s, the challenge of foreign trade reform has been greater than in most developing countries attempting to pursue a more open trade regime. China has gone a long way toward meeting this challenge. Over the decade of the 1980s, the prices of an ever-growing number of commodities were liberalized and determined by the market. By 1988 about half of all commodity prices were determined in the market. The state fixed the prices of only about one fourth of all commodities. The balance of goods were subject to prices that floated within a range specified by the state (World Bank 1990a, 59).

Similarly, there was a rapid expansion of the share of key commodities no longer subject to direct state allocation. By 1988 the number of commodities subject to state allocation had fallen to twenty-seven, about one tenth the number in 1979. By 1988 the shares of four important industrial goods subject to state distribution – steel, timber, coal, and cement – fell by one third or more compared to what they had been in 1979. The share of steel allocated by the state, for example, fell from more than three quarters to less than half. Even many kinds of industrial machinery were sold largely in the market rather than being allocated by the state. For example, three fourths of all metal cutting tools were distributed via markets at the end of the 1980s (World Bank 1990a, 60–1).

The development of these markets and the freeing of prices means that many key decisions are now being made on the basis of prices that reflect opportunity costs. In principle, this should improve the efficiency of resource allocation.

However, in many other critical areas progress has been slow. Despite dramatically increased reliance on bank loans and retained earnings as sources of investment funds, for example, there is little reason to believe that the allocation of investment resources in the state sector has improved. Similarly, labor markets in the state sector are in their infancy and significant future development depends on several key interrelated institutional reforms that will be politically most difficult.

The constraining effects of these underdeveloped markets on the state sector is made evident by examining the sources of export growth in the 1980s. By 1990 exports of foreign-invested firms, at $7.8 billion, and township and village enterprises, at $12.5 billion, accounted for one third of China's exports (Staff Reporter; Xinhua 1990d).[29] Astonishingly they accounted for almost half of the growth of exports over the decade of the 1980s.[30] As previously explained, these firms operate in an environment that is much more subject to market forces than state-owned firms.

The relatively lethargic performance of the state sector is also reflected in the dramatic escalation of state budgetary subsidies to cover financial losses and the expansion of bank credit that also keeps many state-owned enterprises afloat. Given artificially low prices set for some commodities, some of these subsidies may be economically appropriate. But to an unknown degree the state seems to be delaying the structural changes, particularly in industry, that a more complete opening to the world economy will entail. Large portions of the heavy industrial sector built up in the years of import substitution policy may not be economically viable in a more open economy. But instead of propping these firms up through a combination of subsidies and continued protection from competition from imports, the state should be doing more to facilitate the development of markets and providing the economic incentives that would facilitate the redeployment of the labor and other resources currently employed there to other, more efficient manufacturing subsectors and to services (World Bank 1990a, 68). Similarly, the state should rely much less on the programs of export promotion, discussed in Chapter 3, which are directed toward increasing exports from state-owned firms. Those programs appear to entail considerable potential for resource misallocation.

The question posed at the outset of this study was whether China's opening to the world economy had contributed to the acceleration of economic growth evident in the 1980s. The answer seems clearly yes. The infusion by the end of the decade of about $35 billion in some twenty thousand foreign-funded enterprises and the import of some additional tens of billions of technologically advanced machinery and equipment, which was financed by increased export earnings and by borrowing abroad, has contributed significantly to the development of many key manufacturing sectors. Yet the overall conclusion of this study is that further domestic economic reform, including better macroeconomic management, is a prerequisite for sustaining China's increasing participation in the world economy. Absent further domestic reforms and a dismantling of the remaining legacy of decades of import substitution policies, which would stimulate greater efficiency in the state sector, China will continue to forego some of the benefits of international trade.

A second question posed at the outset of this study is whether China's first decade of reform contains any lessons for the Soviet Union or the countries of Eastern Europe. At one time the answer appeared to be no. The pace of China's reforms slowed after mid-1989 and in the absence of significant further political reform many doubt whether it will be possible for economic reform in China to regain the momentum that it enjoyed through much of the 1980s. Simultaneously with these developments in China discussion in the Soviet Union focused on Stanislav Shatalin's proposal for a sweeping economic reform that would be carried out in the space of only five hundred days. And the demise of communist regimes in Eastern Europe in late 1989 appeared to have substantially eased some of the prior constraints to economic reforms there. If the key features of planned economic systems in the Soviet Union and Eastern Europe could be successfully thrown off in only a year or two, what possible lessons could China offer?

The demise of communism in Eastern Europe may have eliminated the ideological factors that still constrain reforms in China. But the early euphoria surrounding these political changes has given way to a more realistic assessment of the economic problems of states in the region, problems that have not been alleviated in any way by the demise of communist ideology. And Shatalin's plan for radical economic reform in the Soviet Union now is remembered as a wistful dream. Perhaps the Chinese experience is of greater relevance to both Eastern Europe and the Soviet Union than it appeared in 1989.

Several points that emerge from China's first decade of reform seem most relevant. First, the legacy of decades of economic planning is not easily overcome. If nothing else the Chinese case demonstrates that prereform pricing of traded goods in socialist states poses an obstacle to increased openness that is at least an order of magnitude greater than that faced by most developing countries. Easing the separation of domestic from foreign prices could not be accomplished overnight in China except at a cost of enormous disruption to the domestic economy. Despite their political revolutions the same economic constraint appears to be relevant in Eastern Europe. Although the reform of pricing of traded goods is still not completed in China, the record of continuing progress on this front, even after mid-1989, is a most promising omen.

Second, the Chinese experience demonstrated the importance of sustained decentralization of control of foreign trade. The virtually continuous expansion in the number of specialized trading companies and export-producing firms authorized to engage directly in international trade seems to have been crucial to the growth of Chinese exports in the decade of the 1980s. Beginning in the fall of 1988, there was a brief period of rationalization of those trading companies. Large numbers of entities that had been unable to live up to the terms of contracts they had signed with foreign partners or had violated various regulations were either closed down or forced to merge. But at the end of the reorganization there were still approximately 4,000 firms authorized to engage in external trade transactions (Lardy 1991). And in a new series of reforms initiated in 1991 the Beijing regime promised to expand the number of firms producing export goods (as opposed to special-ized trading companies) that would be allowed to sell their products directly on the international market (Chang Hong).

By contrast the Hungarian reform of 1968 was unable to sustain its decentral-ization of foreign trade authority. A modest erosion of the monopoly trading rights of the foreign trade corporations was a key feature of the New Economic Mechanism introduced in Hungary in 1968. But the producing firms that were granted trading rights remained administratively isolated and were unable to expand their share of trade turnover beyond 10 percent. By the mid-1970s the state reasserted the traditional principle that foreign trade was a state mo-nopoly, a decision that was not reversed until 1987 (Naray, 88–92).

Third, the Chinese case suggests that the privatization of the state sector is not necessarily a prerequisite for foreign trade liberalization. The Soviets in particular seem to be preoccupied with the question of how to transfer state assets into private hands. Privatization is seen as a means of both raising productivity of these firms and of absorbing some of the excess holdings of rubles of the population. The constraint is that in the absence of working markets for machinery, equipment, and other investment goods privatization could amount to a massive transfer of assets from the state to private buyers at prices that are too low. It would thus benefit those few individuals that would be in a position to scoop up these assets at distressed prices.

By contrast China has not been preoccupied with privatization. Of course, it was discussed intensively in some circles. Although the Communist Party has periodically issued decrees upholding the primacy of state ownership of the means of production, the role of nonstate firms has steadily widened. As already noted these firms by 1990 produced almost half of all output indus-trial goods, traditionally the sector of socialist economies in which the role of the state is preeminent. Even in Poland, more than a year after initiating the "big bang" radical reform program, 90 percent or more of all industrial output was produced in state-owned firms. The transformation has been equally rapid in the service sector in China where private and other nonstate firms have grown dramatically, leaving state firms with an ever shrinking share of service activities.

The contrast between China's dynamic entrepreneurial service and manu-facturing firms and the continued domination of state-owned firms in the Soviet Union, Poland, Czechoslovakia, and Hungary drives home a funda-mental point. Operative markets for factors and outputs cannot be created overnight. Yet without these markets there is little likelihood that either nonstate firms will develop and flourish or that state firms can be privatized without creating windfall profits for the few that successfully exploit the conditions created by markets that either do not exist or are in their infancy. Contrast the painfully slow response to the Soviet law on cooperatives, passed by the Supreme Soviet in July 1988, with the dramatic expansion of nonstate firms in China. By mid-1990 cooperatives employed just 5 million workers. In China almost 100 million Chinese were working in township and village enterprises in rural areas producing, as was noted above, more than one fifth of Chinese exports by 1990. An additional 20 million entrepreneurs were engaged in private service and manufacturing ventures by the end of the 1980s.

None of these new activities in China would have been possible without the gradual but sustained development of markets. The process began in the rural sector where constraints on traditional periodic markets were dramatically eased in the late 1970s. But the process of marketization spread throughout the 1980s. The sanctioning of formal markets for machinery, equipment, and other producer goods in 1983 was critical to this process. It was not simply that some of these goods were distributed by provincial and local governments and did not come under the direct control of the central materials allocation bureaucracy. Increasingly, even state-owned enterprises were allowed to sell significant quantities of their output on the market. Without this process the acquisition of critical capital goods by township and village enterprises and by other entrepreneurial firms would have been difficult and the nonstate sector could not have grown so dramatically. It is for this reason that Janos Kornai (1990) and others have begun to argue that the creation of markets must precede privatization of state firms. McKinnon (1990b) has been even more specific arguing that rapid privatization of state firms while quantitative restrictions on outputs and inputs remain would be counterproductive. He envisions a period in which liberalized firms, mostly small-scale private firms, coexist for a period of years with state ownership of large-scale manufacturing. But the prerequisite for this development is to allow markets for capital goods and intermediate goods to develop. That has been the basis for the rapid growth of the nonstate sector in China.

Thus the key lessons of China's experience are two. First, appropriate exchange rate policy and the provision of other incentives for export are just as important in reforming socialist economies as they have been shown to be in other developing countries. Second, domestic market liberalization is also critical. Without that the reforms of the foreign trade and exchange regime will have only modest effects. The challenge China now faces is to expand the role of the market so that its influence will be more deeply felt in areas where the legacy of economic planning is still strong.

Appendix A.

The yuan–dollar exchange rate, 1952–90

	Year-end rate yuan/$100	Average annual rate yuan/$100
1952	261.70	226.45
1953	261.70	261.70
1954	261.70	261.70
1955	246.76	246.76
1956	246.18	246.18
1957	246.18	246.18
1958	246.18	246.18
1959	246.18	246.18
1960	246.18	246.18
1961	246.18	246.18
1962	246.18	246.18
1963	246.18	246.18
1964	246.18	246.18
1965	246.18	246.18
1966	246.18	246.18
1967	246.18	246.18
1968	246.18	246.18
1969	246.18	246.18
1970	246.18	246.18
1971	226.73	246.11
1972	224.01	224.51
1973	202.02	198.94
1974	183.97	196.12
1975	196.63	185.98
1976	188.03	194.14
1977	173.00	185.78
1978	157.71	168.36
1979	149.62	155.49
1980	153.03	149.84
1981	174.55	170.50
1982	192.27	189.25
1983	198.09	197.57

	Year-end rate yuan/$100	Average annual rate yuan/$100
1984	279.57	232.70
1985	320.12	293.67
1986	372.21	345.28
1987	372.21	372.21
1988	372.21	372.21
1989	472.21	376.59
1990	522.21	478.38

Sources: 1953–87: People's Bank of China Research and Statistics Department (1988, 156–7).
1988–90: State Statistical Bureau (1990a, 101). Xinhua (1989b; 1990b).

Appendix B

A Note on the degree of openness of the Chinese economy

Economists conventionally use the ratio of exports plus imports relative to gross national product or national income as an indicator of the degree of "openness" of an economy. This measure, frequently referred to as the trade ratio, is a convenient method both for measuring how the degree of openness of an economy changes over time and for comparing the degree of openness of different economies. Intercountry comparisons, of course, are somewhat problematic because ceteris paribus "large" countries have lower trade ratios than "small" countries. There are several reasons for this. First, large countries are less likely to depend on imports of minerals and other raw materials. Second, they are more likely to have levels of domestic demand sufficiently large to take advantage of economies of scale, which exist in some types of manufacturing, without exporting part of the output. Finally, relatively higher transport costs in large countries tend to provide domestic producers a greater degree of natural protection against foreign competition (Perkins and Syrquin, 1,705–22).

In the text of this study I have avoided using estimates of China's trade ratio to measure the degree of openness of the Chinese economy. This is because of the uncertainties involved in measuring China's trade volume and its gross national product (GNP) in a common currency. China compiles its trade data in U.S. dollars and its GNP in terms of domestic currency. Although it is a simple matter to convert these to a common currency by dividing the reported GNP in domestic currency by the official exchange rate, it is a dubious procedure, particularly for an economy such as China's in which the relative prices of nontraded goods and particularly services are fixed by the government at unusually low levels.

Even when the degree of government intervention in price formation is more modest, these calculations are likely to mislead because the official

Appendix Table B.1. *A Hypothetical Calculation of the Degree of Openness of the Chinese Economy in 1978, 1980, and 1989*

	1978	1980	1989
1. Trade volume (billions of $)	20.6	38.1	111.6
2. Gross national product (billions of yuan)	358.8	447.0	1,567.7
3. Exchange rate (yuan/dollar)	1.684	1.498	3.766
4. Gross national product (billions of $)	213.1	298.4	416.3
5. Trade ratio (percent)	9.7	12.8	26.8

Sources: Line 1: Table 1.1
Line 2: State Statistical Bureau (1990a, 5).
Line 3: Appendix A.
Line 4: line 2 divided by line 3.
Line 5: line 1 divided by line 4.

exchange rate usually underestimates the true value of the currency as measured by its purchasing power parity. Studies begun by Milton Gilbert and Irving B. Kravis in the 1950s and continued up to the present by their associates, show that official exchange rates for developing countries substantially understate the purchasing power of national currencies. They found real gross domestic product measured in international prices in 1975, for example, was one and one half to two and one half times that calculated by using the official exchange rate to convert output to GNP in dollars. In extreme cases, the differential was as much as 3.5 (Kravis, Heston, and Summers, 12). Thus conventionally calculated trade ratios would typically overstate the degree of openness of developing countries.

However, because they are widely used, hypothetical calculations of the degree of openness of the Chinese economy in several years of the 1980s are presented in Table B.1. These data, which use GNP to measure output, show the degree of openness of the Chinese economy almost tripling to just over one fourth in the first decade or so of reform. Calculations by Chinese authors, which tend to be based on a somewhat narrower net material product concept of output, show trade ratios of one third by 1988 (Hu Dinghe, 34).

For reasons alluded to above and discussed in more detail below, these data almost certainly are quite misleading. Yet, data of this type are frequently used uncritically by both Chinese and Western writers. For example, in 1990 a researcher from China's State Council cited the dramatic increase in the trade ratio to 28 percent by 1987 as evidence that China was actually trading too much (Luo Long in *China Daily*, May 12, 1990, p. 4). The ratio of 28 percent, which was calculated using the methodology of Table B.1, was said to be higher than the average for other countries. Similarly, *The Economist* (2–8 June 1990, 35–6) argued that "foreign trade provides one third of China's national income" and then drew the erroneous conclusion that China was extremely vulnerable to international trade sanctions imposed after the Tiananmen tragedy because of its high dependence on external markets.

Although there are no really satisfactory estimates of China's GNP based on the purchasing power of the yuan, there is widespread agreement that converting the domestic currency measure of GNP to yuan by using the official exchange rate results in a significantly downwardly biased estimate of China's GNP in U.S. dollars. This understatement is particularly obvious if one examines the World Bank's estimates of China's per capita GNP. The World Bank estimated China's 1987 per capita GNP to be $290 and that the average annual rate of growth of real output per capita in the period 1980–7 was 9.2 percent (World Bank 1989, 164). However, consulting the Bank's earlier publications one finds an estimate of per capita GNP for 1980 of $280 (World Bank 1982, 110). This inconsistency is the result of the Bank's procedures for calculating GNP in dollars – dividing the officially reported Chinese figure for national income by the official exchange rate.[1] As reported in Appendix A, the official exchange rate averaged 1.5 in 1980 and 3.7 in 1988. If there had been no change in the real level of output in China over this period, the Bank's procedures would result in an estimate of a 60 percent decline in real output measures in dollars between 1980 and 1987. As it was, the devaluation of the domestic currency and the growth of real output almost exactly offset each other. That led to the inconsistency in the estimated levels of real output in 1980 and 1988 on the one hand, and the estimated rate of real growth of 9.2 percent per annum over the intervening years on the other. Western economists have long commented on this inconsistency and Chinese authors also have begun to criticize the Bank's procedures and have advanced the view that China's per capita output is significantly above $300 (Yu and Li).

The very few purchasing power parity estimates of China's national income in dollars which have been published also support this view. For example, Herbert Block (1981, 43) estimated China's 1980 GNP as $592 billion (measured in 1980 prices), which is twice the dollar value of GNP obtained by dividing the official estimate of GNP in yuan by the exchange rate for the same year. The purchasing power estimate of China's 1980 GNP (measured in 1980 prices) of Summers and Heston (1988, 22) is substantially higher, $1,650 billion. Based on the Block estimate of real GNP, China's trade ratio in 1980 would be 6.4 percent. Calculations based on the Summers and Heston estimate would put the trade ratio at 2.3 percent.

Although I do not believe one can judge accurately China's trade ratio for any point in time, I believe one can say something more conclusive about how the ratio changed over the first decade of reform. This is possible by comparing the growth of China's trade and its GNP. Of course, we need to correct for price inflation by measuring both series in constant prices. Fortunately, for the years since 1978 the Ministry of Foreign Economic Relations and Trade has published annual data on the real volume of both imports and epxorts. Moreover, the State Statistical Bureau now has released estimates of China's GNP based on Western concepts of how to measure the output of an economy. These data can be used in place of the only measure previously published – national income based on the concept of net material product.

This comparison is made in Table B.2. These data show that foreign trade grew faster than GNP after 1978. In the first decade of reform real GNP more than doubled, whereas the real volume of foreign trade more than tripled. Comparing the ratio of the two indices, in the third column of Table B.2, shows how much the trade ratio has increased over time. The entry of 128 for 1988 means that the trade ratio in 1988 was about three tenths higher than that of a decade earlier.

Because the data in the foreign trade column in Table B.2 are based on the measure of trade compiled by the Ministry of Foreign Economic Relations and Trade (MOFERT), they are biased downward. As explained in the notes to Table 1.1, MOFERT data exclude the value of exports produced under compensation trade contracts. They may also undercount the value added in processed exports. These activities had grown to be quite large by the late 1980s and thus should be included in any measure of openness of China's economy. What is lacking is the data necessary to deflate the value of these activities so that they are measured in real rather than nominal terms. If, as an approximation, we assume that the same deflator that MOFERT calculated also applies to the trade activity recorded in the customs data but not in the data released by MOFERT, the index of foreign trade in 1988 would be 408.7. That is real trade quadrupled in the first decade of reform. And the ratio of the growth of trade to the growth of GNP for 1988 would stand at 163. The latter ratio means that the trade ratio rose by a little more than three fifths over the decade. Thus, if the trade ratio were 6 percent in 1978, it

Appendix Table B.2. *Indexes of China's foreign trade and gross national product, 1978–88*

	Foreign trade (1)	GNP (2)	Ratio (3)
1978	100	100.0	100
1979	118	107.6	110
1980	129	116.0	111
1981	135	121.2	111
1982	148	131.8	112
1983	174	145.4	120
1984	203	166.6	122
1985	264	187.8	141
1986	279	203.4	137
1987	315	225.8	140
1988	320	250.2	128

Notes: The index of gross national produce is calculated in what the State Statistical Bureau refers to as "comparable prices." Their procedures may impart a slight upward bias to the growth rate, particularly when measuring growth over a period of several decades. However, for a period of about a decade or so the index may be regarded as providing a close approximation of a measure of growth in constant prices.

The index of foreign trade is a volume index, i.e., a value index deflated to eliminate the effect of price changes. The Chinese publish separate volume indexes for imports and for exports. The index of foreign trade (column 1) is a weighted average of the separate series, where the weights for imports and exports are the respective annual shares of each in China's total trade turnover.

Sources: Column 1 – Ministry of Foreign Economic Relations and Trade (1989, 357).

Column 2 – State Statistical Bureau (1989a, 28).

Column 3 – Column 1 divided by column 2.

would be 10 percent in 1988 and so forth. If Block's calculation of China's GNP in 1980 is taken as meaningful, the index in the third column, adjusted to account for the broader customs based measure of trade, could be used to calculate that the trade ratio in China rose from 5.8 percent in 1978 to 9.4 percent by 1988. If the Summers and Heston estimate is taken as meaningful, the trade ratio rose from 2.1 percent to 3.4 percent over the same period.

A detailed critique of the alternative estimates of China's GNP presented in this appendix lies well beyond the scope of this book. If forced to choose among them, however, I am quite confident that the estimates in Table B.1 substantially overstate both the level of openness of the Chinese economy and the increase in openness over time. They should not be used in any serious economic analysis. On the other hand, the Summers and Heston estimate of real GNP is almost certainly too high. They estimate that per capita income in China in 1980, measured in 1980 prices, was $1,619. That was almost two and two thirds their estimate of per capita real gross domestic product for India in the same year. I believe the estimate for China can be rejected. Block's estimate is clearly preferred to the other two. Thus I would accept, as a rough estimate, that China's trade ratio rose from around 6 percent as reform began to around 10 percent by the late 1980s.

Notes

1. Trade policy and economic development

1. For the most comprehensive and insightful analysis of these developments, see Jacobson and Oksenberg (1990).

2. The current account is the sum of the merchandise and service balances plus net unrequited transfers. The People's Bank of China began to publish these and other balance of payments data, compiled according to standard international conventions, in the journal *Zhongguo jinrong* (Chinese Banking) in the mid-1980s. Retrospective data for the years 1982–6 were published in English in 1987 ("China's Balance of Payments in 1982–86") and data for subsequent years has been published in English annually. The only data I have seen for years prior to 1982 published in a Chinese source are estimates of Wu Jingben (1986, 16).

3. With the average of 1979–80 as the base, China's cumulative incremental imports during the decade ending in 1989, over $170 billion, were more than four times the increase in the value of outstanding external debt over the same period.

4. The Ministry of Foreign Economic Relations and Trade, based on the export data incorporated in Series A in Table 1.1 and GATT data for other countries, regularly reports China's rank among world exporters. This comparison shows China ranked seventeenth in 1987 and fourteenth in 1989 (Ministry of Foreign Economic Relations and Trade 1989, 358; Liu Xiangdong). The GATT data on which this ranking is calculated include reexports. For Hong Kong, one of the countries ranking above China, reexports of goods originating in China comprised a substantial portion of total exports. If one strips the Hong Kong export data of reexports, its rank falls and China ranks sixteenth in 1987 and thirteenth in 1989. If the ranking were calculated on the basis of the customs data, Series B in Table 1.1., China's rank might be another notch higher in most years in the latter part of the 1980s. See notes to Table 1.1. for a brief outline of the differences in the two series.

2. The prereform foreign trade system

1. The remaining portion of the Ministry of Trade, responsible for domestic commerce, was redesignated the Ministry of Commerce.

2. In 1960 a separate Bureau of Foreign Economic Relations was established to manage China's programs of technical and economic assistance in third world countries. In 1964 this bureau was elevated to a commission and later it became a ministry. In March 1982 this ministry and the Ministry of Foreign Trade were merged, along

156

with the Foreign Investment Control Commission (established in 1979) and the State Import and Export Control Commission (established in 1979) to create the Ministry of Foreign Economic Relations and Trade, commonly referred to by its acronym, MOFERT (Lu Jinhao, 43; Xu Jianfeng, 20).

3. The classic descriptions of the material balance system used in the Soviet Union are those of Herbert Levine (1959, 151–76) and J. M. Montias (1959, 968–85).

4. In principle an enterprise might receive a higher (lower) price if the export product was of a higher (lower) quality than the domestically produced good whose price served as the referent. There is no evidence of which I am aware that sheds light on how these quality comparisons and subsequent price adjustments were made in the prereform era. In the postreform era, when the same pricing principles applied in the domestic marketing of a decreasing range of imported goods, the adjustments sometimes were substantial. The domestic price of imported Japanese color television sets in the mid-1980s, for example, was 25 percent higher than the price of domestic color televsions (World Bank 1988a, 113).

5. Calculated based on data in Rawski (1980, 39, 86, 88).

6. Several imported commodities for which the domestic pricing would have changed from an import cost basis to the price of comparable domestic products basis were exempted from the new pricing system. Prices for those goods "are to be determined according to the current method of price formation with no change." That presumably means they continued to be priced on the basis of the import cost converted to domestic currency at the official exchange rate. The exempted imports were grain, oils and fats, chemical fertilizers, insecticides, and military equipment and prototypes ordered directly by the military system (State Council 1963, 1,230).

7. Technically the case of limited domestic production volume applied to goods that were in the stage of trial manufacture for which there was only a "temporary product price" (State Council 1963, 1,230). Once serial production began the state would fix a regular price for the goods, and imports would then be priced on the principle of comparable domestic goods not import cost.

8. For goods imported from the Soviet Union that were not eligible for pricing according to the prices of similar domestic goods, the exchange rate to be used in determining the domestic price was 4.5 yuan per ruble, a 7 percent premium over the then prevailing rate for the trade ruble (State Council 1963, 1,231). That implies the rate for the trade ruble at the time was 4.2 yuan. The rate for foreign trade transactions had been set at 2.222 yuan per ruble in January 1961 when the Soviet Union devalued the external value of the ruble (Wu and Chen, 115). Western writers who have studied the yuan–ruble exchange rate presume that rate continued for several years after 1961 but the State Council document suggests the ruble had been devalued again after January 1, 1961, but before December 17, 1963, the date of the State Council document (Chao and Mah). Curiously, but presumably not coincidentally, a 103 percent premium over the trade rate set in 1961 yields a rate of 4.5 yuan per ruble (i.e., $2.22 \times 2.03 = 4.51$). In any case, Chinese trade with the Soviet Union was declining rapidly during this period.

9. Through the end of 1979, customs revenues were included within the revenues of the foreign trade system. In January 1980, the General Customs Bureau was reestablished as an independent unit directly under the State Council and customs revenue thereafter was accounted for independently (Li Chengxun, 91).

10. Indeed one cannot help but wonder whether the several adjustments of the exchange rate in 1952 were made so that the average rate during the year, 2.26, came out to be the average of 3.08 and 1.43!

11. Because the data for 1936 appear to be exclusive of the trade of Manchuria,

which was then under Japanese occupation, they understate the share of producer goods in imports for China as a whole. Japan at that time was supplying huge quantities of producer goods to Manchuria to build up a heavy industrial base in support of its expansionist aims in the Pacific.

12. The rate of profits (losses) on exports is measured in terms of domestic currency as the ratio of financial profit (loss) to the cost of exports (Zhao Fengchen, 101).

13. In addition to two other classification schemes that are of indigenous origin, the Ministry of Foreign Economic Relations and Trade provides a third breakdown of the commodity composition of foreign trade, which is based on the United Nations Standard International Trade Classification (SITC) system. Primary products include foodstuffs; beverages and tobacco; nonfood items; minerals and fuels; and animal and vegetable oils and fats.

14. The share of manufacturing in China's national income (net material product basis) rose by about half (from 37 to 59 percent) between 1965–6 and 1978 (State Statistical Bureau 1989a, 32). This measure is imperfect for the purposes of this analysis because in China's output statistics manufacturing includes mining – goods that if exported would be reflected in primary products rather than manufactured goods in the classification of China's exports referred to in the text. However, mining accounts for only a few percentage points of the total value of industrial output so any distortion would be quite small.

15. Capital intensity is measured here as the ratio of capital to output. For example, in the 1950s the value of output per unit of fixed assets in the textile industry was from three to four times more than in the First Ministry of Machinery Industry. See *Chinese Economic Statistics, A Handbook for Mainland China*, edited by Nai-ruenn Chen (Chicago: Aldine, 1967), p. 264.

16. What I refer to here and elsewhere as permanent urban residents are those classified by the Chinese as the "nonagricultural population" (feinongye renkou). These individuals, who are entitled to subsidized grain distributed through a system of coupon rationing and a broad range of other income supplements and social and welfare benefits, live predominantly in urban areas (Lardy 1983, 163–5). But this group also includes permanent state employees and party cadres carrying out their functions in rural areas.

17. There was one exception to this. A peasant who managed to become a permanent urban worker could generally pass along to one of his children the right to a job within his enterprise at the time of his retirement. Such a job entitled one child to be reclassified as a permanent urban resident but only on the condition that the father be reclassified as a permanenet rural resident at the time of his retirement (Potter, 483). Such a reclassification would eliminate the worker's entitlement to urban housing and subsidized basic staple foods.

3. Reforming the foreign trade system

1. The text of Deng's report, entitled "Some Problems in Accelerating Industrial Development," never was published officially. It did appear in a Hong Kong magazine *Qishi niandai* (The Seventies) and was translated in Chi Hsin (1977, 239–76).

2. The full text of the report in Chinese is contained in State Council (1984b). Extracts of the report, which lack much critical material, are available in both Chinese and English in Ministry of Foreign Economic Relations and Trade (1985, 29–32, 388–92).

3. The system used through 1963 for importing machinery, equipment, industrial raw materials, and intermediate goods discussed in Chapter 2, also appears to have been an agency system. The agency system was also in limited use in the late 1970s or early 1980s (State Bureau of Commodity Prices 1980, 76). While the agency system was used primarily as a mechanism to handle unplanned trade undertaken at the initiative of firms producing exports, some planned trade also utilized the agency system (World Bank 1988a, 108).

4. "Taking imports to support exports" includes three different types of activities: processing, the export of finished products created by processing imported materials; assembly, the export of assembled products mainly from imported parts or fittings; and export of agricultural or animal husbandry products relying on animals raised or plants grown using imported breeding stock, fodder, seeds, and fertilizer. These three activities are usually referred to as lailiao jiagong, laiyang jiagong, and laizhang yangzhi. Collectively, these are sometimes called "processed and assembled exports (using) materials brought in" (lailiao jiagong zhuangpei chukou). The term used to describe these three types of exports based on imports plus exports produced under compensation trade (buchang maoyi) agreements is "sanlai yibu chukou" (literally "exports [based on] the three come ins and one supplement").

5. The fourteen cities were Tianjin, Dalian, Qinhuangdao, Shanghai, Lianyungang, Nantong, Wenzhou, Ningbo, Fuzhou, Yantai, Qingdao, Guangzhou, Zhanjiang, and Beihai.

6. Although the rise in the magnitude of rebated taxes on exports appears to have been the result of the spread of the rebate program to include more commodites, Jiao and Zhou (1989, 6) argued that the rate of increase in the value of rebates in 1988, twice as fast as the volume of exports, showed that the "center should take steps to strengthen the management of rebates." Again that seems to reflect the strictly financial perspective adopted by these writers in their analysis of foreign trade reform.

7. The new regulations make no reference to the regulations they replace so the 1950 regulations could have been modified prior to 1980. However, I have not found any reference to foreign exchange regulations other than those dated 1950 or 1980.

8. The State General Administration of Exchange Control (Guojia waihui guanli zongju) was first established in March 1979 (Tang Gengyao 1986, 43; Wu and Chen, 12). Originally it was an organization directly under the State Council. In 1982, when it became part of the People's Bank of China, its name was modified to Guojia waihui guanli ju (Yin Ling, 25). Although ju is usually translated as "bureau," English-language Chinese publications usually referred to the organization after 1982 as the State Administration of Exchange Control, but the former name, the State General Administration of Exchange Control, was still used occasionally. In the mid-1980s, the annual reports of the IMF on exchange controls describe the organization as "a government institution under the leadership of the People's Bank of China." Although this formulation is somewhat vague, the Bank's table of organization shows it to be part of the Bank on the same administrative level as a bureau (Chinese Finance and Banking Society 1987, XI–1).

9. The document dealing with nontrade foreign exchange retentions makes clear that a retention system for these sources of foreign exchange earnings already existed. For example, the rate of retention of remittances from overseas Chinese was raised from 6 to 30 percent; for income received from the provision of services to foreign vessels in Chinese ports the rate was to remain unchanged at 20 percent; and so forth. The document makes no reference to when the prior rates were established and I have not discovered any source that sheds light on when the retention of nontrade foreign exchange income began.

10. As can be seen from the many gaps in Table 3.3, information on the quantity of

funds retained annually is incomplete. Even less is known about the distribution of these retentions. However, in the earliest years of the program the great majority of the entitlements were generated by provincial and local governments and their subordinate enterprises. The share accruing to central government ministries and their enterprises was much smaller. In 1979 and 1980 the total quantity of foreign exchange not subject to central allocation was $4.625 billion ($854 million and $1,579 million in retained export earnings; $1,192 in retained nontrade foreign exchange earnings; and $500 million annually allocated to provincial and local governments by the center) of which $3.666 billion were in "local" (difang) hands, that is, provincial and local governments, and $959 million were in the hands of the "ministries" (bumen) (Sun Wenxiu, 54). I have not seen any information that delineates how these shares changed later in the 1980s, but it would be surprising if the "local" share did not expand.

11. Localities had two options with regard to revenues from processing of imported materials. In exchange for assuming the risk of either a part or all of the potential losses, they were allowed to retain either 70 or 100 percent of the foreign exchange income (Yin Ling, 27).

12. The division of the foreign exchange earned in these three sectors, at least in Guangdong, was structured to provide particularly large incentives for the trade corporation handling the export. The firm producing the export good and the local government split 25 percent of the foreign exchange earnings so their 12.5 percent shares were the same as those prevailing in sectors where no preferential arrangements were in place. But the center took only 30 percent of the foreign exchange earned, leaving 45 percent for the trade corporation (Zhou Shude, 13). Because the exports probably were handled by enterprises surbordinate to the local industrial bureaus overseeing the enterprises in these three sectors, these retained funds would have been used for the benefit of the specific sectors in which the foreign exchange earnings were generated.

13. The avoidance of the word "market" (shihchang) in the official name given to these "centers" presumably reflects the political constraints on economic reform. Rather than using their official name in the text, I usually refer to these markets as the parallel market, swap market, or auction market.

14. The volume of transactions at this price appears to have been quite small and the government quickly abandoned its effort to constrain the price in the market to the internal settlement price of foreign exchange.

15. The specific authorization for foreign-invested firms to engage in swap market transactions is contained in article 14 of the State Council's (1986a) directive "Provisions for the Encouragement of Foreign Investment."

16. "Foreign-invested enterprises" is the usual translation for the phrase sanzi qiye. It might be translated literally as "the three types of enterprises with (foreign) capital." The three major types of foreign-invested firms are cooperative ventures, equity joint ventures, and wholly foreign-owned firms (Jiang Xiang).

17. Although the wholesale "borrowing" of retained foreign exchange by central authorities appears to have begun in 1985, Song's statement implies that such "borrowing" may have begun almost from the outset of the foreign exchange retention system.

18. According to one source the regulations allow the purchased foreign exchange to be used only for one of the following four purposes: (1) to import advanced machinery and equipment and spare parts for technical transformation projects; (2) to purchase apparatus and scientific and technicial materials and books and periodicals for scientific, medical, and educational purposes; (3) to purchase various raw and

processed materials and spare parts; and (4) for repatriation of profits by equity joint ventures, contractual joint ventures, and wholly foreign-owned subsidiaries (Yan Xiaoqing and Shen Mei, 18). However, the first and third purposes are rather elastic and difficult to enforce. In the Shenzhen Special Economic Zone it was said that no controls were exercised on the use of funds purchased in the zone's foreign exchange center in 1988. That resulted in a rate as high as 9 yuan per dollar and the import, in contravention of central regulations, of quantities of luxury consumer products (Liu Hong 1989a). In some cases approval must actually come from the ministry that produces or might produce the import substitute product.

19. In Shenzhen, for example, foreign exchange purchased on the swap market was to be used within three months. The Shenzhen branch of the State Administration of Exchange Control (SAEC), upon petition, was authorized to grant an additional three months to complete a transaction involving the expenditure of the funds ("Temporary Methods of Managing Shenzhen's Foreign Exchange Adjustment"). Disposition of funds not spent, according to the official document, was to be handled according to means specified in other regulations. I have not been able to locate the latter. According to article 46 of the regulations of the Shanghai swap market, the foreign exchange was to be used within six months although a six-month extension could be requested from the Shanghai branch of the SAEC. If the funds were not used at the end of the year, the original buyer had to sell them back to the Shanghai branch of the People's Bank of China. However, the regulations specified that in the event the foreign exchange increased in value, the price (in yuan) received would be the original price paid, not the higher price prevailing when the foreign exchange was sold back ("Shanghai Foreign Exchange Adjustment Center Business and Management Regulations," 7).

20. Brokers are the Chinese and foreign financial institutions authorized to deal in foreign currency. Dealers are major domestic and foreign-funded enterprises as well as foreign trade companies. In mid-1989 there were fifteen brokers and forty-three dealers. Dealers are allowed only to sell foreign currency in their own possession or buy to finance their own imports. Brokers can enter buy and sell orders on behalf of clients whom they charge a modest commission to cover their costs (Shen Feiyue 1989a).

21. In October 1989 when the official exchange rate was .63 rubles per dollar, the black market rate was about 10 rubles per dollar in Moscow and as high as 20 rubles, more than thirty times the official rate, in Leningrad and the Baltic republics (Esther B. Fein, "Ruble is Devalued in Some Cases; Step to Spur Soviet Economy Seen," *New York Times*, October 26, 1989, p. A1, C2).

22. Moreover, the change in the value of the Chinese currency vis-à-vis some other currencies was significantly different than the change against the dollar. For example, in 1970–9 the yuan depreciated significantly against the deutsche mark and the Swiss franc. However, it was revalued upward against the British pound, the French franc, and the Hong Kong dollar (Wu and Chen, 141).

23. The foreign trade system also sustained financial losses in 1975–6 but their magnitude appears to have been relatively small.

24. The original plan was that the foreign trade corporations would transfer commodities in this category to the relevant ministries at domestic prices derived by converting the world market price to yuan at the internal settlement price of foreign exchange. The objective was to make the ministries using the imported goods more sensitive to the cost of imports and thus lead to a more rational utilization of imported commodities. Under this plan state financial subsidies to cover losses would be negotiated between the central government and its Finance Ministry on the one hand and

the ministries using the imports on the other. As of mid-1982 this system had not been adopted and the users of these imports, as explained in the text, were insulated from exchange rate changes. And subsidies were provided to the foreign trade corporations, not the ministries using the imports (Hu Changnuan, 504).

25. The judgment that the doubling of price subsidies in 1981 was due to the introduction of the internal settlement rate is based on the relatively small change in the physical quantities of the five imported goods and the relative stability of world prices for the goods. The change in the physical quantities of imports in 1981 compared to 1980 was as follows: grain, +10 percent; sugar, +19 percent; chemical fertilizer, −7 percent; and cotton, −15 percent. Imports of agricultural pesticides are not reported in physical terms but the dollar value of imports fell 8 percent (Ministry of Foreign Economic Relations and Trade 1984, IV-114–IV-118). World prices of wheat and sugar fell while the price of cotton rose slightly. See World Bank, *Commodity Trade and Price Trends August 1981* (Balitmore: The Johns Hopkins University Press, 1981), pp. 46, 48, 70.

26. A central feature of the most widely publicized State Council (1984) decision on reform of the foreign trade system was the promotion of the agency system in foreign trade transactions. Because of the prominence the agency system was given, some authors have assumed that the system was first introduced in 1984. In fact it was in use by 1980, if not earlier. See the directive of the State Bureau of Commodity Prices (1980, 76) discussing foreign trade corporations undertaking import transactions on an "agency" (daili) basis.

27. These proportions are based on the share of imports not under the direct administration of the foreign trade corporations of MOFERT.

28. There are conflicting statements on the extent to which the use of the principle of "foreign trade agent price formation" was used to determine the price of imports. A source cited later gives the share as 43 percent in 1984 as compared to the 20 percent figure cited here. Chen is a researcher in the Finance and Trade Research Institute of the Chinese Academy of Social Sciences, and the Academy was responsible for the volume in which the higher figure was published so the discrepancy is puzzling. However, there is no doubt that the pass-through of international prices into the domestic market via imports at least doubled between 1984 and 1986.

29. The twenty-eight commodity categories were pig iron, timber, plywood, wood pulp, refined naphthalene, soda ash, caustic soda, chemical fertilizer, nonferrous metals, tallow, coconut oil, sulphur, cocoa beans, grain, phosphorus ore, glycerine, titanium dioxide, and intermediates used to make agro-chemicals, aniline, butanol, acyl alcohol, cattle hides, alkyl benzene, steel products, nonionic surface active agents, dimethylbenzene, five sodiums (possibly sodium bichromate, sodium cyanide, sodium tripolyphospate, and other sodium compounds), nitrobenzene, and rubber.

30. For example, wool, chemical fibers, and chemical industry monomers were not on the 1986 list but apparently were sold to domestic end users at subsidized prices until 1988. Cotton and sugar were not included in the list of twenty-eight imported commodities that would be subsidized so they could be sold at the same price as comparable domestic goods. Imports of cotton and sugar traditionally had been subsidized (Table 3.4) and some specialists told me in mid-1990 that they continued to be sold at subsidized prices even though they were not listed. Since the retail price of sugar was raised at least twice, in 1988 and 1990, perhaps subsidies for imports were eliminated by 1991.

31. Four steel products continued to be exempt from pricing based on import cost − ordinary cold steel of less than 4.5 mm thickness, hot rolled sheet steel plate, strip steel, and tinplate. In the nonferrous metals category, aluminum was exempt.

32. The eight commodities that the central government continued to subsidize so that they could be sold on the domestic market at the same price as comparable domestically produced goods were chemical fertilizer, wood pulp, alkyl benzene, five sodiums, nonionic surface active agents, grain, phosphorous ore, and intermediates for agro-chemicals.

33. Interview, State Bureau of Commodity Prices Foreign Price Office, April 23, 1990.

34. As described earlier, as part of the decentralization of foreign trade authority in the 1980s, most provincial branches of the twelve specialized national foreign trade corporations were converted to provincially run foreign trade corporations. However, national foreign trade corporations responsible for category one export commodities appear to have retained direct control of their subordinate provincial branches in key provinces. For example, the China National Chemical Industry Import and Export Corporation (Sinochem) retained control of its branches in Heilongjiang and Liaoning, the location of major oil production facilities.

35. The figure of 25–30 percent is my estimate based on adding up the value of exports of the twenty-one products. Uncertainty arises because the categories in which the export value data are reported do not correspond precisely with the list of twenty-one commodities. At the outset of this chapter another source was cited stating that these category one exports accounted for 20 percent of China's total exports. My higher figure may result because the value of national export of these commodities includes decentralized, above-plan export of these products whereas the 20 percent refers to the value of the twenty-one products exported under the centrally stipulated plan.

36. Interview, State Bureau of Commodity Prices Foreign Price Office, April 23, 1990.

37. The Industrial and Commercial Bank of China was established in 1984 by the divestiture of the commercial banking activities of the People's Bank of China. The latter name was assigned to the central bank, formally created in the same year (World Bank 1988b, 246–7).

4. The efficiency of China's foreign trade

1. Zhang and Wu's statement is that "At present China's foreign trade export management system has the structure of relying mainly on the mandatory plan and supplementarily on the guidance plan; mandatory plan exports comprise 70 percent of the total and must be exported regardless of the cost of earning foreign exchange." Because their article appeared in a newspaper in mid-1987, I presume the 70 percent figure applies to 1987 or 1986. The share is roughly consistent with the discussion in Chapter 3 of the shrinking scope of the trade plan during the 1980s.

2. In the original source, the export earnings from international sales were converted from dollars to yuan at the official exchange rate, which in 1983 averaged 1.976 yuan per dollar (see Appendix A). I recalculated earnings based on the internal settlement rate of 2.8 yuan per dollar since this is the rate that exporters received from the Bank of China. The original data show aggregate export losses of 25.9 billion yuan.

3. The input–output table is for eighteen sectors. But these included one sector, electric power, with no exports.

4. Exports totaled 43.8 billion yuan in 1983 (State Statistical Bureau 1984, 381). Note that the loss figure of 14.1 billion yuan is more than the amount of export subsidies financed through the government budget for two reasons. First, since a significant portion of exports in 1983 were handled by the national foreign trade corporations, some of the profits on the export of coal, petroleum, and building materials (totaling 5.037 billion yuan) could have been transferred by the Ministry of Foreign Economic Relations and Trade within these corporations to offset some of the losses. Second, some portion of foreign exchange earnings was retained and converted to yuan through the swap centers at rates more favorable than 2.8 yuan per dollar. The losses calculated in Table 4.1 assume that all foreign exchange earnings were converted to domestic currency at the prevailing internal settlement rate of 2.8 yuan per dollar.

5. Sinopec apparently was allowed to export one or two minor petroleum products, but the annual export earnings from these sales were only about $100 million on average, in the 1980s.

6. I say perhaps the Ministry of Petroleum industry, despite the evidence that its largest field received no direct benefits from the increased international sales of petroleum. The reason is that the State Planning Commission may have directed Sinochem to transfer part of its extra profits from international sales to the domestic industry. Also other smaller fields possibly may have been allowed to sell petroleum directly on the international market starting in 1983. That would reduce the financial pressure on the industry and thus on the Ministry of Petroleum Industry.

7. The Chinese periodically publish data on the share of domestic manufacturing capacity that is shut down because of insufficient electricity. For example, in 1987, according to one estimate, the shortage of electric power was 70 billion kilowatt-houts, idling one fourth of industrial capacity (Li, Xie, and Li, 3). Undoubtedly if large increases in electricity become available in a limited time period, industrial output would not rise proportionately since shortages of other inputs would emerge. Nonetheless there is little doubt the shortage of electric power has widespread repercussions. The export of crude and petroleum products contributed to the electricity shortage because a significant portion (about one fifth) of China's thermal power generating capacity was oil-fired. Thermal generating capacity accounted for about 70 percent of China's total electric power generating capacity (World Bank 1983, vol. 2, 373). Moreover, refined petroleum products were widely used as fuels in small generators in the countryside. It is sometimes argued that shortages of refining capacity made exports of petroleum rational, at least in the short run. That may be true for crude oil, although as just noted some crude was burned in thermal plants. Moreover, exports of significant and rising quantities of crude occurred over a period of more than a decade, a time more than sufficient to invest in and bring additional refining capacity on stream. Moreover, that explanation does not apply to the export of refined petroleum products, including gasoline and diesel. Domestic shortages of these fuels hampered both transportation and agricultural development.

8. Because the average exchange rate during 1984 was 2.33 yuan per dollar (Table 2.1), the 5-yuan ceiling was equivalent to saying that losses could not exceed 53 percent $[(5 - 2.33) / 5) = .53]$. Thus this regulation appears to be somewhat more stringent than the earlier 70 percent loss ceiling. However, two points should be noted. First, Zhu and Bai state that the inclusion in the plan and the export of products exceeding this limit were to be "basically eliminated," implying that there was some discretion in the implementation of the rule. Second, it is not clear how long this regulation was in effect. As shown in Table 2.1, the cost of earning foreign exchange did fall by almost 8 percent in 1984. But the domestic currency cost of earning a dollar in foreign exchange subsequently rose quite sharply. Despite a substantial cumulative devaluation of the domestic currency, losses per dollar of exports were also sharply higher by the end of the decade.

9. According to Chinese customs data, crude oil exports jumped by about half from 14.82 million metric tons in 1983 to 22.01 million metric tons in 1984 (State Statistical Bureau 1985, 502). Because of the artificially low price of crude on the domestic market and the relatively high share of crude oil in total exports (about 36 percent in 1984), the increase in the quantity of crude oil exports in 1984 reduced the average cost of earning a dollar on the international market significantly.

10. Jing Ji (1987, 38) places export losses in 1986 at 6.4 billion yuan. However, his article was dated January 1987, a time of the year when data on export losses for the previous year would only be available in preliminary form. His figure on import losses must also be regarded as preliminary.

11. Xiao's statement was "Central government budgetary subsidies of foreign trade in 1987 exceeded $20 billion and the cost of earning foreign exchange exceeded the nominal exchange rate by more than 20 percent." Given Chinese conventions in rounding off, the statement "more than 20" could be as small as 21 or range as high as 29. A very rough estimate leads me to believe the actual figure was approximately 23 to 24 million yuan. The estimate is the sum of separate estimates for exports and imports.

It is unlikely that export subsidies could have risen by more than one third in 1987 as compared with 1986. The value of exports measured in dollars rose by almost 30 percent. But the unit cost of export earnings in 1987 rose only slightly as compared to the previous year (Table 2.1). And since the yuan was devalued by about 15 percent in July of 1986, the need for subsidies to cover domestic currency losses would be reduced somewhat in 1987 as compared to 1986 when the more favorable rate for exporters applied to only half of the year. Thus export losses were probably 9–10 billion yuan.

The value of imports, measured in dollars, was almost unchanged in 1987. Because some portion of these imports was sold at low fixed domestic prices, the need for import subsidies would have been slightly higher in 1987 than 1986. And for a small proportion of imports sold at high fixed domestic prices, financial profits would have been somewhat lower. These changes on the import side would have occurred because the lower value of the yuan, about 3.7 per dollar, applied to the full calendar year, whereas in the first half of 1986 the official exchange rate was only 3.2 yuan per dollar. In addition, the prices of Chinese imports rose about 6 percent on world markets. That would have increased domestic currency losses or reduced domestic currency profits on those imports for which the domestic sale price was not based on import cost. Altogether these factors probably increased the need for import subsidies by about 15 percent or by about 2 billion yuan.

12. These include provinces, autonomous regions, municipalities administered directly by the central government (Beijing, Shanghai, and Tianjin) and so-called "separately planned municipalities" that have been granted increased autonomy from the provinces in which they are located. The first group of cities in the latter category – Chongqing, Wuhan, Shenyang, Xian, and Harbin – was designated in 1985. In 1987 the state expanded the group to include Dalian, Guangzhou, Qingdao, and Hainan Island.

13. All of the sources I have found refer specifically to the abolition of the system. None suggest that the funds previously frozen and spent by the central government (see Chapter 3) were restored. In this respect the freeze of foreign exchange was similar to the central government's "borrowing" of fiscal revenues from the provinces when the revenue-sharing system was found to provide inadequate revenues for the central government's needs. According to the World Bank (1988b, 436), most of these loans by localities "in fact appear to be uncollectable."

5. Integrated versus partial reforms

1. Pudong was designated as a new development zone in a joint decision of the Central Committee and the State Council on April 15, 1990. The preferential policies to apply in the region were sketched out in *Beijing Review* no. 29, 1990, p. 30 and no. 43, 1990, pp. 16–19.

The law on joint ventures was amended at the Third Session of the Seventh National People's Congress on July 4, 1990. It liberalized the original 1979 joint-venture law in three respects. First, it states that joint ventures will not be nationalized but that if this were to occur it would be in accordance with legal procedures and that compensation would be paid. Second, it allows the chairman of the board of directors of a joint venture to be a foreigner. Third, it removed legal restraints on the duration of joint ventures. The full text of the amended law was carried in *Beijing Review* no. 19, 1990, pp. 31–2.

2. Technically, export-producing firms were to receive the rebated taxes only when the foreign trade corporation handled the transaction for a commission – a so-called agency transaction in which the enterprise assumed the risks of the transaction (Sun Wenxiu, 56). The rebated taxes were to go to the trade corporation in traditional transactions in which it procured the goods from the producer and sold them abroad on its own account. As discussed in Chapter 3 the spread of the agency system in exporting was very slow. Thus it may well have been that local governments really were withholding the rebated taxes from the local FTCs, not the producing enterprises. Enterprises, however, felt that they were entitled to the rebates.

3. The three targets stipulated in the contract were classified as "mandatory plan targets" (State Council 1988, 388). That category of plan target is said to be legally compulsory.

4. According to Hu Keli (1989, 12), the average rate in the foreign exchange adjustment centers was 5.7 yuan per dollar at the beginning of 1988 and 7 yuan toward the end of the year, with rates greater than 7 in a few markets, for example, Zhuhai. He estimated the average annual swap market rate was 6. Hu quotes the average official exchange rate as 3.73 (the 3.72 rate in Appendix A is the average of the Bank of China's buy and sell prices; Hu's rate is the selling price), so the spread is 2.27 yuan, making the swap rate a premium of 61 percent over the official rate.

5. The ex-factory price of pig iron in the mid-1980s ranged between 260 and 314 yuan per ton (Ma and Sun, 385). If that price range still prevailed at the time of the particular case cited, the value of the license was equal to as much as 6–8 percent of the ex-factory price of the pig iron.

6. This measure was based on the financial rather than the economic cost of earning foreign exchange. Because, for reasons discussed earlier, there were incentives to export underpriced goods, the financial cost of earning foreign exchange probably understated its economic cost. However, moving the price of foreign exchange close to its average financial cost was almost certainly the correct direction in which to move the official exchange rate.

7. Although some observers at the time speculated that the big one-time devaluation was in response to IMF advice, the first confirmation I saw of this came in a study by Wu and Chen (1989, 239–45). They recount in detail the May 1986 consultations between China and the IMF, providing specific information on IMF recommendations, including a substantial devaluation of the yuan in one step, as opposed to the policy of devaluing in small steps that was pursued in 1985 and the first half of 1986. Wu and Chen also summarize the empirical evidence the Fund advanced to support its contention that the yuan remained significantly overvalued.

8. In principle the calculation of the real effective exchange rate should be based on the ratio of changes in China's domestic price level to changes in world prices. However, available indices of Chinese domestic prices suffer from severe methodological shortcomings. Thus I prefer to use the Chinese index of export goods prices as a proxy for changes in the level of domestic prices. The index of import prices should serve as a reasonable proxy for world prices. A caveat should be added – little or nothing is known about how the Chinese calculate their published indices of import and export prices.

9. Chen Gongyan's (1989, 69) figure for 1987 was 27.9 percent. Chen was a member of the State Council's Economic, Technical, and Social Development Research Center. This center, headed by Ma Hong, was widely regarded in the late 1980s as the single most influential and prestigious institution in the field of economic research. See Appendix B for the reasoning underling the estimate of 10 percent for China's trade ratio in the late 1980s.

10. There may even have been some who actually believed, erroneously in my view, that the effect on domestic prices from this course of action would be less than from an equivalent explicit devaluation of the official exchange rate.

11. If there was no government intervention in the swap market the equilibrium exchange rate would be higher than the official rate but less than the swap rate. However, in conditions prevailing in China the assumption that the higher swap market rate may be closer to the equilibrium rate might not be unreasonable. Several reasons underlie that judgment. Recall that entry into the market, even for acquiring foreign exchange for trade transactions, was limited by the system of import licenses. Second, regulations precluded entry into the market to those who might have wished to speculate on the value of the domestic currency or to finance capital account transactions. Finally, there was government intervention in the swap market in the form of direct sales and induced sales of foreign exchange to prevent the price of foreign exchange from rising too high.

12. Hu Keli's calculation is based on the assumption that retained foreign exchange was 30 percent of the value of exports as reported by the Chinese Customs General Administration, or $14.3 billion. In fact, the amount of retained foreign exchange in 1988 was $18.5 billion (Table 3.3). Correcting for this would reduce the estimate of the subsidy to imports to 83.4 billion yuan, or 6 percent of gross national product.

13. Chinese sources state that export subsidies were equal to 4 percent of exports in 1988 (Qu Yingpu 1991). Exports in 1988 were 177 billion yuan, which would put subsidies at about 7 billion yuan.

14. In total 2,473,959 individuals left their jobs in 1988. Chinese data disaggregate this total into twelve different subcategories depending on the specific cause for the departure (State Statistical Bureau Social Statistics Office and Ministry of Labor Comprehensive Planning Office 1989, 206–7). Well over half of these departures involved death or retirement. Also excluded from my calculation are around 110,000 who took leave without salary. These individuals generally cannot seek new jobs and their employers are not allowed to fill their positions, so no turnover is created by a worker moving into this category. I also excluded about 98,000 workers who worked for state enterprises that were reclassified as collective enterprises because this involved no change of jobs. Thus 849,168 is the number of people who left their jobs (both voluntarily and involuntarily) to take up or potentially to seek other employment. It is thus what is sometimes called a quit rate.

15. Not all observers are as pessimistic. For example, Jefferson, Rawski, and Zheng (forthcoming) argue that the gap separating marginal returns to both labor and fixed capital in state and collective industries has fallen significantly during the 1980s. They

attribute this pattern of convergence to the development of more efficient institutions for allocating these inputs, as one would expect in an increasingly more marketized economy.

16. I have not been able to construct a time series of exports of goods produced in Shanghai that begins as early as in the late 1970s. Exports can be estimated as $2.9 billion in 1981 based on a statement by Yu Zhoggen (1986,31) that $2.6 billion in export earnings in 1985 was a decline of nearly 10 percent compared with 1981. Exports in 1983 were $2.85 billion (Shanghai Municipal Government Staff Office Secretariat, VI–82). The figure for 1986 can be estimated as $2.8 billion on the basis of reported total exports of $3.582 billion of which 68 percent were goods produced in Shanghai (Shanghai Municipal Foreign Economic Relations and Trade Commission 1987, 242). Of total exports of $4.16 billion through the port in 1987, about $3 billion were produced in the city according to a report citing the Director of the Shanghai Municipal Commission on Foreign Economic Relations and Trade (Xie Songxin 1988). Exports of the municipality in 1988 can be estimated as $3.1 billion on the basis of a statement that two thirds of Shanghai's total exports of $4.602 billion were goods produced in the city (Chen Zhiguang, 367; Shi Yongxiang, 376).

17. The drop in Guangdong's conventional exports in 1989 appears to have been caused by the loss of the preferential foreign exchange retention rates that applied in the special economic zones through 1988. Because retained foreign exchange could be converted to domestic currency on the swap market for a premium over the official rate, trade corporations in Shenzhen and the other special zones (two of which in addition to Shenzhen were in Guangdong Province) could earn more in terms of domestic currency for every dollar's worth of sales in international markets than could corporations based in other provinces. Thus these trading companies outbid corporations, for example, in Hunan and Guangxi, for export goods produced in those provinces (Zweig). However, even in 1990, the second year in which Shenzhen operated without the advantage of its preferential retention rate, $863 million of the Zone's total exports of $2.996 billion were products from outside the zone. Shenzhen Municipal Statistical Bureau, "Statistical Report on National Economic and Social Development in 1990," *Shenzhen Special Zone Newspaper* (Shenzhen tequ bao), March 21, 1991, p. 2. In a visit to the zone in March 1991 I was told that the great majority of these products from outside the zone were purchased by Shenzhen trading companies outside of Guangdong Province.

18. The Ministry of Foreign Economic Relations and Trade historically has classified exports into three categories: agricultural and sideline products, processed agricultural and sideline products, and industrial and mineral products. In 1985, the first category accounted for 17.5 and 32.6 percent of the exports of China and Guangdong, respectively (Guangdong Statistical Bureau 1989, 333; Ministry of Foreign Economic Relations and Trade 1989, 359).

19. The Chinese State Statistical Bureau for decades has classified light industry into two types – one depending on agricultural raw materials and the other on industrial raw materials. In 1988 the former type accounted for 50 percent of light industrial output in Shanghai (Shanghai Municipal Statistical Bureau, 150) and 53 percent in Guangdong (Guangdong Statistical Bureau 1989, 139).

20. Shanghai received agricultural and subsidiary products used as raw materials in industrial production from other regions valued at 835 million yuan in 1977. By 1978 this fell 11 percent to 746 million yuan. In 1979 it dropped a further 23 percent to 573 million yuan. The supply of fuels and other nonagricultural raw material fell by roughly comparable amounts.

21. The article by Rong, Zhong, and Dai reports only the expenditures on cotton imports, not the quantity. My estimate of 11,000 tons is based on the assumption that the price of cotton imported into Shanghai was the same as the average price paid for all cotton imported into China in 1988. Total Chinese cotton imports of 34,773 tons in 1988 cost $58.85 million implying a price of about $1,690 per ton (State Statistical Bureau 1989a, 642).

22. The declines in the quantities of these goods produced in the city and purchased by foreign trade corporations for export in 1988 compared to 1987 were as follows: textiles, a decline of 180 million yuan; cotton cloth, 27 percent; and printed cotton cloth, 17 percent. The annual Shanghai Statistical Yearbook includes time series data on the export of cotton piece goods, but these data include goods transshipped through the municipality and thus overstate the decline in the role of Shanghai as an exporter.

23. The World Bank's figures are for the quota of revenues remitted to the center by Guangdong Province. Part of any over-plan revenues would also have been forwarded to Beijing. In addition in the early 1980s the central government also "borrowed" some domestic revenues from the province. These funds appear not to have been repaid directly although no doubt the province sought to use this as a lever in its efforts to obtain other concessions from the central government.

24. Chris Yeung, "Warning to Provinces, Guangdong, Shanghai to Pay Treasury More," *South China Morning Post,* March 27, 1991, p. 10.

25. The main difficulty is to understand why actual revenue collections in Guangdong were so far below those of Shanghai. Their industrial sectors, the major source of fiscal revenue, were roughly comparable. The answer appears to lie in differences in patterns of ownership. Most of Shanghai's industry was state-owned and rules of taxation and profit remission in that sector are well established and presumably somewhat difficult to avoid. By contrast, a much larger share of Guangdong's manufacturing establishment was comprised of enterpreneurial establishments that were not state-owned. The enterpreneurial sector, as part of national policy, benefited from tax concessions. Thus while one could calculate Guangdong's remissions to the central government as a percentage of revenues collected, that would significantly overstate the fiscal burden imposed on the province by the central government.

26. In January 1989 the official exchange rate was 506 zlotys per U.S. dollar, a substantial devaluation compared to the average official exchange rate in 1986 of 175 zlotys per dollar. The auction market price of a dollar in January 1989 was 2,705 zlotys, more than five times the official rate. By November 1989 the official rate was 3,275 zlotys per dollar and the auction market rate was 5,113 zlotys, a premium of more than 50 percent. Internal convertibility was introduced in January 1990 with a unified rate of 9,500 zlotys per dollar. Peter Havlik, "Die Vechselkurspolitik der RGE-Länder und Problem der Konvertibilität," Vienna Institute for Comparative Economic Studies, Research Report no. 162, March 1990, p. 8. *Poland, Economic Management for a New Era.* (Washington, D.C.: The World Bank, 1990), p. iv.

27. In principle these "subsidies of enterprise losses" (qiye kuisun butie) differed from "price subsidies" (jiage butie), which were also financed from state revenues. The latter were to cover the losses associated with the sale of three broad categories of products at less than their cost: the sale of rationed grain and vegetable oil to the nonagricultural population; the sale of certain agricultural producer goods to the rural population; and the sale of five imported goods (grain, cotton, sugar, fertilizer, and pesticides). Because the state specifically approved these price subsidies in order to achieve certain objectives, they were sometimes called "policy losses" (zhengcexing kuisun). Enterprise subsidies, by contrast, were to cover operating losses occurring for other reasons. In fact this distinction is quite artificial because a significant portion of enterprises losses are the direct result of state price policy. The financial losses in the coal and petroleum sectors, for example, are due primarily to the low state-fixed prices for the products of these sectors. But the losses are covered under the category of enterprise subsidies rather than price subsidies. Data on subsidies and losses is particularly confusing for the first half of the 1980s when these programs were treated as a reduction to the state's fiscal revenues and were not explicitly listed in the state budget. In an effort to gain some greater control over these expenditures, they have been listed as separate budgetary expenditure items since the mid-1980s.

28. The distinction between losses in industry as opposed to commerce is not meaningful in economic terms because transactions between the two sectors occur largely at state-fixed prices. For any given set of prices paid by final users of goods, if goods are transferred from manufacturers to wholesalers at higher prices, industrial sector losses (profits) will fall (rise) while commercial sector losses (profits) will rise (fall).

29. It is possible that there is some double counting in these two categories of exports because township and village enterprises are engaged in processing and assembly operations involving imported parts and components and some of these exports may already be included in exports of foreign-funded firms. On the other hand, Sung Yun-wing (1990, 29) estimated exports of foreign ventures to be substantially higher than the figure I cite, which was attributed to the General Administration of Customs. Sung's estimate of $26.28 billion in 1989 is based on export earnings of foreign-funded firms of $4.92 billion (reported by MOFERT) plus an estimate of $21.9 billion for processing and assembly operations. In principle the value added in exports of processing operations is included in MOFERT export data. However, as explained in the notes to Table 2.2, if such processing operations are carried out under compensation trade contracts, the value of exports would not be included in MOFERT data on exports. Further research is required to refine the estimate provided in the text to see whether it is overstated because of double counting between foreign-funded firm's exports and township and village enterprise exports or understated because it does not include the value of some processing and assembly exports.

30. Exports rose by $43.95 billion, from $18.12 billion in 1980 to $62.07 billion in 1990. If there were no exports from township and village enterprises (TVEs) and foreign-invested firms in 1980, they would account for 46 percent of export growth over the ten-year period. There is little doubt that foreign-invested firms were negligible exporters in 1980. The total amount of foreign capital actually invested in China by the end of 1980 was only a few hundred million dollars. Although foreign-directed investment expanded rapidly in the first half of the 1980s, in 1985 exports of foreign-invested firms were only $320 million according to MOFERT data (Qu Yingpu 1990b). TVE exports also were likely to have been quite small in 1980. The estimate that almost half the growth of exports can be accounted for by TVE and foreign-invested enterprises may understate the relatively poor export performance of the state sector. Roughly an additional 10 percent of the growth of exports in the decade was accounted for by increased sales of agricultural goods on world markets.

Appendix B

1. The inconsistency is even worse than it appears because $280 in 1980 was measured in 1980 prices while $290 in 1987 was measured in 1987 prices. The implicit national income deflator for 1987 (1980 = 100), which can be estimated from published Chinese indices of national income in nominal and real terms, was 132.35 (State Statistical Bureau 1988, 51–2). Thus 1987 national income in 1980 prices would be $220. Thus the Bank's data imply that China's per capita real output fell at an annual rate of 4.2 percent from 1980 through 1987 while their explicit estimate of real per capita growth was a positive 9.2 percent.

References

The following abbreviations are used in the References:

BR	*Beijing Review*
CD	*China Daily*
CDBW	*China Daily Business Weekly*
CJYJ	*Caijing yanjiu* (Finance and Economics Research)
CMJJ	*Caimao jingji* (Finance and Trade Economics)
CZ	*Caizheng* (Finance)
CZJR	*Caizheng, jinrong* (Finance, Banking)
DWJMYJ	*Duiwai jingmao yanjiu* (Research on Foreign Economics and Trade)
FBIS	Foreign Broadcast Information Service
GC	*Gaige* (Reform)
GJMY	*Guoji maoyi* (International Trade)
GJMYLT	*Guoji maoyi luntan* (International Trade Forum)
GJMYYF	*Guoji maoyi yu fa* (International Trade and Law)
GJMYWT	*Guoji maoyi wenti* (Issues in International Trade)
GJMYYJ	*Guoji maoyi yanjiu* (International Trade Research)
GJSB	*Guoji shangbao* (International Business)
GZDWMYXYXB	*Guangzhou duiwai maoyi xueyuan xuebao* (Canton Foreign Trade University Bulletin)
JGLLYSJ	*Jiage lilun yu shijian* (Price Theory and Practice)
JHJJYJ	*Jihua jingji yanjiu* (Planned Economy Research)
JFRB	*Jiefang ribao* (Liberation Daily)
JJCK	*Jingji cankao* (Economic Reference)
JJDB	*Jingji daobao* (Economic Reporter)
JJGL	*Jingji guanli* (Economic Management)
JJLLYJJGL	*Jingji lilun yu jingji guanli* (Economic Theory and Economic Management)
JJRB	*Jingji ribao* (Economic Daily)
JJSHTZBZ	*Jingji shehui tizhi bijiao* (Comparative Economic and Social Systems)
JJYJ	*Jingji yanjiu* (Economic Research)
JJYJCKZL	*Jingji yanjiu cankao ziliao* (Reference Materials on Economic Research)
JJYGLYJ	*Jingji yu guanli yanjiu* (Research on Economics and Management)

JPRS	Joint Publications Research Service
JRSB	*Jinrong shibao* (Banking News)
JRYJ	*Jinrong yanjiu* (Banking Research)
LNDXXB	*Liaoning daxue xuebao* (Liaoning Univeristy Bulletin)
LW	*Liaowang* (Outlook)
MYJJ	*Maoyi jingji* (Trade Economics)
NKJJYJ	*Nankai jingji yanjiu* (Nankai Economic Research)
RMRB	*Renmin ribao* (People's Daily)
SHJJ	*Shanghai jingji* (Shanghai's Economy)
SHJJYJ	*Shanghai jingji yanjiu* (Research on Shanghai's Economy)
SHKX	*Shehui kexue* (Social Science)
SJJJDB	*Shijie jingji daobao* (World Economic Herald)
SSIC	Social Sciences in China
TQYKFCSJJ	*Tequ yu kaifeng chengshi jingji* (Economics of Special Zones and Open Municipalities)
TJCJXYXB	*Tianjin caijing xueyuan xuebao* (Tianjin Finance and Economics Institute Bulletin)
TJSHKX	*Tianjin shehui kexue* (Tianjin Social Science)
WMJJGJMY	*Waimao jingji, guoji maoyi* (Foreign Trade Economics, International Trade)
XHYB	*Xinhua yuebao* (New China Monthly)
ZGDWMY	*Zhongguo duiwai maoyi* (Chinese Foreign Trade)
ZGJR	*Zhongguo jinrong* (Chinese Banking)
ZGTXS	*Zhongguo tongxun she* (Chinese Information Service)
ZGWJ	*Zhongguo wujia* (China Price)
ZNCJDXYJSXB	*Zhongnan caijing daxue yanjiusheng xuebao* (South China Finance and Economics University Graduate Student Bulletin)
ZSDXXB:ZSB	*Zhongshan daxue xuebao: zheshe ban* (Zhongshan University Bulletin: Philosophy and Social Sciences Edition)

Chinese institutional authors

Unless published by the Foreign Languages Press, appearing in an English language periodical (such as *China Daily* or *Beijing Review*), or in a source of translated materials (such as FBIS or JPRS), or specifically indicated as being published in English, all publications originating in the People's Republic of China listed in the references are in Chinese. To facilitate locating these materials in library catalogs, the names of all institutional authors, in pinyin romanization, are given below.

Bank of China Staff Office *Zhongguo yinghang bangongshi*
China International Trade Society Editorial and Publishing Commission *Zhongguo guoji maoyi xuehui bianji chuban weiyuanhui*
Chinese Academy of Social Sciences Law Institute *Zhongguo shehui kexueyuan faxue yanjiusuo*
Chinese Economic Yearbook Editorial Committee *Zhongguo jingji nianjian bianji weiyuanhui*
Chinese Finance and Banking Society *Zhongguo jinrong xuehui*
Compilation Group *Zhongguo shehui zhuyi wujia xue bianxiezu*
Contemporary China Series Editorial Board *Dangdai zhongguo congshu bianji weiyuanhui*

General Administration of Customs Tariffs Office *Haiguan zongshu guanshuisi*
Guangdong Statistical Bureau *Guangdongsheng tongjiju*
Guangzhou Municipal Industrial and Commerical Administration and Management Society *Guangzhoushi gongshang xingzheng guanli xuehui*
Hubei Provincial Bureau of Commodity Prices *Hubeisheng wujiaju*
Liaoning Economic and Statistical Yearbook Editorial Committee *Liaoning jingji tongji nianjian bianji weiyuanhui*
Ministry of Finance Foreign Affairs Finance Bureau *Caizhengbu waishi caiwusi*
Ministry of Finance General Planning Department *Zhonghua renmin gongheguo caizhengbu zonghe jihuasi*
Ministry of Finance Legal Bureau *Caizhengbu tiaofasi*
Ministry of Foreign Economic Relations and Trade *Duiwai jingji maoyibu*
Ministry of Foreign Economic Relations and Trade Education Bureau *Duiwai jingji maoyibu jiaoyuju*
People's Bank of China Research and Statistics Department *Zhongguo renmin yinghang diaocha tongjisi*
People's Bank of China State Office *Zhongguo renmin yinghang bangongting*
Sea and Sky Publishers *Haitian chubanshe*
Secretariat of the Chinese International Trade Society *Zhongguo guoji maoyi xuehui mishuchu*
Shanghai Academy of Social Sciences *Shanghai shehui kexueyuan*
Shanghai Statistical Bureau *Shanghaisheng tongjiju*
State Bureau of Commodity Prices *Guojia wujiaju*
State Bureau of Commodity Prices Commodity Price Research Institute *Guojia wujiaju wujia yanjiusuo*
State Bureau of Commodity Prices Foreign Price Office *Zhonghuarenmin gongheguo guojia wujiaju shewai jiagesi*
State Bureau of Supplies Price Office *Guojia wuzi zongju wujiasi*
State Council Staff Office Bureau of Legal Affairs *Guowuyuan bangongting fazhiju*
State Council Bureau of Legal Affairs *Guowuyuan fazhiju*
State Economic Commission Economic System Reform Bureau *Guojia jingji weiyuanhui jingji tizhi gaigeju*
State Planning Commission Economic Laws and Regulations Office *Guojia jihua weiyuanhui jingji tiaofa bangongshi*
State Planning Commission Legal Staff Office *Guojia jihua weiyuanhui tiaofa bangongshi*
State Planning Commission System Reform and Laws and Regulations Departments *Guojia jiwei tizhi gaige he faguisi*
State Statistical Bureau *Guojia tongjiju*
State Statistical Bureau National Economic Balance Statistics Department *Guojia tongjiju guomin jingji pingheng tongjisi*
State Statistical Bureau Social Statistics Office *Guojia tongjiju shehui tongjisi*
State Statistical Bureau Social Statistics Office and Ministry of Labor Comprehensive Planning Office *Guojia tongjiju shehui tongjisi; Laodongbu zonghe jihuasi*

Balassa, Bela. 1970. "The Economic Reform in Hungary." *Economica*, 145:1–22.
1989. "Outward Orientation." In Chenery and Srinivasan, eds. (1989, 1,645–89).
Bank of China Staff Office. 1986. *A Compilation of Important Documents on 1984 Foreign Exchange Work.* Beijing: Chinese Banking Publishing House.
Bhattacharya, Amarendra and Linn, Johannes F. 1988. "Trade and Industrial Policies in the Developing Countries of East Asia." Discussion Paper 27. Washington, D.C.: The World Bank.

Block, Herbert. 1981. *The Planetary Product in 1980: A Creative Pause?* Washington, D.C.: United States Department of State Bureau of Public Affairs.

Brada, Josef C., Hewett, Ed A., and Wolf, Thomas A. 1988. *Economic Adjustment and Reform in Eastern Europe and the Soviet Union.* Durham, N.C.: Duke University Press.

Bruton, Henry. 1989. "Import Substitution." In Chenery and Srinivasan, eds. (1989, 1,601–44).

Byrd, William A. 1987. "The Impact of the Two-Tier Plan/Market System in Chinese Industry." *Journal of Comparative Economics* 11, 3:295–308.

Byrd, William A. and Lin Qingsong. 1990. *China's Rural Industry: Structure, Development, and Reform.* New York: Oxford University Press.

Cao Wushu. 1988. "A Discussion of the Differential Between Domestic Prices and International Prices." *GJMY*, 11:26–9.

Chan, Yvonne. 1987. "Understanding the Tariff System." *The China Business Review*, November–December, 46–9.

Chan, Yvonne and Levy, Mimi. 1987. "The New Customs Law." *The China Business Review*, November–December, 44–6.

Chang Hong. 1991. "Enterprises Given Right in Foreign Trade Deals." *CD*, February 8, p. 1.

Chao Kang and Mah Feng-hwa. 1964. "A Study of the Rouble-Yuan Exchange Rate." *China Quarterly*, 17:192–204.

Chen Dongsheng and Wei Houkai, 1989. "Some Reflections on Interregional Trade Friction." *GG*, 2:79–83. In JPRS-CAR-89-077, July 24, pp. 5–9.

Chen Gongyan. 1989. "Trade Expansion and Structural Changes." *JJYJ*, 3:69–74.

Chen Jiaqin. 1989. "Marxist Exchange Rate Theory and China's Exchange Rate Policy." *JJLLYJJGL*, 6:51–6.

Chen Jiaqin, Huang Zheng, Wang Baochen, and Yang Zhongguang. 1981. "Give Full Play to Superiority, Expand Exports." *CMJJ*, 12:55–8.

Chen Jianliang. 1987. "Theory on Exchange Rates and Renminbi's Exchange Rate System." *SSIC*, March:9–22.

Chen Mingxing, Feng Gufeng, and Yang Hua. 1990. "The Way Out of the Predicament of Foreign Trade Reform." *GJSB*, April 21, p. 3.

Chen Suning and Gong Genfu. 1989. "A New Fiscal Contract System Is Beginning to Take Form." In Shanghai Academy of Social Sciences (1989, 475–7).

Chen Weihua. 1988a. "Losses Flow from China's Largest Oil Field." *CDBW*, May 23, p. 2.

   1988b. "Shanghai Sees Money Trade Boost." *CD*, September 30, p. 1.

   1989. "Dollar Up Only Slightly in Shanghai Money Mart." *CD*, December 19, p. 2.

Chen Ying. 1984. "An Exploration of the Problem of Losses in Foreign Trade in Recent Years." In Secretariat of the Chinese International Trade Society (1984, 47–56).

Chen Zhiguang. 1989. "A Summary of Foreign Economics and Trade." In Shanghai Academy of Social Sciences (1989, 367–70).

Chenery, Hollis and Srinivasan, T. N., eds. 1989. *Handbook of Development Economics*, vol. 2. Amsterdam: Elsevier Science Publishers.

Chi Hsin. 1977. *The Case of the Gang of Four.* Hong Kong: Cosmos Books.

China Daily News. 1990. "Foreign Debts Amount to $45 Billion." *CD*, November 28, p. 2.

China International Trade Society Editorial and Publishing Commission. 1988. *Development and Reform of China's Foreign Trade.* Beijing: China International Trade Society.

"China's Balance of Payments in 1982–86." 1987. *BR*, 36:28.

China's Foreign Economic Legislation. Vol. 1, 1982; vol. 2, 1986; vol. 3, 1987. Beijing: Foreign Languages Press.

Chinese Academy of Social Sciences Law Institute. 1982. *A Compendium of Economic Laws and Regulations of the People's Republic of China, Oct. 1979–Dec. 81.* Beijing: Chinese Finance and Economics Publishing House.

1983. *A Compendium of Economic Laws and Regulations of the People's Republic of China (1982).* Beijing: Chinese Finance and Economics Publishing House.

Chinese Economic Yearbook Editorial Committee. 1984. *Almanac of China's Economy 1984.* Beijing: Economic Management Publishing House.

1987. *Almanac of China's Economy 1987.* Beijing: Economic Management Publishing House.

Chinese Finance and Banking Society. 1987. *Almanac of China's Finance and Banking 1986.* Beijing: Chinese Banking and Finance Publishing House.

1989. *Almanac of China's Finance and Banking 1989.* Beijing: Chinese Banking and Finance Publishing House.

Chu Lanfen. 1991. "City's Export Trend Sees Industrial Goods Boost." *CD*, March 4, East China Supplement.

Clark, M. Gardner. 1973. *Development of China's Steel Industry and Soviet Technical Aid.* Ithaca, N.Y.: Committee on the Economy of China of the Social Science Research Council.

Clarke, Christopher M. 1987. "Two Views of China's Foreign Trade." *China Business Review*, July–August, pp. 15–16.

Compilation Group. 1982. *Studies of China's Socialist Prices.* Xian: Shaanxi People's Publishing House.

Contemporary China Series Editorial Board. 1989. *Contemporary China Commodity Prices.* Beijing: Social Sciences Publishing House.

Corden, W. M. 1971. *The Theory of Protection.* London: Oxford University Press.

Da Chansong. 1987. "Ministry Adjusts License List to Improve Exports." *CDBW*, January 21, p. 1.

Donnithorne, Audrey. 1967. *China's Economic System.* New York: Praeger.

Ericson, Richard E. 1989. "Soviet Economic Reforms: The Motivation and Content of Perestroika." *Journal of International Affairs*, 2:317–31.

Feder, Gershon. 1983. "On Exports and Economic Growth." *Journal of Development Economics*, 1/2:59–73.

Feng Yiling, Li Huayun, and Zhou Xiaochuan. 1987. "A Discussion of Reform of the Foreign Trade System and the Coordination of External and Departmental Relations." *CMJJ*, 8:13–20, 54.

Fenwick, Ann. 1980. "Chinese Foreign Trade Policy and the Campaign Against Deng Xiaoping." In *China's Quest for Independence: Policy Evolution in the 1970s*, edited by Thomas Fingar, pp. 199–224. Boulder, Colo.: Westview Press.

Feuerwerker, Albert. 1983. "Economic Trends, 1912–1949." In *The Cambridge History of China*, edited by John K. Fairbank, vol. 12, pt. I, pp. 28–127. Cambridge: Cambridge University Press.

Field, Robert Michael, Emerson, John Philip, and Lardy, Nicholas R. 1975. *A Reconstruction of the Gross Value of Industrial Output by Province in the People's Republic of China: 1949–1973.* Foreign Economic Report No. 7. Washington, D.C.: U.S. Department of Commerce.

Fu Zhongxin. 1986. "We Must Gradually Establish an Export Production System." *ZGDWMY*,8:6–7.

Fu Ziying. 1988. "Reflections on Establishing a Foreign Exchange Tax System and

Reform Making Foreign Trade Enterprises Responsible for Their Own Profits and Losses." *GJMYWT*, 9:27–9.

1989. "A Review of and the Prospects for the Foreign Trade Contract Management Responsibility System." *GJMYWT*, 4:17–19.

Gao Guangyu. 1986. "Gradually Open Up Shenzhen Special Economic Zone's Foreign Exchange Market." JRYJ, 6:50–3. In *TQYKFCSJJ*, 7:31–4.

GATT. 1979. *Agreement on Interpretation and Application of Articles VI, XVI, and XXIII of the General Agreement on Tariffs and Trade.* Geneva: GATT.

General Administration of Customs Tariff Office. 1989. *A Handbook of the Import Tariffs and the Commodity Taxes Levied by the Customs.* Beijing: The General Administration of Customs Tariff Office.

Geng Shuhai. 1990. "Policies and Problems We Face in Further Stabilizing Prices." *JHJJYJ*, 3:73–8.

Gerschenkron, Alexander. 1951. *A Dollar Index of Soviet Machinery Output, 1927– 28 to 1937.* Santa Monica, Calif.: The RAND Corporation.

Granick, David. 1986. "Prices and the Behavior of Chinese State Industrial Enterprises: Focus on the Multi-Price System." Unpublished manuscript.

Guangdong Statistical Bureau. 1989. *Guangdong Statistical Yearbook 1989.* Beijing: Chinese Statistical Publishing House.

1990. *Guangdong Statistical Yearbook 1990.* Beijing: Chinese Statistical Publishing House.

Guangzhou Municipal Industrial and Commercial Administration and Management Society. 1985. *A Compendium of Economic Laws and Regulations, 1978–1984.* 2 vols. Guangzhou: Zhongshan Economic and Technical Consultative Center.

Harding, Harry. 1987. *China's Second Revolution: Reform After Mao.* Washington, D.C.: The Brookings Institution.

Holzman, Franklyn D. 1966. "Foreign Trade Behavior of Centrally Planned Economies." In *Industrialization in Two Systems: Essays in Honor of Alexander Gerschenkron,* edited by Henry Rosovsky, pp. 237–65. New York: John Wiley & Sons.

Hsiao, Katherine Huang. 1971. *Money and Monetary Policy in Communist China.* New York: Columbia University Press.

Hsu, Immanuel C. Y. 1990. *China Without Mao: The Search for a New Order.* Oxford: Oxford University Press.

Hsu, John C. 1989. *China's Foreign Trade Reforms: Impact on Growth and Stability.* Cambridge: Cambridge University Press.

Hu Changnuan. 1982. *Price Studies.* Beijing: Chinese People's University Publishing House.

Hu Dinghe. 1990. "Ideas About the Internationalization of the Renminbi." *GJMYWT*, 6:32–5.

Hu Keli. 1989. "An Estimate of the Value of Rents in China in 1988." *JJSHTZBJ*, 5:10–15.

Hubei Provincial Bureau of Commodity Prices. 1987. *A Compendium of Documents on Commodity Prices 1985.* N.p.

International Monetary Fund. *Annual Report on Exchange Arrangements and Exchange Restrictions.* Washington, D.C.: International Monetary Fund.

International Monetary Fund et al. 1990. *The Economy of the USSR.* Washington, D.C.: The World Bank.

Jacobson, Harold K. and Oksenberg, Michel. 1990. *China's Participation in the IMF, the World Bank, and GATT: Toward a Global Economic Order.* Ann Arbor: University of Michigan Press.

Jefferson, Gary H., Rawski, Thomas G., and Zheng Yuxin. Forthcoming. "Growth,

Efficiency, and Convergence in China's State and Collective Industry." *Economic Development and Cultural Change*.

Ji Chongwei. 1984. "Strive to Increase the Economic Benefits of Foreign Trade." In Secretariat of the Chinese International Trade Society (1984, 1–6).

Ji Chongwei and Yang Mu. 1988. "A Comprehensive and Accurate Understanding and Implementation of the Development Strategy of an Externally Oriented Economy." *RMRB*, July 18, p. 5.

Jia Huaiqin. 1986. "Customs and MOFERT Statistics: Two Parallel Systems of Foreign Trade Statistics." GJMYWT, 5:51–6. In JPRS-CEA, March 4, 1987, pp. 31–40.

Jiang Xiang. 1987. "Shanghai's Foreign Exchange Market Has Suddenly Arisen." *SJJJDB*, July 13.

Jiao Wuling and Zhou Zhuangen. 1989. "An Analysis of the Financial Beneficial Factors of Foreign Trade." *JHJJYJ*, 10:59–62.

Jin Weizu and Min Yi. 1986. "Strategic Concepts for Promoting Shanghai's Export Trade." *CJYJ*, 5:21–4.

Jing Ji. 1987. "Successes and Failures in 1986 Price Reform Measures." *JJYJCKZL*, 99:32–41.

Kornai, Janos. 1990. *The Road to a Free Economy Shifting from a Socialist System: The Example of Hungary*. New York: W. W. Norton.

Kravis, Irving, Heston, Alan, and Summers, Robert. 1982. *World Product and Income: International Comparisons of Real Gross Product*. Baltimore: The Johns Hopkins University Press.

Kreuger, Anne O. 1978. *Liberalization Attempts and Consequences*. Cambridge, Mass.: Ballinger Publishing Co.

1988. "The Relationships between Trade, Employment, and Development." In Ranis and Schultz, eds. (1988, 357–83).

Lardy, Nicholas R. 1978. *Economic Growth and Distribution in China*. Cambridge: Cambridge University Press.

1983. *Agriculture in China's Modern Economic Development*. Cambridge: Cambridge University Press.

1987. "The Chinese Economy Under Stress, 1958–1965." In *The Cambridge History of China*, edited by Roderick MacFarquhar and John K. Fairbank, vol. 14, pt. I, pp. 360–97. Cambridge: Cambridge University Press.

1989. "Dilemmas in the Pattern of Resource Allocation in China, 1978–1985." In *Remaking the Economic Institutions of Socialism: China and Eastern Europe*, edited by Victor Nee and David Stark, pp. 278–305. Stanford, Calif.: Stanford University Press.

1991. *Redefining U.S.-China Economic Relations*. Analysis no. 5. Seattle, Washington. National Bureau of Asian and Soviet Research.

Levine, Herbert S. 1959. "The Centralized Plannning of Supply in Soviet Industry." In *Comparisons of the United States and Soviet Economies*, pt. I, pp. 151–76. Washington, D.C.: U.S. Government Printing Office.

Li Boxi, Xie Fuzhan, and Li Peiyu. 1988. "An Analysis of Policy Toward the Development of Bottleneck Industries." *JJYJ*, 12:3–9.

Li Chengxun, ed. 1989. "The Situation of, Problems in, and Policy Toward China's Economic Gains." *JJYJCKZL*, November 12, pp. 1–96.

Li Lanqing. 1988a. "Reform of China's Foreign Trade System." ZGDWMY, 1:6–7.
1988b. "Reform of the Foreign Trade System and the Development of Foreign Trade." *JJYJCKZL*, December 16, pp. 1–20.

Li Yafei, Meng Zijun, and Liu Jingyue. 1989. "What is the Way to Bring Order to Our Chaotic Foreign Trade?" *LW*, 10:28–9.

Li Yang. 1989. "An Analysis of Financial Subsidies of Foreign Economic Activity." *GJMY*, 12:19–24, 57.

Liaoning Economic and Statistical Yearbook Editorial Committee. 1987. *Liaoning Economic and Statistical Yearbook 1987*. Beijing: Chinese Statistical Publishing House.

Lieberthal, Kenneth. 1978. *Central Documents and Politburo Politics in China*. Michigan Papers in Chinese Studies no. 33. Ann Arbor, Mich.: Center for Chinese Studies.

Lieberthal, Kenneth and Oksenberg, Michel. 1988. *Policy Making in China: Leaders, Structures, and Processes*. Princeton, N.J.: Princeton University Press.

Lin Yifu, Cai Fang, and Shen Minggao. 1989. "China's Economic Reform and Development Strategy." *JJYJ*, 3:28–35.

Little, Ian M. D. 1982. *Economic Development: Theory, Policy, and International Relations*. New York: Basic Books.

Liu Dizhong. 1988. "State Sets List of 100 Products to Cut Imports." *CD*, April 29, p. 2.

Liu Hong. 1989a. "Foreign Exchange Markets Hope to Escape Wild Fluctuations." *CDBW*, February 20, p. 1.

1989b. "More Scope for Cash Trading by Individuals." *CD*, February 20, Autumn Fair Supplement, p. 1.

Liu Xiangdong. 1990. "Past Decade Registered Steady Trade Growth." *CD*, October 15.

Liu Yaoyu. 1985. "Foreign Trade Pricing." In Min, Liu, and Qiu, eds., (1985, 101–13).

Liu Yun. 1989. "We Must Attach Importance to and Appropriately Implement the Strategy of Import Substitution." *JJYJCKZL*, 185:2–22.

Liu Zewei and Bao Feng. 1990. "Steadfastly Carry Out the Policy of Retrenchment." *JHJJYJ*, 1:7–12.

Lu Jinhao. 1987. "A Discussion on the Reform of China's Foreign Trade Macroeconomic Management Structure." *CJYJ*, 110:43–7.

Lu Libin. 1989. "Gradually Perfecting the Foreign Trade Contract Management Responsibility System." *GJMYWT*, 4:20–2.

Lubman, Stanley B. 1988. "Investment and Export Contracts in the People's Republic of China: Perspectives on Evolving Patterns." *Brigham Young University Law Review*, 3:543–65.

Luo Guang. 1990. "Reflections on the Aftermath of a Devaluation of the Renminbi." *ZGJR*, 3:54–5.

Luo Jingfen. 1990. "How to Gradually Eliminate the 'Dual Track System' for Producer Goods Prices." *JHJJYJ*, 2:17–22.

Ma Hong and Sun Shangqing. 1988. *Studies on China's Price Structure*: Shanxi: Shanxi People's Publishing House and the Chinese Social Sciences Publishing House.

Mah, Feng-hwa. 1968. "Foreign Trade." In *Economic Trends in Communist China*, edited by Alexander Eckstein, Walter Galenson, and Ta-chung Liu, pp. 671–738. Chicago: Aldine Publishing Company.

1971. *The Foreign Trade of Mainland China*. Chicago: Aldine Atherton, Inc.

Martin, Will. 1990. "Modelling the Post-Reform Chinese Economy." National Centre for Development Studies, China Working Paper No. 90/1. Canberra: The Australian National University.

McKinnon, Ronald I. 1982. "The Order of Economic Liberalization: Lessons from Chile and Argentina." In *Economic Policy in a World of Change*, edited by

Karl Brunner and Allan H. Meltzer, pp. 159–86. Carnegie-Rochester Conference Series on Public Policy, vol. 17. Amsterdam: North-Holland Publishing Company.

1990a. "Liberalizing Foreign Trade in a Socialist Economy: The Problem of Negative Value Added." Unpublished manuscript.

1990b. "Stabilizing the Ruble: The Problem of Internal Currency Convertibility." Unpublished manuscript.

Meng Zijun, et al. 1989. "Export of Low Priced, Import of High Priced (Goods)." *JJCK*, January 17, p. 2.

Michaely, Michael, Papageorgiou, Demetris, and Choksi, Armeane M. 1991. *Liberalizing Foreign Trade: Lessons of Experience in the Developing World*. Cambridge, Mass.: Basil Blackwell.

Min Zongtao, Liu Jianchu, and Qiu Jianmin, eds. 1985. *Reference Materials on Commodity Price Study*. Beijing: Central Broadcasting and Television University Publishing House.

Ministry of Finance Foreign Affairs Finance Bureau. 1982. *A Compilation of Laws and Regulations on Finance of Foreign Affairs and Foreign Nationals*. Beijing: Chinese Finance and Economics Publishing House.

Ministry of Finance General Planning Department. 1987. *Chinese Financial Statistics 1950–1985*. Beijing: Finance and Economics Publishing House.

1989. *China Finance Statistics (1950–1988)*. Beijing: Finance and Economics Publishing House.

Ministry of Finance Legal Bureau. 1987. *A Compilation of Financial Laws and Regulations in the People's Republic of China*. Beijing: Chinese Finance and Economics Publishing House.

Ministry of Foreign Economic Relations and Trade. 1984. *Almanac of China's Foreign Economic Relations and Trade 1984*. Beijing: Ministry of Foreign Economic Relations and Trade Publishing House.

1985. *Almanac of China's Foreign Economic Relations and Trade 1985*. Beijing: Ministry of Foreign Economic Relations and Trade Publishing House.

1986. *Almanac of China's Foreign Economic Relations and Trade 1986*. Beijing: Ministry of Foreign Economic Relations and Trade Publishing House.

1987. "Memorandum on China's Foreign Trade Regime." Submitted to the General Agreement on Tariffs and Trade.

1989. *Almanac of China's Foreign Economic Relations and Trade 1989* (English Edition). Hong Kong: China Resources Advertising Co., Ltd.

Ministry of Foreign Economic Relations and Trade and the Customs General Administration. 1984. "Detailed Rules for the Implementation of the Interim Regulations on Licensing System of the People's Republic of China." In Ministry of Foreign Economic Relations and Trade (1985, 435–39).

Ministry of Foreign Economic Relations and Trade and the State Bureau of Commodity Prices. 1987. "Notice on Strengthening the Management of Procurement Prices for Export Commodities." In State Bureau of Commodity Prices Commodity Price Research Institute (1989, 623–4).

Ministry of Foreign Relations and Trade Education Bureau. 1988. *The Theory and Practice of China's Foreign Economic Relations and Trade*. Beijing: Foreign Trade Education Publishing House.

Ministry of Foreign Trade. 1980. "Notice Concerning the Use by Various Ministries of Non-trade Retained Foreign Exchange to Import Commodities." In Chinese Academy of Social Sciences Law Institute (1982, 541–2).

Ministry of Textile Industry. 1988. "Notice Concerning the Implementation of Agent

Pricing for Imported Chemical Fibers, Chemical Monomers, and Wool." In State Bureau of Commodity Prices (1989, 25).

Montias, J. M. 1959. "Planning with Material Balances in Soviet-Type Economies." *American Economic Review*, 5:963–85.

Murrell, Peter. 1990. *The Nature of Socialist Economics: Lessons from Eastern European Foreign Trade*. Princeton, N.J.: Princeton University Press.

Na Cheng and Wu Yanmin. 1988. "The Black Hole of Subsidies: The Existing Situation, Appraisal, and Policy." *TJSHKX*, 4:45–8. In *CZJR*, 9:23–6.

Naray, Peter. 1989. "The End of the Foreign Trade Monopoly: The Case of Hungary." *Journal of World Trade*, vol. 23, no. 6, pp. 85–97.

Naughton, Barry. 1988a. "Industrial Planning and Prospects in China." In *U.S.–China Trade: Problems and Prospects*, edited by Eugene K. Lawson, pp. 179–93. New York: Praeger.

1988b. "The Third Front: Defence Industrialization in the Chinese Interior." China Quarterly, 115:351–386.

1990. "Macroeconomic Obstacles to Reform in China: The Role of Fiscal and Monetary Policy." Unpublished manuscript.

"News in Brief." 1991. *BR*, 5:43.

Ni Yijin. 1988. "Expanding Exports of Machinery and Electronic Products Is an Important Strategic Responsibility." In Ministry of Foreign Economic Relations and Trade Education Bureau (1988, 302–16).

Nordhaus, William D. 1990. "Soviet Economic Reform: The Longest Road." *Brookings Papers on Economic Activity* 1, 287–318.

Nuti, D. Mario and Sengupta, Jayshree. 1988. "Trade Regimes, External Adjustment, and Industrialization: Hungary, Poland, and Yugoslavia." Unpublished manuscript.

Oksenberg, Michel. 1982. "Economic Policy Making in China: Summer 1981." *China Quarterly*, 90:165–94.

Oksenberg, Michel and Tong, James. Forthcoming. "The Evolution of Central-Provincial Fiscal Relations in China, 1971–84: The Formal System." *China Quarterly*.

People's Bank of China Research and Statistics Department. 1988. *Chinese Financial Statistics 1952–1987*. Beijing: Chinese Financial Publishing House.

People's Bank of China Staff Office. 1984. *A Compilation of Rules and Regulations on Banking 1982*. Tianjin: Chinese Banking Publishing House.

Perkins, Dwight. 1966. *Market Control and Planning in Communist China*. Cambridge: Harvard University Press.

Perkins, Dwight and Syrquin, Moshe. 1989. "Large Countries: The Influence of Size." In Chenery and Srinivasan, eds. (1989, 1,693–1,753).

Plowiec, Urszula. 1988. "Economic Reform and Foreign Trade in Poland." In Brada, Hewett, and Wolf (1988, 340–69).

Potter, Sulamith Heins. 1983. "The Position of Peasants in Modern China's Social Order." *Modern China*, 4:465–99.

Poznanski, Kazimierz Z. 1987. *Technology, Competition, and the Soviet Bloc in the World Market*. Berkeley, Calif.: Institute of International Studies.

Qin Xiaoli. 1989. "Imports of Steel Under Supervision." *CD*, December 30, p. 1.

Qiu Jie. 1987. "The Foreign Trade Contract System and Reform of the Foreign Trade System." *GJMYWT*, 6:8–11, 32.

Qu Yingpu. 1989. "More Rules for Imports, Exports." *CD*, December 22, p. 2.

1990a. "Foreign Funded Firm Exports to Reach $6 Billion." *CD*, August 3, p. 2. In FBIS-CHI, August 9, p. 42.

1990b. "Foreign Funds Flow In." CDBW, December 24, p. 1.

1991. "Reform Detailed in Foreign Trade," *CD*, February 8, p. 2.

Ranis, Gustav and Schultz, T. Paul, eds. 1988. *The State of Development Economics: Progress and Perspectives.* Oxford: Basil Blackwell.

Rawski, Thomas G. 1980. *China's Transition to Industrialism: Producer Goods and Economic Development in the Twentieth Century.* Ann Arbor: University of Michigan Press.

Ren Kan. 1990. "Machinery Goal is 20% Sales Boost." *CD*, February 27, p. 2.

Ren Long. 1988. "The Progress and the Future of Reform of the Foreign Trade System." *JHJJYJ*, 12:Supplement no. 1, pp. 20–5.

Reporter, 1988. "Export Licensing Defended." *CD*, November 14, p. 2.

1989a. "Initial Steps in the Establishment of China's Foreign Exchange Market." *JRSB*, February 15, p. 1.

1989b. "Township Enterprises See Boom in Exports." *CD*, Octrober 25.

1990. "We Must Firmly Grasp and Carry Out the Work of Rectifying the Various Kinds of Foreign Trade Corporations." *GJSB*, March 21, p. 1.

Rong Licheng, Zhong Tiehua, and Dai Haiping. 1989. "Shanghai's Cotton Textile Industry Encounters Raw Materials Difficulties." *JFRB*, April 24, p. 5.

Sea and Sky Publishers. 1988. *China's Special Economic Zones and Foreign Economic Laws*, vol. 2, April 1986–April 1987. Shenzhen: Sea and Sky Publishing Company.

Secretariat of the Chinese International Trade Society. 1984. *Collected Papers on the Economic Benefits of Foreign Trade.* Beijing: Prospects Press.

Shanghai Academy of Social Sciences. 1987. *Shanghai Economic Yearbook 1987.* Shanghai: Sanlian Bookstore Publishing House.

1989. *Shanghai Economic Yearbook 1989.* Shanghai: Sanlian Bookstore Publishing House.

"Shanghai Foreign Exchange Adjustment Center Business and Management Regulations." Mimeographed, n.d., 8 pages.

Shanghai Municipal Foreign Economic Relations and Trade Commission. 1987. "Shanghai's 1986 Foreign Economic Relations and Trade." In Shanghai Academy of Social Sciences (1987, 242–4).

Shanghai Municipal Government Staff Office Secretariat. 1984. "New Economic Development in Shanghai Municipality." In Chinese Economic Yearbook Editorial Committee (1984, VI81–VI85).

Shanghai Municipal Statistical Bureau. 1989. *Shanghai Statistical Yearbook 1989.* Beijing: Chinese Statistical Publishing House.

Shen, Frank. 1989. "Price of Dollars Slips as Enterprises Buy Needed Renminbi." *CD*, August 24, Shanghai Focus, p. 1.

Shen Feiyue. 1989a. "Exchange Plan Draws Praise." *CD*, April 27.

1989b. "Foreign Exchange Center Praised." *CD*, May 8, Shanghai Focus, p. 2.

Shen Juren. 1988. "Carry Out the Foreign Trade Contract Management System Taking the Localities as the Main (Element)." *GJMY*, 9:4–6.

Shi Fu. 1989. "The Worrisome Problems of the 'Feudal Lord Economy' in China." *ZGTXS*, August 11. In FBIS, August 18, pp. 30–1.

Shi Yongxiang. 1989. "An Analysis of Current Sources of Exports." In Shanghai Academy of Social Sciences (1989, 376–7).

Shirk, Susan. 1984. "The Domestic Political Dimensions of China's Foreign Economic Relations." In *China and the World: Chinese Foreign Policy in the Post-Mao Era*, edited by Samuel S. Kim, pp. 57–81. Boulder, Colo.: Westview Press.

Song Gongping. 1989. "Abuses of and Policy Toward Our Current Foreign Trade System." *GJMYYF*, 1:18–22. In *WMJJGJMY*, 2:51–55.

Song Hai. 1988. "Macroperspective Reflections on the Reform of China's Foreign Exchange Management System." *JJYGJYJ*, 1:7–11. In *CZJR*, 3:143–7.

Staff Reporter. 1991. "Exports Boom for Foreign Funded Firms." *CD*, January 21, p. 1.

State Administration of Exchange Control. 1985. "Promulgation of Detailed Punishment Measures for the Violation of Exchange Controls." In State Economic Commission System Reform Bureau (1986, 1,004–7).

State Bureau of Commodity Prices. 1980. "Notice Concerning Issues in Domestic Price Formation for Imported Commodities." In State Bureau of Supplies Price office (1981, 76–7).

 1985a. "A Notice on Issures Concerning the Domestic Prices of Imported Goods." In Hubei Provincial Bureau of Commodity Prices (1987, 874).

 1985b. "Notice on an Opinion on the Domestic Pricing of Goods Imported from Capitalist Countries in 1985." In Hubei Provincial Bureau of Commodity Prices (1987, 878–82).

 1989. *Chinese Commodity Price Yearbook 1989*. Beijing: Chinese Commodity Price Publishing House.

State Bureau of Commodity Prices Commodity Price Research Institute. 1986. *A Compilation of Selected Documents on Prices (1979–1983)*. Beijing: Chinese Finance and Economics Publishing House.

 1989. *A Compilation of Selected Documents on Prices (1987–1988)*. Beijing: Chinese Commodity Price Research Institute.

State Bureau of Commodity Prices Foreign Price Office. 1988. *A Handbook of China's Policy and Laws on Foreign Prices*. Hong Kong: Hong Kong Main Culture Company, Ltd.

 1989. "Foreign Prices." In State Bureau of Commodity Prices (1989, 158–62).

State Bureau of Commodity Prices, Ministry of Foreign Economic Relations and Trade, and Ministry of Finance. 1986. "Notice on Issues in the Domestic Price Formation of Centrally Financed Imports." In State Bureau of Commodity Prices Foreign Price Office (1988, 117).

State Bureau of Commodity Prices, State Council, et al. 1988. "Notice on Implementing Agent Pricing for the Chemical Fiber, Chemical Monomers and Wool Imported by the Ministery of Textile Industry." In State Bureau of Commodity Prices (1989, 25).

State Bureau of Supplies Price Office. 1981. *A Compilation of Selected Documents on Commodity Prices (1963–1981)*. Beijing: State Bureau of Supplies Price Office.

State Commodity Price Bureau Heavy Industrial Products Price Office. 1989. "The Prices of Products in Heavy Industry." In State Bureau of Commodity Prices (1989, 143–8).

State Council. 1963. "Provisional Regulations on Carrying Out Uniform Price Formation Methods for Imported Commodities." In State Planning Commission Legal Staff Office (1987, 1,229–30).

 1965. "Interim Regulations on Uniform Price Formation Methods for Commodities Supplied for Export." In State Council Bureau of Legislative Affairs (1987, 701–3).

 1975. "Report on Opinions on Revising the Method of Pricing Imported Commodities." In State Bureau of Supplies Price Office (1981, 72–5).

 1979a. "Approval and Transmittal of the State Bureau of Commodity Prices Report Requesting Instructions on Several Issues in Determining the Supply Prices for Industrial Export Goods." In State Bureau of Commodity Prices Commodity Price Research Institute (1986, 40–3).

1979b. "Methods of Implementing Retention of Export Products Foreign Exchange Earnings," In Guangzhou Municipal Industrial and Commercial Administration and Management Society (1985, 1,021–4).

1979c. "Methods of Implementing Retention of Nontrade Foreign Exchange Earnings." In Guangzhou Municipal Industrial and Commercial Administration and Management Society (1985, 1,024–6).

1980a. "Interim Regulations on Foreign Exchange Control of the People's Republic of China." In *China's Foreign Economic Legislation* (1982, 118–29).

1980b. "Report on the Methods of Implementing the Foreign Exchange Internal Settlement Price in Foreign Trade." In State Bureau of Supplies Price Office (1981, 77–85).

1982. "Notice on the Report Concerning Revisions in Methods of Carrying Out the Foreign Exchange Retention System for Export Commodities." In Chinese Academy of Social Sciences Law Institute (1982, 566–9).

1984a. "Interim Regulations on Licensing System for Import Commodities of the People's Republic of China." In Ministry of Foreign Economic Relations and Trade (1985, 433–5).

1984b. "Notice Concerning the Report of Opinions on Reforming the Foreign Trade System." In Bank of China Staff Office (1986, 170–80).

1985a. "Notice Approving and Transmitting the Ministry of Finance Report Concerning the Levy and Rebate of the Product Tax and Value Added Tax on Import and Export Commodities." In State Economic Commission Economic System Reform Bureau (1986, 630–4).

1985b. "Notice Promulgating the Report of the State Bureau of Commodity Prices Concerning the Domestic Pricing of Goods Imported from Korea, Romania, and Other (Socialist) Countries." In Hubei Provincial Bureau of Commodity Prices (1987, 824–6).

1985c. "Regulation on Carrying Out Proportionate Sharing of Increased Profits or Reduced Losses on the Self-Managed Exports of Foreign Trade Enterprises." In Ministry of Finance Legal Bureau (1987, 225–7).

1985d. "Decision on Strengthening Foreign Exchange Management." In State Economic Commission Economic System Reform Bureau (1986, 613–14).

1986a. "Provisions for the Encouragement of Foreign Investment." BR, 43:26–8.

1986b. "Regulations on the Question of Balancing Foreign Exchange Revenues and Expenditures of Chinese Foreign Joint Ventures." In Chinese Economic Yearbook Editorial Committee (1987, X41–4).

1988. "Regulation on Various Issues Concerning Accelerating and Deepening Reform of the Foreign Trade System." In State Planning Commission System Reform and Laws and Regulations Departments (1989, 385–94).

State Council Bureau of Legal Affairs. 1987. *A Compendium of Current Laws and Regulations of the People's Republic of China 1949–1985.* Foreign Affairs and Foreign Economics and Trade Volume. Beijing: People's Publishing House.

State Council Staff Office Bureau of Legal Affairs. 1986. *Compendium of Laws and Regulations of the People's Republic of China (January–December, 1979).* Beijing: Legal Publishing House.

State Economic Commission Economic System Reform Bureau. 1985. *A Selection of Policies and Laws on China's Economic Management, July 1984–June 1985.* Beijing: Economic Science Publishing House.

1986. *A Selection of Policies and Laws on China's Economic Management, July 1985–June 1986.* Beijing: Economic Science Publishing House.

State Import and Export Commission and Ministry of Foreign Trade. 1980. "Interim

Procedures of the People's Republic of China Concerning the System of Export Licensing." In Ministry of Foreign Economic Relations and Trade (1985, 407–14).

State Planning Commission, Ministry of Foreign Economic Relations and Trade, and State Bureau of Foreign Exchange Control. 1987a. "Notice Concerning the Adjustment of the Foreign Exchange Retention Rate for Enterprises Producing Textile Products for Export." In State Planning Commission Economic Laws and Regulations Office (1989, 699–700).

1987b. "Notice Concerning the Adjustment of the Foreign Exchange Retention Rate for Enterprises Producing Light Industry Products for Export." In State Planning Commission Economic Laws and Regulations Office (1989, 700–2).

State Planning Commission, State Economic Commission, and Ministry of Foreign Trade. 1979. "Implementing Methods for Taking Imports to Support Exports." In State Council Staff Office Bureau of Legal Affairs (1986, 181–4).

State Planning Commission Economic Adjustment Bureau. 1989. "The Reasons for and Suggestions for Bringing Under Control the Present Surge in Currency in Circulation in China." *ZGWJ*, 4:20–6.

State Planning Commission Economic Laws and Regulations Office. 1989. *A Compilation of Planning Laws and Regulations of the People's Republic of China (1986–1987)*. Beijing: Chinese Finance and Economics Publishing House.

State Planning Commission Legal Staff Office. 1987. *A Compilation of Selected Materials on Important Economic Laws 1977–1986*. Beijing: Chinese Statistical Publishing House.

State Planning Commission System Reform and Laws and Regulations Departments. 1989. *An Overview of Ten Years of Reform of the Planning System*. Beijing: Chinese Planning Publishing House.

State Price Commission. 1964a. "Notice on Draft Detailed Regulations for Implementing Uniform Price Formation Methods for Imported Commodities." In State Bureau of Supplies Price Office (1981, 64–71).

1964b. "Supplementary Notice on Draft Detailed Regulations for Implementing Uniform Price Formation Methods for Imported Commodities." In State Bureau of Supplies Price Office (1981, 71–2).

State Statistical Bureau. 1982. *Chinese Statistical Yearbook 1981*. Beijing: Statistical Publishing House.

1984. *Chinese Statistical Yearbook 1984*. Beijing: Statistical Publishing House.

1985. *Chinese Statistical Yearbook 1985*. Beijing: Chinese Statistical Publishing House.

1987. *Chinese Statistical Yearbook 1987*. Beijing: Chinese Statistical Publishing House.

1988. *Chinese Statistical Yearbook 1988*. Beijing: Chinese Statistical Publishing House.

1989a. *Chinese Statistical Yearbook 1989*. Beijing: Chinese Statistical Publishing House.

1989b. *Economic Research and Statistical Materials on Coastal Economic Open Areas*. Beijing: Chinese Statistical Publishing House.

1990a. *Chinese Statistical Abstract 1990*. Beijing: Chinese Statistical Publishing House.

1990b. *Chinese Statistical Yearbook 1990*. Beijing: Chinese Statistical Publishing House.

1991. "Report on National Economic and Social Development in 1990." *CDBW*, March 4, p. 4.

State Statistical Bureau National Economic Balance Statistics Department. 1985. *1983 National Input-Output Tables*. Beijing: Statistical Publishing House.

State Statistical Bureau Social Statistics Office. 1987. *Statistical Materials on Chinese Labor and Wages 1949–1985*. Beijing: Chinese Statistical Publishing House.

State Statistical Bureau Social Statistics Office and Ministry of Labor Comprehensive Planning Office. 1989. *Chinese Labor and Wages Statistical Yearbook 1989*. Beijing: Labor and Personnel Affairs Publishing House.

Stoltenberg, Clyde D. 1986. "Trends in PRC Import Cases Under U.S. Trade Law." *The Columbia Journal of World Business*, vol. 21, no. 1, pp. 41–8.

Sullivan, Lawrence R. 1988. "Assault on the Reforms: Conservative Criticism of Political and Economic Liberalization in China, 1985–86." *China Quarterly*, 114:198–222.

Summers, Robert and Heston, Alan. 1988. "A New Set of International Comparisons of Real Product and Price Levels Estimates for 130 Countries, 1950–1985." *Review of Income and Wealth*, 1:1–25.

Sun Wenxiu. 1989. "A Review and Forecast of the Reforms of the Foreign Trade System." *JHJJYJ*, 8:53–9.

Sun Yong. 1989. "Last Year Our Balance of Foreign Exchange Income and Expenditure Showed a Surplus; This Year We Can Establish a Foreign Exchange Adjustment Fund." *JJRB*, February 14.

Sung Yun-wing. 1990. "Explaining China's Export Drive: The Only Success Among Command Economies." Unpublished paper.

Tang Gengyao. 1985. "China's Foreign Exchange Control Policies." *BR*, 43:20–2.

   1986. "The Basic Situation and Important Issues in China's Management of Foreign Exchange." *ZGJR*, 9:43–5.

"Temporary Methods of Managing Shenzhen's Foreign Exchange Adjustment." In Sea and Sky Publishers (1988, 56).

Tong Shuguang and Hua Xiaohong. 1990. "A Discussion of the Foreign Trade Contract Management Responsibility System." *GJMY*, 2:9–12.

Van Brabant, Josef M. 1985. *Exchange Rates in Eastern Europe: Types, Derivation, and Application*. World Bank Staff Working Papers No. 778. Washington, D.C.: The World Bank.

Vogel, Ezra. 1989. *One Step Ahead in China: Guangdong Under Reform*. Cambridge: Harvard University Press.

Walder, Andrew. 1986. *Communist Neo-Traditionalism: Work and Authority in Chinese Industry*. Berkeley: University of California Press.

Wang Bingqian. 1981. "Report on the State's 1980 Final Account and on Conditions of Implementation of the 1981 State Budget." *XHYB*, 12:28–38.

   1989. "Current Fiscal Problems." *RMRB*, September 2, p. 2.

   1990. "Report on the Implementation of the State Budget for 1989 and on the Draft State Budget for 1990." *BR*, 17:ix–xiv.

   1991. "Report on the Implementation of the State Budget for 1990 and on the Draft State Budget for 1991." *BR*, 16:34–9.

Wang Dacheng and Yang Shubing. 1990. "Price Reform Must Be Taken Seriously During the Course of Carrying Out Rectification." *JHJJYJ*, 3:25–30.

Wang Deyun. 1989. "Create Conditions of Fair Competition; Deepen the Reform of the Foreign Trade System." *GJMY*, 2:35–9.

Wang Dongmin. 1985. "The Reform of the Renminbi Exchange Rate and the Reform of the Price System." *LNDXXB*, 2:21–4.

Wang Fenji. 1990. "An Introduction to China's Financial Subsidy Situation in Recent Years." *NKJJYJ*, 1:79–80.

Wang Jian. 1990. "Comments on the Development of Township and Village Enterprises in China in the Past Decade." *LW*, 22:20–1. In FBIS, June 19, pp. 37–9.

Wang Juhua. 1989. "New Developments in the Foreign Exchange Adjustment Market." In Shanghai Academy of Social Sciences (1989, 495).

Wang Liewang. 1986. "A Discussion of the Renminbi Price of Foreign Exchange and Issues in Fixing the Price of Foreign Exchange." *GJMY*, 2:16–18.

Wang Ping and Che Delong. 1989. "Enhanced Export Role Envisioned for Coastal Township Enterprises." JJYGLYJ, 5:11–13. In JPRS-CAR-90-010, February 7, pp. 57–60.

Wang Shaoxi. 1989. "A Review of Ten Years of Reform of the Foreign Trade System." *GJMYWT*, 12:2–7.

Wang Xiangwei. 1990a. "Rein Kept on Currency." *CD*, February 13, p. 2.

1990b. "U.S. Dollar May Face Tumble in China." *CD*, November 20, p. 2.

Wang Yiqian. 1988. "Implementing the Contract Management Responsibility System Is a New Solution in the Reform of the Foreign Trade Management System." In China International Trade Society Editorial and Publishing Commission (1988, 257–67).

Wang Zhenzhi and Qiao Rongzhang, eds. 1988. *A Review and Forecast of China's Price Reform.* Beijing: Chinese Commodities Publishing House.

Wang Zhenzhong. 1985. "The Relationship Between Domestic Prices and International Market Prices." *JJYJ*, 9:38–45.

White, Lynn T. 1989. *Shanghai Shanghaied? Uneven Taxes in Reform China.* Center of Asian Studies Occasional Papers and Monographs no. 84. Hong Kong: University of Hong Kong.

Wong, Christine. 1985. "Material Allocation and Decentralization: Impact of the Local Sector on Industrial Reform." In *The Political Economy of Reform in Post-Mao China,* edited by Elizabeth J. Perry and Christine Wong, pp. 253–78. Cambridge: Harvard University Press.

Working Party on China's Status as a Contracting Party. 1987. "Questions and Replies Concerning the Memorandum on China's Foreign Trade Regime." Geneva: General Agreement on Tariffs and Trade.

1988. "China's Foreign Trade Regime: Note by the Secretariat." Geneva: General Agreement on Tariffs and Trade.

World Bank. 1982. *World Development Report 1982.* New York: Oxford University Press.

1983. *China's Socialist Economic Development.* 3 vols. Washington, D.C.: The World Bank.

1985. *China: Long Term Issues and Options.* Baltimore: The Johns Hopkins University Press.

1987. *World Development Report 1987.* New York: Oxford University Press.

1988a. *China: External Trade and Capital.* Washington, D.C.: The World Bank.

1988b. *China: Finance and Investment.* Washington, D.C.: The World Bank.

1989. *World Development Report 1989.* New York: Oxford University Press.

1990a. *China: Between Plan and Market.* Washington, C.D.: The World Bank.

1990b. *World Development Report 1990.* New York: Oxford University Press.

1990c. *China Financial Sector Review: Financial Policies and Institutional Development.* Washington, D.C.: The World Bank.

Wu Jingben. 1989. "China's Foreign Economic and Trade Performance from the Perspective of International Revenue and Expenditure." ZSDXXB:ZSB, 4:27–37. In *WMJJGJMY*, 6:15–25.

Wu Jinglian and Zhao Renwei. 1987. "The Dual Price System in Chinese Industry." *Journal of Comparative Economics,* 3:309–18.

Wu Jingquan. 1988. "Current Restrictive Factors Which Are Unfavorable with Respect to Devaluation of the Renminbi." *GJMY*, 2:23–5.

Wu Nianlu and Chen Quangeng. 1989. *Studies on the Exchange Rate of the Renminbi.* Beijing: Chinese Finance Publishing House.

Wu Nianlu and Zhang Ying. 1987. "Reforming the Exchange Rate for the Renminbi: Results, Influence, and Policy." *SJJJDB*, June 1, pp. 10–11.

Wu Zesong. 1988. "Further Strengthen the Foreign Trade Financial Accounting Work; Perfect the Foreign Trade Contract Management Responsibility System."*GJMYWT*, 11:9–13.

Xiang Yin. 1985. "A Discussion of the Issues of the Speed of Development of China's Foreign Trade and Management Profits and Losses." *GJMYWT*, 3:15–20.

Xiao Qu. 1990. "Private Foreign Money Deposits Up." *CDBW*, September 10, p. 1.

Xiao Xiru. 1989. "China's inflation in 1987 and 1988 – A Systematic Explanation." *JGLLYSJ*, 1:22–7.

Xie Songxin. 1986. "Oil Undisputed Trade Champ." *CD*, January 7, p. 2.

1988. "Shanghai Clinches First Foreign Exchange Centre." *CD*, February 11, p. 2.

Xie Songxing. 1989. "Oil Exporting Strategy Under Fire." *CDBW*, August 21, p. 2.

Xinhua. 1989a. "Money Changed for Individuals." *CD*, September 5.

1989b. "The Renminbi Exchange Rate Is Devalued Today." *RMRB*, December 16, p. 1.

1989c. "U.S. Dollar Appreciates Against Renminbi." In FBIS, December 19, p. 28.

1990a. "Central Bank Increases Export-Oriented Loans." In FBIS, January 22, p. 31.

1990b. "Adjustment of the Renminbi Exchange Rate Will Benefit Economic Development." *RMRB* (overseas edition), November 20, p. 3.

1990c. "Shanghai Exchange Sees Record Cash Deals." *CD*, November 21, p. 2.

1990d. "China Sees Good Years in Rural Industry." *CD*, December 7, p. 1.

Xu Jianfeng. 1988. "The Objective Pattern of China's Foreign Trade System Reform." *GJMYWT*, 12:18–22.

Xu Xuehan and Meng Xianggang. 1984. "A Preliminary Discussion of the Problem of False Losses on Exports in Foreign Trade." *CMJJ*, 2:5–9.

Xu Yi, Chen Baosen, and Liang Wuxia. 1982. *Socialist Price Issues.* Beijing: Finance and Economics Publishing House.

Xu Yu and Zhu Mingxia. 1988. "The Separation of Authority (of Governments and Enterprises) and the Foreign Trade Contract Management Responsibility System." *GJMYWT*, 12:22–5,6.

Xue Muqiao. 1986. "A Discussion of the Reform of the Foreign Trade Management System." *GJMY*, 3:4–8.

Yan Xiaoqing and Shen Mei. 1988. "Current Problems in China's Foreign Exchange Market and Steps for Reform." *CJYJ*, 12:17–18.

Yang Jianhua. 1988. "Disadvantages in Our Present Exchange Rate Policy and Suggestions for Reform." *GJMYYJ*, September 30, pp. 2–14.

Yang Keqin and Song Shuguang. 1989. "A Review and Forecast of Reforms of the System of Comprehensive Planning." *JHJJYJ*, 6:29–35.

Yang Peixin. 1988a. "Reform the Foreign Exchange System To Stimulate Foreign Trade." SJJJDB, March 28, p. 3. In JPRS-CAR, May 23, pp. 26–9.

1988b. "On the Large Contract for Finance, Trade, Foreign Exchange, and Credit." *CMJJ*, 6:18–21.

Yang Xiaowei, Hua Xiaohong, and Zhu Guoxing. 1989. "An Investigation of Certain Issues Related to the Development of China's Externally Oriented Economy." *GJMYWT*, 3:4–12.

Yang Xiong. 1986. "Reforming the System of Proportionate Retention of Foreign Exchange Earned through Trade." *SHKX*, 7:36–7.

Yao Jianguo. 1990. "Foreign Trade Increase in 1989." *BR*, 7:43.

Yao Jinguan, ed. 1989. *An Introduction to Market Price Studies.* Beijing: Finance and Economics Publishing House.

Ye Dongfeng. 1990. "An Analysis of and Suggestions Concerning a Plan for the Reform of Crude Oil Prices." *JGLLYSJ*, 10:30–7.

Ye Jizhuang. 1957. "A Discussion of Foreign Trade." *XHYB*, 16:90–4.

Ye Xiangzhi and Xu Yunren. 1984. "A Further Discussion of the Problem of False Losses on Exports in Foreign Trade." *CMJJ*, 5:15–20.

Yin Ling. 1988. "An Exploration of the Reforms of the Foreign Exchange Management System." *JHJJYJ*, 12:Supplement no. 1, pp. 25–30.

Ying Pu. 1991. "China Tightens Control over Foreign Debt." CDBW, March 4, p. 1.

Yu Xingfa. 1982. "The Domestic Market Prices of Import and Export Commodities and Foreign Commodity Prices." *JGLLYSJ*, 2:50–64.

Yu Quanyu and Li Xiaogang. 1990. "An Analysis of 'Per Capita Gross National Product of $300 U.S.' " *RMRB*, January 22, p. 2.

Yu Zhonggen. 1986. "Strategy for Shanghai's Industrial Exports During the Seventh Five-Year Plan." *SHJJ*, 3:14–17. In JPRS-CEA, February 27, 1987, pp. 31–8.

Yuan Zhou. 1988. "Stricter Licensing to be Adopted for Exports." *CDBW*, December 5, p. 1.

Zhang Gang. 1987. "A Summary of the Professional Work of the Bank of China." In Chinese Finance and Banking Society (1987, III62–III65).

Zhang Guanghua and Wang Xiangwei. 1990. "Swap Centers Will Be Updated." *CDBW*, May 7, p. 1.

Zhang Jiren. 1989. "Some Thoughts on the Establishment of a New Order for Foreign Trade Administration." GJSB February 18, p. 3. In JPRS-CAR-89-038, April 28, pp. 20–2.

Zhang Weiying. 1985. "On the Role of Prices." *SSIC*, 4:177–4.

Zhang Wenzhong. 1990. "Ideas on the Structural Reform of the Oil Industry." JJGL, 4:24–7. In FBIS June 18, pp. 44–8.

Zhang Yuan. 1989. "Industrial Losses Pose Problem." *CDBW*, February 27, pp. 1–2. In FBIS-CHI, March 1, pp. 45–6.

Zhang Zuoqian. 1990. "The Development of China's Foreign Trade in 1989." *GZDWMYXYXB*, 1:20–7. In *WMJJGJMY*, 3:23–30.

Zhao Fengchen. 1982. "China's Foreign Trade Business Accounting." TJCJXYXB, 3:41–5. In *MYJJ*, 10:99–103.

Zhao Shengting. 1987. "The Influence of Renminbi Devaluation on China's Foreign Trade." *CMJJ*, 3:53–5, 6.

  1988. "On the System of Export Promotion." ZNCJDXYJSXB, Supplement:62–68. In *WMJJGJMY*, 6:44–9.

Zhao Ziyang. 1988. "Coastal Areas' Development Strategy." *BR*, 6:18–23.

Zheng Jifang. 1987. "The Form and Reform of China's Oil Pricing System." *JGLLYSJ*, 5:25–8.

Zheng Jianjing. 1982. "A Discussion Meeting on Issues in Foreign Trade Losses and Subsidies Opens in Shanghai." *CZ*, 10:32.

Zheng Tuobin. 1988. "Excerpts of a Speech by the Minister of Foreign Economic Relations and Trade to the National Foreign Trade Export Planning Meeting." *GJMYYJ*, November 25, pp. 1–11.

Zhong Pengrong. 1988. "The Foreign Trade System Must Achieve Four Transformations." *CMJJ*, 7:56–9.

Zhong Zhengyan. 1990. "Research on Issues of the Appropriate Scope and Speed of China's Development of Exports." *GJMYLT*, 1:16–23.

Zhou Chuanru. 1988. "Specific Measures for Reforming China's Foreign Trade System." *JJDB*, 16:11–12.

Zhou Hongqi. 1989. "Exports of Some Metals Banned." *CDBW*, February 20, p. 2.

Zhou Jianming. 1986. "The Structure of Imports and Exports and Economic Efficiency." *SHKX*, 9:31–3.

Zhou Jianping and Zhao Kaitai. 1983. "Several Opinions on Solving Current Foreign Trade Losses." *CMJJ*, 1:45–8.

Zhou Shude. 1988. "To Carry Out the Foreign Trade Contract Economic Management Responsibility System We Must Implement a Series of Policy Measures." *DWJMYJ*, November 25, pp. 12–16.

Zhou Xiqiao. 1984. "A Preliminary Discussion of the Changing Trend and Rational Adjustment of the Prices of Industrial Raw Materials." *CJYJ*, 2:29–33.

Zhou Xiaochuan. 1987. "Establish a System of Indirect Regulation of Foreign Trade; Promote Change in the Structure of Export Commodities." *GJMYWT*, 5:5–10.

1988a. "A Discussion of the Overall Demand of and Difficult Problems in the Direction and Stages of Foreign Trade System Reform." *GJMY*, 2:12–18.

1988b. "Seriously Implement and Further Improve the System of Rebating Taxes on Exports." In Ministry of Foreign Economic Relations and Trade Education Bureau (1988, 57–72).

1990a. *An Exploration of the Reform of the Foreign Trade System*. Beijing: Outlook Publishing House.

1990b. "The Speech of the Assistant to the Minister of Foreign Economic Relations and Trade." *GJMYLT*, 2:5–82.

Zhu Bisheng and Bao Haiyou. 1986. "A Discussion of the Reform of Export Commodity Prices." *GJMY*, 3:45–7.

Zhu Yunhai and Lu Guanxu. 1988. "A Critical Evaluation of the Results of Exchange Rate Devaluation in China." *SHJJYJ*, 1:32–4. In *CZJR*, 3:148–50.

Zou Siyi. 1990. "Reflections on Several Issues in Deepening Foreign Trade System Reform." *GJMYLT*, 1:14–15, 23.

Zweig, David. "Internationalizing China's Countryside: The Politics of Exports from Rural Industry." *China Quarterly* (forthcoming).

Index